DISTRIBUTED AND PARALLEL SYSTEMS

*From Instruction Parallelism
to Cluster Computing*

THE KLUWER INTERNATIONAL SERIES
IN ENGINEERING AND COMPUTER SCIENCE

DISTRIBUTED AND PARALLEL SYSTEMS

From Instruction Parallelism
to Cluster Computing

Edited by

Peter Kacsuk
MTA SZTAKI, Budapest, Hungary

Gabriele Kotsis
University of Vienna, Austria

KLUWER ACADEMIC PUBLISHERS
Boston / Dordrecht / London

Distributors for North, Central and South America:
Kluwer Academic Publishers
101 Philip Drive
Assinippi Park
Norwell, Massachusetts 02061 USA
Telephone (781) 871-6600
Fax (781) 681-9045
E-Mail <kluwer@wkap.com>

Distributors for all other countries:
Kluwer Academic Publishers Group
Distribution Centre
Post Office Box 322
3300 AH Dordrecht, THE NETHERLANDS
Telephone 31 78 6392 392
Fax 31 78 6546 474
E-Mail <services@wkap.nl>

 Electronic Services <http://www.wkap.nl>

Library of Congress Cataloging-in-Publication Data

Distributed and parallel systems : from instruction parallelism to cluster computing /
edited by Peter Kacsuk, Gabriele Kotsis.
    p. cm. -- (Kluwer international series in engineering and computer science ; SECS 567
Includes bibliographical references and index.
ISBN 0-7923-7892-X (alk. paper)
    1. Electronic data processing--Distributed processing. 2. Parallel processing (Electronic
computers) I. Kacsuk, Peter. II. Kotsis, Gabriele, 1967 - III. Series.

QA76.9.D5 D48552 2000
004'.36--dc21   00-044778

Printed on acid-free paper.

Printed in the United States of America

The Publisher offers discounts on this book for course use and bulk purchases.
For further information, send email to <scott.delman@wkap.com>.

Contents

Preface

This is the third Austrian-Hungarian Workshop on Distributed and Parallel Systems organized jointly by the Austrian Computer Society and the MTA SZTAKI Computer and Automation Research Institute. The series of workshops started in 1992 in Sopron, then the second one was held in 1994 in Budapest as a really regional meeting of Austrian and Hungarian researchers focusing on the transputers as a hot research topic of that time. Since then transputers became historical show-pieces but the scope of the workshop has been widened to parallel and distributed systems attracting more and more participants every second year. Since 1996 the workshops have been organized under a new name showing the transition to new challenging research areas. DAPSYS'96 held in Miskolc, and DAPSYS'98, held in Budapest, proved the viability of this new concept.

This time the proceedings contain 18 full papers and 12 short papers from 14 countries around the world including Japan, Korea and Brasil. The paper sessions cover a broad range of research topics in the area of parallel and distributed systems, including software development environments, performance evaluation, architectures, languages, algorithms, web and cluster computing.

DAPSYS 2000 is held together with the 7th Euro PVM/MPI conference. Participants of the two events share invited talks, tutorials, vendor session and social events while contributed paper presentations are going on in separate tracks in parallel. While EuroPVM/MPI is dedicated to the latest developments of PVM and MPI, DAPSYS is expected to be a major event to discuss general aspects of distributed and parallel systems. In this way the two events are complement to each other and participants of the DAPSYS2000 workshop can benefit from the joint organization of the two events.

Invited speakers of DAPSYS 2000 are Domenico Laforenza, Jack Dongarra, and Günter Haring whille those of Euro PVM/MPI are Al Geist, Miron Livny, Rusty Lusk, Bernard Tourancheau, and Thomas Sterling.

Preceeding both conferences, a tutorials day is organized. Tutorials will be given by on timely topics such as Network Computing (Alois Ferscha), MPI-

2 (Rusty Lusk), Globus and Metacomputing (Carl Kesselman), and Parallel Programming on Supercomputers (Silicon Graphics).

We would like to express our gratitude for the kind support of Silicon Computers Ltd and the Foundation for the Technological Progress of the Industry.

Also, we would like to say thanks to the members of the Programme Committee and to the reviewers for their work in refereeing the submitted papers and ensuring the high quality of DAPSYS 2000. Finally, we are grateful to Scott Delman and Melissa Fearon from Kluwer Academic Publishers for their valuable support in producing this volume.

Peter Kacsuk   Gabriele Kotsis
Workshop Chair   Program Chair

Program Committee and List of Referees

Program Committee Members

M. Amamiya (Kyushu University, Japan)
L. Böszörményi (University Klagenfurt, Austria)
L. Brunie (INSA-Lyon, France)
Y. Cotronis (University of Athens, Greece)
J. Cunha (Universita Nova de Lisboa, Portugal)
A. Ferscha (University of Vienna, Austria)
W. Gentzsch (Genias, Germany)
A. Goscinski (Daekin University, Australia)
G. Gupta (New Mexico State University, USA)
G. Haring (University of Vienna, Austria)
Z. Juhász (University of Veszprem, Hungary)
P. Kacsuk (MTA SZTAKI, Hungary)
K. Kondorosi (Technical University of Budapest, Hungary)
H. Kosch (University Klagenfurt, Austria)
G. Kotsis (University of Vienna, Austria)
D. Laforenza (CNUCE-CNR, Italy)
E. Luque (Universita Autonoma de Barcelona, Spain)
W. Schreiner (University of Linz, Austria)
V. Sunderam (Emory University, USA)
G. Terstyánszky (University of Miskolc, Hungary)
F. Vajda (MTA SZTAKI, Hungary)
S. Winter (Westminster University, UK)
R. Wismüller (Technische UniversitäT München, Germany)

Referees

Jemal Abawajy
Mokhled Al-Tarawneh
Vibhas Aravamuthan
Balász Goldschmidt
Karl E. Grosspietsch
Hermann Hellwagner
Helmut Hlavacs
Karin Hummel
Rushed Kanawati
Masud Hassan Khan
Elsa Mara Macas López
Qusay H. Mahmoud
Allen Malony
Pedro Medeiros
Zsolt Németh
Alvaro Suárez Sarmiento
Markus Schordan
Stephen Scott
Pavol Sestak
Kurt Stockinger
Imre Szeberényi

Part I

SOFTWARE DEVELOPMENT ENVIRONMENTS AND PERFORMANCE EVALUATION

THE DIWIDE DISTRIBUTED DEBUGGER ON WINDOWS NT AND UNIX PLATFORMS

J. Kovács and P. Kacsuk
MTA SZTAKI
H1518 Budapest, P.O. Box 63, Hungary
{smith,kacsuk}@sztaki.hu

Abstract   This paper introduces two versions of DIWIDE distributed debugger and gives an overview about platform specific solutions and the recent developments. DIWIDE has been designed for debugging parallel and distributed applications created by VisualMP programming environment running on Unix-based platforms and by WINPAR environment running on Windows NT workstations. The main goal of DIWIDE is to provide distributed debugging operations for the user through an easy-to-use graphical interface. New debugging techniques Macrostep and Replay debugging has been also implemented in DIWIDE in order to provide a great help for finding parallel programming bugs.

Key words: Distributed debugging, message-passing programs, graphical programming environment, replay, systematic debugging.

1.   INTRODUCTION

With the increasing amount of computational work development of parallel applications is getting more and more significant. In the life cycle of parallel development, the weakest point is the application debugging due to the inherently non-deterministic execution of these programs. This paper presents and compares two versions of an existing debugger namely DIWIDE distributed debugger, which has been integrated in WINPAR [1] and *Visual*MP parallel programming environments.

The first version of DIWIDE has been developed in the framework of an ESPRIT project and aimed at debugging WMPI message-passing applications created by TRAPPER [5] in the WINPAR environment running on a network of Windows NT workstations. Accordingly, DIWIDE uses stand-alone graphical user interface and gives some extra support for inspecting message queues and for controlling the application processes together by providing operations concerning each process.

The other version of DIWIDE has been developed for *Visual*MP parallel programming environment to provide debugging operations. *Visual*MP is a new graphical programming environment integrating several tools to support building Message-Passing applications running on Unix based homogeneous/heterogeneous clusters. One of its essential feature is providing a high level graphical support for each step of development. Tools of *Visual*MP are the GRAPNEL [3] graphical parallel programming language, GRED graphical editor [6] to design the application, GRP2C pre-compiler to generate source code using PVM or MPI function calls extracted from the graphical layout in GRED, the DIWIDE distributed debugger and the PROVE performance visualisation tool [7] with the distributed monitor, GRM [8]. This new environment had an early prototype, called GRADE [4] aiming at supporting the development of high-performance computing applications, using PVM. VisualMP is the new commercial version of GRADE including many novel features and tools that were missing in the predecessor. Meanwhile GRADE supported only PVM and the development of small size parallel programs, VisualMP provides the same visual program development environment both for PVM and MPI, and is able to support the development of large, real-life application programs, too.

The main goal of DIWIDE is to provide not only the pure debugging functions existing in traditional distributed debuggers, but supporting high-level debugging like stepping on graphical items in GRED, putting breakpoints on communication channels to inspect messages. Moreover, DIWIDE provides a new mechanism to ease parallel debugging by adopting the so-called Macrostep [9] method. This new technique gives the user the ability to debug parallel applications as easy as sequential ones by executing the application from communication point to communication point and in addition by supporting replay technique. With this extension DIWIDE became one of the most powerful debugger, providing a good support for systematic parallel debugging.

The following section summarises the services of DIWIDE. Next section is about the concrete implementation of Windows NT version of DIWIDE. Section 5 details the integration and the implementation work of DIWIDE on UNIX platform. In section 6 the user interface of both version are detailed. Finally, some other existing debuggers are compared in section 7.

2.   SERVICES OF DIWIDE

As a distributed debugging tool DIWIDE provides a wide set of operations concerning one process or each process of the application. These are the well-known debugging functions existing in sequential debuggers like control operations (e.g. stop, continue, step, stop all, continue all), breakpoint handling, variable and stack inspection. Both versions of DIWIDE have some prominent features.

DIWIDE on Windows NT has the ability of accessing the message queues of WMPI. In this case the user can check the state of the message-passing layer at any time and examine the contents of messages both in the send and in the receive queues. A new breakpoint type has been introduced, called global breakpoint. Hitting global breakpoint causes the whole application to stop and the user can examine what the other processes were doing when this process hit this breakpoint.

The DIWIDE integrated into *Visual*MP gives the user a high-level graphical debugging support. In *Visual*MP a process is represented by a flowchart built by the user and DIWIDE is able to associate debugging information to the graph and vice versa. User can put breakpoint to any item in the flowchart, moreover it is also possible to make debugging operations (e.g. step, set breakpoints) on source level generated by GRP2C in *Visual*MP. An intelligent structure browser is also provided, which helps the user to examine huge compound structures, blocks or chained lists. The structure is represented as a tree, where every compound leaf can be expanded or collapsed.

The main benefits of DIWIDE concerning the parallel features of the debugger are the Macrostep method and Replay technique. DIWIDE is able to discover the connections between processes and to stop the application before each communication. After all the processes are standing on a communication point DIWIDE is able to detect the communications which can be realised and is able to continue these ready processes until the next communication point. At macrostep-by-macrostep execution the debugger records all the send-receive pairs to replay the application to the same point. During replay DIWIDE is able to force the process to select the appropriate branch at the alternative receive instructions. Different states of the application are represented as a graph in the macrostep control panel where the user can select any point to which the application should run. With this support the application can be tested for all execution paths i.e. for all timing conditions.

3.   DIWIDE ON WINDOWS NT PLATFORM

Windows NT version of DIWIDE was planned to be a standalone distributed debugger with its own graphical user interface. In this case MD and GUI was implemented together as one module as it is depicted on Figure 1. Start-up phase starts with loading an MPI application. After extracting the host names from the corresponding mapping file, MD starts establishing the connections to DIWIDE services installed on the remote hosts. After successful connections, MD requests all the services to start Debug Controller on their hosts, waits for status report ("Start DC" and "Result" on Figure 1). After every DCs have been launched, they establish connections to MD using IP sockets. DIWIDE is ready for debugging the

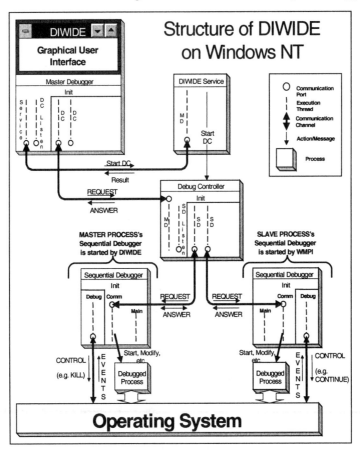

Figure 1. Inner structure and start-up scheme of DIWIDE on NT

application when every DC has registered itself at MD. Starting the application to debug begins with launching the first Sequential Debugger with the Master Process inside (SD on the left on Figure 1). When the SD has loaded its executable, it connects to the Debug Controller running on the host. Each SD downloads the breakpoints and the variables of the process stored in Master Debugger before they execute their process. As each process reaches the initialisation point the message-passing subsystem starts the next instance of Sequential Debugger with the slave-process (SD on the right side on Figure 1). The initialisation ends when every instance of SD registers at MD.

The Sequential Debugger has been implemented from scratch, since the operating system has a good support to develop debuggers with a collection of

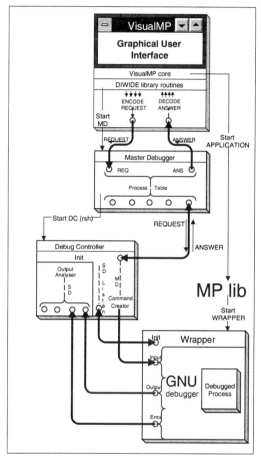

Figure 2. Inner structure and start-up scheme of
DIWIDE on UNIX

WIN32 system calls. Discovering the internals of the processes is also supported by "imagehlp" library routines. Moreover, own development has the advantage of providing the information in the right format and does not require a recognition module in the Debug Controller. The detailed description of developing a sequential debugger is out of scope of this paper.

The communication between DIWIDE components are implemented by pipe between local processes (DC - SD, MD – DC on console host) and by sockets between remote processes (MD – DCs on remote hosts). In every component every communication end-point is handled by a new thread as it is shown in Figure 1 by dotted lines.

4.   DIWIDE UNDER THE CONTROL OF VISUALMP

Unix version of DIWIDE (see Figure 2) was planned to be an integrated distributed debugging engine as a part of the *Visual*MP parallel programming environment. In this case the general layout should be complemented by a so called "diwide library" which hides the system specific features and provides exact functions to access debugging operations. At startup *Visual*MP initialises DIWIDE system through library routines to start MD on local host. After the connection established, Master Debugger requests the list of hosts from *Visual*MP and launches DCs. The DIWIDE subsystem in *Visual*MP

is ready to start debugging when all Debug Controller have registered in Master Debugger. *Visual*MP detects the ready state of Debug Controllers and starts the user application in debugging mode. In this case PVM or MPI starts the "Wrapper" processes which connect to the local Debug Controller and load GDB. After the connection between GDB and DC is fully operable the actual process is ready to be controlled by DIWIDE system and *Visual*MP sends the run application request to DIWIDE. When a sequential debugger has connected to DC it downloads the list of breakpoints and variables from *Visual*MP.

The communication in DIWIDE is implemented by pipes between local processes (DC - SD, MD – DC on console host) and by sockets between remote processes (MD – DCs on remote hosts). MD and DC uses "select" system call to scan for new messages through the connections. The lowest level is provided by GDB.

At the design phase of a distributed debugger we expect some support from the lowest layer we employ, especially from sequential debuggers. We have to take into account their behaviour when implementing the Debug Controller that is responsible for handling the SDs. They should be well controllable and the output needs to be provided in a strict format for recognition. After studying the behaviour of some existing command-line debugger, we notice that we lose control of the sequential debugger when the debugee is running. In other words GDB does not return control and does not accept any command after continuing the process until it hits a breakpoint or exits. During this time the debugger system is not able to affect these processes, which is not acceptable. The Debug Controller should recognise this state, because it is implemented in one execution thread and hence the Controller would not be able to receive the information coming from the other SDs.

5.   USER INTERFACE OF DIWIDE

The first version of DIWIDE on Windows NT has been developed for WMPI and with Stand-alone Graphical User Interface. On Figure 3 all types of windows are shown to demonstrate DIWIDE during work. DIWIDE consist of Main window

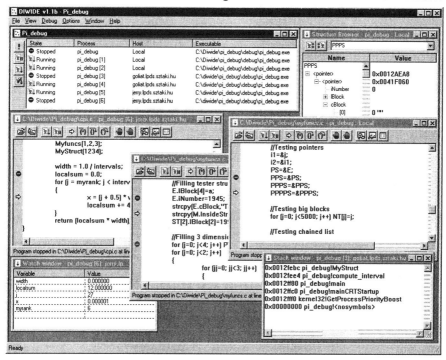

Figure 3. Screenshot of DIWIDE on Windows NT

as a frame for all, Application window to contain the list and state of processes, Process window to examine the source, Stack window to show the current state of stack, Watch window to inspect simple type variables and Structure Browser to display compound type variables. Structure window provides a toolbar with "Send Queue" and "Receive Queue" buttons to show the message queues. All commands and settings can be accessed from the menu of the Main window, furthermore toolbars on windows are also available for quick access.

In *Visual*MP the whole life-cycle of the parallel program development is supported by the same graphical view designed as a GRAPNEL program. GRAPNEL is a hybrid language providing graphics for the parallel activities and textual language (currently C) for defining the sequential activities. Accordingly, three programming layers are used to support a top-down style parallel program design. At the top level the Application Window (see Figure 4) provides graphics to define the processes and their interconnections via ports and channels. The Process Window at the second level serves for the detailed internal design of processes supporting graphically the design of those program structures that include communication activities. Other program structures are hidden by the so-called text boxes and these are defined at the third level which is the textual code level placed at the bottom part of Process Window.

The Macrostep Control Panel (see Figure 4) provides the operations required for systematic parallel debugging and replay support. The panel contains three main parts:

Graph window shows the Execution Tree, where each branch represents an alternative receive instruction and each node means the next communication point in the application. Red node signs the current position in the graph, green

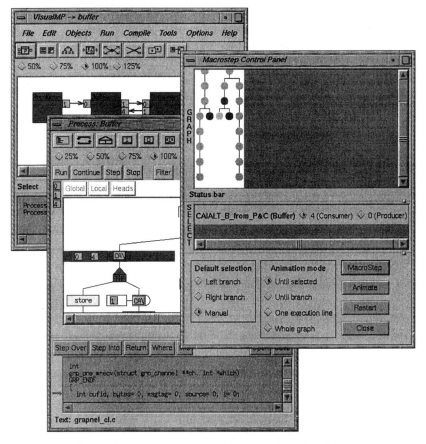

Figure 4. Screenshot of DIWIDE integrated in *Visual*MP

is the selected one, orange node is the exit point of the application, blue is undiscovered and gray is a discovered node. The graph is built automatically by DIWIDE.

Selection window is used for choosing the direction in the execution tree, when a process is standing on an alternative receive. In this case the selectable ports (to receive from) are listed in a box, which immediately maps its selections to the graph i.e. the corresponding node becomes selected. The selection can also be made in the graph window by clicking on the node which immediately set the choice in the box(es).

Control buttons and settings provide the Macrostep and Replay operations. "Macrostep" button performs one "step" in the application i.e. continues the execution of each process until the next communication point. "Animate" button automatically steps through the nodes depending on the "Animation mode" setting. "Restart" button reinitialises the application and "Close" button kills the application, finish the Macrostep debugging and VisualMP turns to "READY" state.

The panel provides the replay technique by allowing the user to reanimate the whole application to a selected point in the Execution Tree graph, i.e., to execute each process to a specific state. The replay method also enables to discover all the states of the application by restarting the application after an execution path has been completed, and by selecting an untraversed execution path originating from a choice point of the Execution Tree. With this support the user can do the test for all inherently different timing conditions and is able to find the bugs caused by concurrent behaviour. The details of the systematic debugging methodology based on the macrostep and replay techniques can be found in [9].

6.   RELATED WORK

TotalView [10] distributed debugger – developed by Etnus Inc. - is one of the most accepted commercially available debuggers. TotalView is a complex and huge debugging tool and the current version fails to satisfy the heterogeneous criterium. Unfortunately Totalview does not provide a systematic debugging method, either.

P2d2 [11] has been designed and developed by NASA and aimed at portability and scalability. In p2d2 a similar idea was realised as in DIWIDE by using gdb as a sequential debugger. Unlike DIWIDE it does not give the possibility to be driven from another environment. To highlight graphical items (e.g. processes, channels, and items in the process graph) *Visual*MP needs special support from the underlying distributed debugger. Moreover, DIWIDE gives a new technique namely Macrostep-debugging to support systematic debugging.

The distributed debugger, DDBG [6] (previously used in GRADE) had also a strong limitation corresponding the message-passing support. The debugger was implemented in a way that strongly relies on PVM features i.e. DDBG is only a PVM debugger. In *Visual*MP we need a communication library independent distributed debugger to support any present and future message-passing libraries.

7.   CONCLUSION

In the paper we presented two implementations of DIWIDE. On Windows NT operating system DIWIDE supports PaTENT MPI (previously WMPI) and gives a Stand-alone graphical user interface. On UNIX platforms DIWIDE has been developed for *Visual*MP parallel programming environment to support high-level graphical debugging and to provide Macrostep and Replay debugging. Macrostep debugging as a new method gives an extra support for systematic parallel debugging by allowing the user to debug the application on a higher abstraction level. DIWIDE with some additional support is able to Replay the application to any predefined point in the Execution Tree. Moreover, the macrostep technique gives the possibility to systematically traverse the whole Execution Tree of the application program and in this way supports the systematic debugging of parallel programs.

References

[1]   Bäcker, A., Ahr, D., Krämer-Fuhrmann, O., Lovas, R., Mierendorff, H., Schwamborn, H., Silva, J.G. and Wolf, K.: WINPAR, Windows-Based Parallel Computing. in Proc. of the ParCo'97 Conference, Bonn, 1997

[2]   PaTENT, Parallel Tools Environment for NT, http://www.genias.de/products/patent/index.html

[3]   Kacsuk, P., Dózsa, G. and Fadgyas, T.: Designing Parallel Programs by the Graphical Language GRAPNEL, Microprocessing and Microprogramming, No. 41 (1996), 625-643

[4]   Kacsuk, P., Dózsa, G., Fadgyas, T. and Lovas, R.: The GRED Graphical Editor for the GRADE Parallel Program Development Environment, Future Generation Computer Systems, No. 15 (1999), pp. 443-452.

[5]   Schaefers, L., Scheidler, C. and Kraemer-Fuhrmann, O.: TRAPPER: A Graphical Programming Environment for Parallel Systems, Future Generations Computer Systems, Vol. 11 (4-5), August 1995

[6]   Cunha, J.C., Lourenco, J., Duarte V.: Using DDBG to Support Testing and High-Level Debugging Interfaces, Computers and Artificial Intelligence, Volume 17, 1998

[7]   Kacsuk, P: "Performance Visualization in the GRADE Parallel Programming Environment", HPCN Asia, Beijing, China, 2000.

[8]   Podhorszki, N., Kacsuk, P.: Design and Implementation of a Distributed Monitor for Semi-on-line monitoring of VisualMP applications, proceeding of DAPSYS'2000.

[9]   Kacsuk, P.: Systematic Debugging of Parallel Programs Based on Collective Breakpoints Proceedings International Symposium on Software Engineering for Parallel and Distributed Systems, May 17-18, 1999 Los Angeles, California

[10]   TotalView Multiprocess Debugger, http://www.etnus.com/products/totalview/index.html

[11]   P2D2: Portable Parallel Distributed Debugger, http://www.nas.nasa.gov/Groups/Tools/Projects/P2D2/index.html

COBRA – THE LIBRARY FOR BUILDING RELIABLE APPLICATIONS IN DISTRIBUTED ENVIRONMENT

Jerzy Brzeziński, Anna Kobusińska, Jacek Kobusiński, Michał Szychowiak
Institute of Computing Science,
Poznań University of Technolog, Poland
{Jerzy.Brzezinski, Anna.Kobusinska, Jacek.Kobusinski, Michal.Szychowiak}@cs.put.poznan.pl

Abstract   The requirement for high level of dependability is crucial in many important domains. In this paper we present the concept and implementation of Cobra - the Common Object Library for Building Reliable Application. This library consists of a set of protocols and algorithm objects that allow to structure fault tolerant distributed applications and simplify the composition of complex protocols in a flexible manner. Cobra library guaranties the proper behaviour of protocols even in the presence of network partitions. Moreover, it is implemented totally in Java, which allows benefiting form all Java characteristics. Furthermore, the Cobra library objects are accessible for wide range of applications, by making them available through CORBA.

Keywords: java-CORBA systems, middlewares, programming tools, reliability

1.   INTRODUCTION

Today's computer technologies are well mastered and highly reliable. Nevertheless, when hundreds or sometimes thousands of machines constitute a distributed system, the probability of at least one failure occurring is too large for many distributed applications. Especially in mission critical systems where failures might result in potential loss of lives or financial hardship, it is unacceptable. Thus, the requirement for high level of dependability, i.e. reliability and availability, which will allow clients to have a justified confidence in services delivered in a distributed system is continually increasing in domains such as finance, booking-reservation, industrial control, telecommunication, etc ([1], [12], [13], [14], [15], [17]).

One approach to achieve fault-tolerance is to build software on top of fault-tolerant (replicated) hardware. This may indeed be a viable solution for some application classes, however it is expensive and does not cope with software errors [12].

Another approach for achieving high level of dependability is to provide programmers with a set of software components (modules, libraries) that solve basic problems like reliable massage passing, failure detection, consensus, and so support building reliable distributed applications.

Several solutions have already been proposed for structuring dependable distributed applications, but none has fully succeeded in bringing power and simplicity, together with adaptability ([5], [10], [13], [14]). Only one of them, BAST ([9]), does provide ready-to-use components that, on the one side, hide the complexity of underlying distributed protocols, and on the other, allow to build fault-tolerant distributed software.

Although BAST provides several abstractions helpful in building distributed software, it does not behave properly in case of network partitions. Therefore, in this paper we propose concept and implementation of Common Object Library for Building Reliable Application (Cobra) that overcomes problems found in BAST. The Cobra library allows building reliable distributed applications able to cope with network partitions. According to our best knowledge, such a feature has not been offered by the systems proposed till now.

The Cobra library is implemented totally in Java. Hence we can benefit from all Java features among which are: simplicity, robustness, security, architecture neutrality, portability and multithread execution.

Furthermore, we want the Cobra library objects to be available for possibly wide range of applications. Thus the protocol object classes are made accessible through CORBA [19] and the corresponding IDL interfaces are added to each object. It means that any CORBA client, independently of the programming language, may invoke them through the ORB. There are several advantages coming from choosing CORBA environment. Among other things, this middleware allows objects to communicate, independently of the specific platforms and techniques used to implement these objects. What more, classical objects only live in a single program and the outside world does not know anything about them, whereas CORBA objects, in contrast, can live anywhere on the network. They can also be accessed by local or remote clients via operations invocations.

The paper is organised as follows. It starts by presenting definitions of problems and mechanisms considered in the project. In Section 4 a general concept of Cobra project is described. Section 5 presents Cobra components. Finally, concluding remark and future lines of investigation are discussed.

2. BASIC DEFINITIONS AND PROBLEM FORMULATION

To ensure higher availability and reliability, distributed systems usually use replication of components or services ([1], [10], [14]). In this solution multiple copies of each server participating in the service are located on distinct network nodes. As long as there are enough copies around, faulty nodes are unable to prevent the overall service from working. A replicated server can be implemented as a group of replicas. Although replication is a very intuitive idea, the design and verification of it in distributed environment is yet a very complex or sometimes even impossible task. This is not surprising, as the implementation of the group abstraction often requires dealing with many non-trivial issues, among which are: reliable communication, failure detection, consensus, etc. ([1], [5], [7], [16]).

In 1985 it was shown by Fisher, Lynch and Paterson that the Consensus problem[1] has no deterministic solution in asynchronous distributed systems that are subject to even a single process crash failure. This assertion is widely known as the Fisher-Lynch-Paterson (FLP) impossibility result [7]. The FLP impossibility result implies that not much can be guaranteed in such a purely asynchronous system, as far as fault-tolerance is concerned. The consequences of this result has been enormous, because most real distributed systems today can be characterised as asynchronous, and Consensus is an important problem to be solved if the system is to tolerate failures. As a result, a Consensus problem has frequently been used as a yardstick of computability in asynchronous fault-tolerant distributed systems.

To circumvent this impossibility, Chandra and Toueg have augmented the system with the theoretical notion of failure detector [6].

A failure detector is a module located on each node and does not necessarily agree with its peers. It monitors a subset of the processes in the system and maintains the list of those that it currently suspects to have crashed. Since some failure detectors are characterised as partially unreliable, erroneous failure detection might occur, i.e. a process might be suspected to be faulty, although it is not.

Table 1. Eight classes of failure detectors

Completeness	Accuracy			
	Strong	Weak	Eventual Strong	Eventual Weak
Strong	Perfect P	Strong S	Eventually Perfect ◊P	Eventually Strong ◊S
Weak	Q	W	◊Q	Eventually Weak ◊W

By restricting the domain of mistakes distributed failure detectors make, several classes of failure detectors may be defined. Formally, Chandra and Toueg

---

[1] Because of equivalence also Total Order Multicast cannot be solved deterministically in an asynchronous system that is subject to even one crash failure.

characterised in [6] failure detectors by two completeness and four accuracy properties. By selecting one of completeness and one of accuracy properties eight classes of failure detectors may be obtained. Their definitions in terms of accuracy and completeness are shown in Table 1.

The suspicions made by the failure detector classes introduced in Table 1 concern all processes in the system. However, sometimes we want only subset of all processes to make suspicions. This is motivated by the fact, that nowadays systems are often subject to wide-area network partitions, in the presence of which the accuracy property considered by Chandra and Toueg simply does not hold. The solution of this problem was shown in [11]. It consists in introducing a new class of failure detectors, described by accuracy property, which restrict the false suspicions made by a subset Γ of the processes. The difference between failure detectors introduced in [6] and Γ-failure detectors lies in the accuracy property, the completeness property is not changed (see Table 2).

Table 2. Γ-accurate failure detector classes

Completeness	Accuracy			
	Strong Γ	Weak Γ	Eventual Strong Γ	Eventual Weak Γ
Strong	Perfect Γ $P(\Gamma)$	Strong Γ $S(\Gamma)$	Eventually Perfect Γ $\Diamond P(\Gamma)$	Eventually Strong Γ $\Diamond S(\Gamma)$
Weak	$Q(\Gamma)$	$W(\Gamma)$	$\Diamond Q(\Gamma)$	Eventually Weak Γ $\Diamond W(\Gamma)$

Although the failure detector abstraction permits us to solve many problems connected with asynchronous distributed systems, there is no means to ensure safe process failure detection. Intrinsically, such detection is at best approximate.

In this paper $\Diamond S(\Gamma)$ failure detector has been chosen and implemented to be a base for Cobra library.

3.   COBRA - THE GENERAL CONCEPT

The Cobra library is placed between application layer and transport layer, as it is shown at Figure 1. The library consists of the protocol modules, which are implemented as object classes and structured as in Figure 2.

The layered architecture resulted from the fact that fault-tolerant distributed protocols often involve many other underlying protocols. Consensus, for example, is itself based on failure detection, reliable point-to-point communication and reliable multicast. The latter also relies on reliable point-to-point communication. Such relationships may result in complex dependencies. A good solution to this problem is subclassing [9] the appropriate protocol modules. Subclassing allows to customise and optimise existing protocols, and to create new ones with minimal effort.

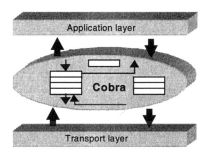

Figure 1. COBRA library

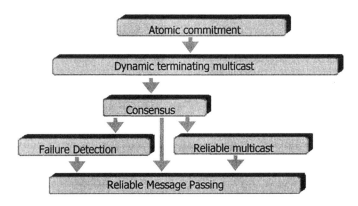

Figure 2. Protocol modules

According to this fact, there are two ways of building new protocol objects, either by customising a protocol class implementing a distributed pattern, or by composing existing protocols using the strategy design pattern ([2], [3], [4], [8]). The first method is adequate when the newly built protocol can be seen as an instance of another, more general protocol. The second method is adequate when the new protocol relays on protocols that are already available in the library. Thus, using protocols as objects allows to structure distributed systems according to the needs and simplifies building new, complex protocols.

Furthermore, protocol objects are separated from their implementations and manipulate the corresponding distributed algorithms, which are also implemented as objects. Consequently, each protocol object is independent of the algorithm supporting this protocol, making protocol composition fully flexible (see Figure 3).

An algorithm object always executes within a protocol object, and they are thus tightly coupled. Furthermore, applications only deal with protocol objects, i.e., they know nothing about algorithm objects.

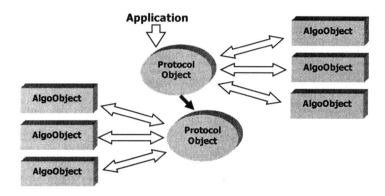

Figure 3. Protocol and Algorithm objects composition

Because of flexibility, extensibility, and possibility of code reuse we have taken advantage of interactions and dependencies between protocol classes introduced in BAST and we implement them in the similar manner. Furthermore, we also use similar notation, so every person familiar with BAST can easily analyse our project. Below there are described protocols and dependencies between them. At present our project provides components supporting the reliable implementation message passing, failure detection, multicast and consensus.

4.   DESIGN ISSUES

While designing protocol and algorithms objects described in the previous section, two basic ceasing issues concern the choice of failure detector and implementation platform.

4.1   The choice of failure detector

The failure detection in Cobra and in BAST is wired in the underlying transport layer. Nevertheless in BAST failure detection scheme is implemented using timeouts and assumed to behave as a failure detector of type $\Diamond S$. The failure detector class $\Diamond S$ is defined by eventual weak accuracy and strong completeness. Such failure detector class is said to be unreliable because they can make false suspicions and moreover they do not behave properly in the presence of network partitions. Thus, to ensure the proper behaviour of protocols even in the presence of network partitions in the Cobra, the mechanism of failure detector of $\Diamond S(\Gamma)$ class was applied. The choice of this class was motivated by the fact that nowadays systems are often subject to network partitions, in the presence of which the accuracy property considered by Chandra and Toueg simply does not hold.

4.2 The implementation platform

While choosing the implementation language for Cobra several languages such as C, C++, Pascal, SmallTalk, and Java were considered. We paid attention to many features, among which the most important were the platform independence and easy distribution of software. Only Java from all mentioned above languages fulfils these requirements in a satisfactory way. Hence, the Cobra project was implemented totally in Java and we can benefit from all Java features among which are: simplicity, robustness, security, architecture neutrality, portability and multithread execution.

5. COBRA COMPONENTS

Below we characterise in shortened way the architecture of protocol objects offered in Corba library.

5.1 Reliable message passing module

There are several libraries developed during past years: PVM, MPI, MPL, but none of them is suitable for Cobra project. There are several disadvantages, which restrain us from using the above mentioned libraries. First of all, none of these libraries is implemented in Java. Moreover they are not object - oriented, which is enough to leave them behind our scope of interest. So we decided to build Cobra communication layer using implemented in Java library called JMPL [18].

The JMPL library is dedicated to Java environment, which makes it very interesting from our point of view. The library uses possibilities offered by Java language and is not limited by any platform-specific elements, moreover it is fully object-oriented. The programmer interface consists of a few classes instead of dozen of functions and procedures. This fact makes JMPL library easy to extend without modification of the source code. Creating the library, an emphasis has been placed on algorithmic simplicity, which resulted in "fast-executed" code.

The JMPL library provides peer-to-peer model, which means that all the processes have the same status, and they are all parts of the system. One of the features of such model is its simplicity. The end-user can easily start remote processes because almost everything is done automatically after execution of the primary copy of the program.

The main disadvantage of proposed model lies in the fact that it is impossible to exclude a process that finishes its execution from the system, as this process becomes an integral part of the system.

To adjust JMPL library to Cobra project, we made a few modifications and extensions that needed to be implemented. First of all the communication layer should provide information about availability of processes. This information will be used in the higher layer to implement failure detector. This requirement results in a new routing sub-layer responsible for collecting and updating information about availability of processes and the optimal routes between them.

5.2   Failure detection module

Protocol objects of class FailureDetObject have the possibility of monitoring other objects through operations startMonitoring() and stopMonitoring(). The monitoring is performed by reliable message passing layer. Each protocol object possesses so-called routing table, where it is marked whether other objects are suspected by a given protocol object or not. Such tables are created on the basis of information received from JMPL subsystem. The table is sent to other instances of FailureDetObject class. Consequently, the given object also receives routing tables from other protocol objects. The information included in such tables affects the modification of the local routing table. When a given protocol object suspects or ceases to suspect any object it modifies its routing table through operations doSuspect() and doNotSuspect(). Actually, every routing table is a private set of objects the given protocol object suspects to be faulty.

Failure detection scheme is implemented using time-outs. Instances of FailureDetObject are assumed to behave as a failure detector of class $\Diamond S(\Gamma)$, so it fulfills strong completeness and eventual weak Γ-accuracy. As for protocol classes supporting point-to-point communication, class FailureDetObject does not relay on an algorithm class. The failure detection protocol is wired in the underlying transport layer.

5.3   Reliable multicast module

Class ReliableMultiObject provides operations rmcast() and rmDeliver(), which enable the sending and receiving of a message to a set of protocol objects referenced in the set of destination objects. Such operations are performed in a way that enforces reliable multicast properties. The class ReliableMultiAlgo implements the algorithm described by Chandra and Toueg in [6].

5.4   Consensus module

The solution of Consensus problem is based on Chandra and Toueg algorithm [6] that assumes the presence of a rotating co-ordinator. In a crash-stop model this algorithm was proved not to block as long as there is a majority of correct participant objects that are able to reach the agreement.

Protocol class ConsensusObject relies on algorithm class ConsensusAlgo. This algorithm class defines two operations: propose() and decide(). When several non-concerned objects join the same consensus execution, they propose the initial value through operation propose(). On contrary, when agreement is reached the decision value is delivered to each participant through operation decide().

Protocol class ConsensusObject also defines operations propose() and decide(), which merely forward their work to the corresponding operations of class ConsensusAlgo. Besides consensus, protocol object aConsensusObject is also able to execute any protocols inherited by its class, i.e., reliable point-to-point communication, failure detection and reliable multicast.

As ConsensusObject class is a key class in our project. As long as no agreement is reached the object aConsensusAlgo performs only reliable point-to-point communication and failure detection. Before taking a decision class aConsensusAlgo invokes a reliable multicast communication to all protocol objects taking part in consensus algorithm by calling the rmcast() operation.

6. CONCLUSIONS

This paper brings up some aspect of achieving fault-tolerance in distributed systems. The method described in this work is based on the failure detection mechanism proposed by Chandra and Toueg. The main emphasis was put on solving consensus problem being key problem in building reliable distributed application.

The aim of this work was to design and implement the Cobra library that consists of set of protocol and algorithm objects, which support development of fault-tolerant application. We describe the way the Cobra library was designed and point out some issues in reusing and composing distributed protocols.

The library is written totally in Java that offers some new useful mechanisms for building parallel and distributed application. But the most important advantages, that Cobra library also inherited from Java, are platform-independence and portability. It follows that the Cobra library can be used on almost every platform on which Java Virtual Machine exists. Cobra library also uses CORBA to make protocol objects available through the ORB. As a result, protocol objects offered by the Cobra library can be used extensively.

Nothing stands in the way to increase functionality of this library either by adding new objects or by extending the existing ones. As an example, currently the Cobra library is being developed to be integrated with distributed, shared memory system Jash. Thus, DSM system combining scalability, ease of programming and efficiency with fault-tolerance will be offered.

References

[1] Bazzi R., Neiger G., Simplifying fault-tolerance. Providing the abstraction of crash failures, College of Computing, Georgia Institute of Technology, (1993)
[2] Benoît Garbinato, Pascal Felber, Rachid Guerraoui. Protocol Classes for Designing Reliable Distributed Environments. In European Conference on

Object-Oriented Programming Proceedings (ECOOP 96), volume 1098 of Lectures in Computer Science, Linz , July 1996, Springer Verlag.

[3] Benoît Garbinato, Rachid Guerraoui. Flexible Protocol Composition in Bast. In Proceedings of the 18th International Conf. on Distributed Computing Systems (ICDCS-18), Amsterdam, May 1998.

[4] Benoît Garbinato, Rachid Guerraoui. Using the Strategy Design Pattern to Compose Reliable Distributed Protocols. In Proceedings of the 3rd USENIX Conference on Object-Oriented Technologies and Systems (COOTS'97), Portland (Oregon), June 1997.

[5] Birman K., Cooper R., Joseph T., Marzullo K., Makpangou M., Kane K., Schmuck F., Wood M., The Isis System Manual, Dept. Of Computer Science, Cornell University, Sept 1990

[6] Chandra T.D, Toueg S., Unreliable Failure Detectors for Reliable Distributed Systems, In Proceedings of the 10th Annual ACM Symposium on Principles of Distributed Computing, pages 325 - 340, Montreal, Quebec, Canada, (1991).

[7] Fisher M. J., Lynch N. A., Paterson M. S., Impossibility of distributed Consensus with one faulty process, Journal of ACM, 32(1985),374-382.

[8] Gamma E., Helm R., Johnson R., Vlissides J., Design Patterns, Elements of Reusable Object-Oriented Software, Addison-Wesley (1995)

[9] Garbinato B., Protocol objects and patterns for structuring reliable distributed systems, Ph.D.Thesis 1801, Operating Systems Laboratory (Computer Science Department) of the Swiss Federal Institute of Technology, Laussane,(1998)

[10] Guerraoui R., Garbinato B., Mazouni K., GARF: A Tool for Programming Reliable Distributed Applications, Technical Raport, Operating Systems Laboratory (Computer Science Department) of the Swiss Federal Institute of Technology, Laussane,(1996)

[11] Guerraoui R., Schiper A., G-Accurate Failure Detectors, Technical Raport,

[12] Laprie J.C. Reliability - basic definitions and terminology, EDCC-2 Workshop on Dependable Computing IEEE Comp. Society Press

[13] Malloth C., Conception and implementation of a toolkit for building fault-tolerant distributed applications in large scale networks, Ph.D. Thesis 1557, Operating Systems Laboratory (Computer Science Department) of the Swiss Federal Institute of Technology, Laussane,(1996)

[14] Malloth C., Felber P., Schiper A., Wilhelm U., A Toolkit for Building Fault-Tolerant Distributed Applications in Large Scale, (1995)

[15] Mishra S., Peterson L, Schlichtig R, Consul: A communication substrate for fault-tolerant distributed programs, Distributed systems Engineering Journal, 1(2): 87-103, 1993

[16] Schiper A., Guerraoui R., The Generic Consensus Service, Technical Raport, Operating Systems Laboratory of the Swiss Federal Institute of Technology, Laussane,

[17] Schneider F. B., Implementing Fault-Tolerant Services using the State Machine Approach. A tutorial. ACM Computing Surveys, 22(4): 299-320, (1990)

[18] Sobaniec C., Oborzyński K., JASH - Java distributed shared memory system, Master thesis at Operating Systems Laboratory, University of Technology, Poznań 1997

[19] The Common Object Request Broker: Architecture and Specification, Object Management Group, Framingham, MA, 1998.

DESIGN AND IMPLEMENTATION OF A DISTRIBUTED MONITOR FOR SEMI-ON-LINE MONITORING OF *VISUAL*MP APPLICATIONS[1]

Norbert Podhorszki and Peter Kacsuk
MTA SZTAKI
H-1518, Budapest, P.O.Box 63, Hungary
{pnorbert, kacsuk}@sztaki.hu

Abstract   A new application-level, software tracing monitor is designed and implemented for the *Visual*MP graphical parallel programming environment to support semi-on-line monitoring of message-passing programs in heterogeneous environments. We present the design aspects of the monitor and the main implementation issues.

Key words: Distributed monitor, message-passing programs, graphical programming environment, performance visualisation.

1.   INTRODUCTION

*Visual*MP is a graphical programming environment integrating several tools to support the life-cycle of building parallel applications. Its major goal is to provide an easy-to-use, integrated set of programming tools for development of message-passing applications to be run in heterogeneous computing environments consisting of computers with different UNIX operating systems, such as SGI IRIX, SUN SOLARIS, LINUX and DEC ALPHA machines as well as the CRAY T3E and the Hitachi SR2201 supercomputers. Its main benefits are the visual interface to define all parallel activities in the application, the syntax independent graphical definition of message passing instructions, full support of compilation and execution on heterogeneous environment and the integrated use of the debugger and performance visualiser. Tools of the *Visual*MP program development environment [[2]] are the

---

[1] The work presented in this paper was supported by the National Science Research Fund OTKA T032226.

GRAPNEL graphical parallel programming language, GRED graphical editor to write parallel applications in GRAPNEL, the GRP2C pre-compiler to produce the C code with PVM or MPI function calls from the graphical program, the DIWIDE distributed debugger, the PROVE execution and performance visualisation tool and the GRM distributed monitor. For detailed overview of the tools of *Visual*MP, see [[2]] and [[3]]. PROVE is presented in [[4]].

The ancestor of *Visual*MP, the GRADE environment supported only the PVM message-passing library and relied on the Tape/PVM monitor [[6]] which is an off-line monitoring tool and its clock synchronisation method and its trace collection techniques are off-line, too. PROVE was a post-mortem performance visualiser.

In off-line monitoring, trace events are stored in local or global storages (memory and files) and are processed after the execution. In on-line monitoring trace events are sent immediately to a tool that processes (visualises or evaluates) them. Instead of sending each individual trace event to the tool, events can be buffered in local storage and collected into a global trace only when they are needed for processing. We call this method *semi-on-line* monitoring (and visualisation). One end of this method is off-line monitoring (i.e. buffering is used and traces are collected only when the application is finished). The other end of this method is on-line monitoring (no buffer is used).

In order to support the examination of long running or cyclic applications PROVE is modified for semi-on-line visualisation. For this purpose we need a distributed monitor that supports trace collection and provides a consistent global time reference at any time during execution. Since Tape/PVM is not an appropriate tool for this purpose we created a new monitor, the GRM. Other reasons to create GRM are that *Visual*MP tools should support also MPI applications, and the execution visualisation should support debugging, too. During execution the user (or the debugger) can force trace collection at any time. Events locally buffered until that time are collected by the monitor and the trace is presented in PROVE.

In this paper we present the design and implementation issues of the GRM monitor designed for semi-on-line monitoring of GRAPNEL programs. In the next section we present the design goals of our new monitor. Section 3 describes the structure of the monitor while in Section 4 we discuss important issues of design and implementation.

2.   DESIGN GOALS OF GRM

The main goals in the design of a new monitor were strongly related to the *Visual*MP environment. They were:
1. To support monitoring and visualising parallel programs at GRAPNEL level.
2. To be part of an *integrated* development environment.

3. *Portability*. To be used on heterogeneous clusters on UNIX operating systems (Irix, Solaris, Linux, DEC-Alpha, etc.)
4. *Semi-on-line* monitoring and visualisation to support the evaluation of long-running programs and debugging in *Visual*MP with execution visualisation.
5. *Dynamic instrumentation* to support evaluation of long-running programs and automatic performance analysers integrated into *Visual*MP in the future.
6. To support the collection of both statistics and event trace.
7. Trace data *should not be lost* at program abortion. The execution to the point of abortion should be visualised.
8. The execution of the application and the development environment should be *separate*. Thus, an application can be developed on a local host while it is executed on a remote cluster (and visualised semi-on-line on the local host).

The goals 1. and 2. simplify the expectations on the monitor. There is no need for monitoring, visualisation or performance bottleneck determination of situations that cannot be improved in the graphical level of the application. The interfaces among the different tools (*Visual*MP, monitor and PROVE) can be far more specific and simpler than for stand-alone monitors that should comply to a complex specification, like the OMIS specification [[5]]. The tight integration of GRM into *Visual*MP enabled us to put several functionalities of a stand-alone monitoring tool into other tools of *Visual*MP. For example, instrumentation is naturally done in the graphical editor; trace events of different processes are not sorted into time order since the pre-processing phase in PROVE does not need a globally sorted trace; local monitors are started on the hosts defined by the environment; the monitor is started and stopped by GRED; the monitor does no bookkeeping of processes, it does not even recognise the completion of the application.

Dynamic instrumentation in *Visual*MP means that during execution the user can modify the instrumentation of the application in the graphical editor. The application code is not modified at all. It is fully instrumented while the local monitors store instrumentation flags in shared-memory. The instrumentation routines in the application check these flags to decide whether an event should be generated or not.

The design goals, however, gave constraints on the monitor, too. The high portability requirement forced us to use only *standard UNIX solutions* for every problem related to monitoring. Operating system or hardware specific solutions, counters or performance analysis tools should have been avoided. Fortunately, keeping us only on GRAPNEL level we could implement GRM in standard UNIX.

The monitoring is *event-driven*, both *trace collection* and *counting* are supported. The collection is fully *software tracing* and the instrumentation method is *direct source code instrumentation*. For a classification of monitoring techniques see [[1]]. Direct source code instrumentation is the easiest way of instrumentation. Since *Visual*MP keeps in hand the whole cycle of application building, and source code instrumentation is supported by graphics, we chose this option.

Both trace collection and statistics are supported by the same monitor and the same instrumentation of the application. Trace collection is needed to give data to PROVE for execution visualisation. Statistics have less intrusion to the execution by generating fixed amount of data and they support initial evaluation of long-running programs. Sophisticated tools, like Paradyn [[7]], go further in this technique. Statistics collection is controlled automatically and the application code is instrumented dynamically on-the-fly.

The first version of the GRM implementation achieves the design goals except for two features: statistics collection and dynamic instrumentation. These features are missing from GRM only due to time constraints.

2.1   Trace event types

GRAPNEL is a hybrid language, i.e. it supports by graphics only the parallel processing activities and inherently sequential parts of the program should be written textually. The nodes of a program graph of a process are graphical blocks representing sequential computation, receiving messages, sending messages, loops and conditional branches. A subgraph of the program graph can be put into one graphical block. PROVE supports the visualisation of such events thus, GRM is designed for the monitoring of these types of events.

Sequential and communication blocks are represented by colored line segments in the space-time diagram of PROVE (see *Figure 1*). Send and receive library calls of the underlying message passing library are represented by arrows between two process lines in the space-time diagram. If the window size makes it possible, communication ports are also displayed as numbered boxes on the process lines. Certain points or sections in the process code can be selected as user events for trace event generation. They are represented by colored line segments in the diagram.

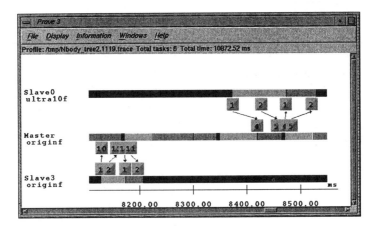

Figure 1. Space-time diagram in PROVE

3.   STRUCTURE OF GRM

GRM is a distributed monitor where one main monitor (MM) process co-ordinates the work of the local monitors (LM) placed on each host participating in the execution. An instrumented GRAPNEL library should be linked to the application processes. The event generation is done by the library functions. *Figure 2*a shows the communication structure of the tools working together in *Visual*MP. *Figure 2*b shows the communication structure of a local monitor and the monitored processes on one host.

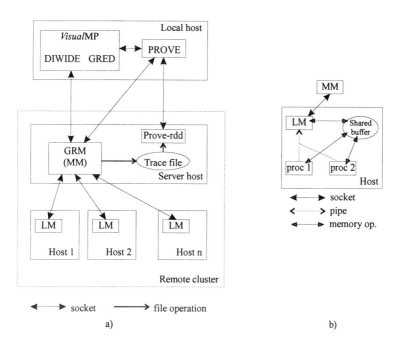

Figure 2. a) Communication of tools in *Visual*MP
         b) Communication structure of LM and the monitored processes

MM collects trace data from local monitors and writes them into a global trace file adjusting the local time of events according to a global clock. MM is connected to GRED and PROVE. An LM process on a host provides a shared memory segment to processes to store trace events and communicates with MM. The application process (through functions of the instrumented library) connects to the local monitor at process start, generates trace events and puts them into the shared-memory segment. It recognises when the buffer is full (reaches a certain limit in the shared buffer) and notifies LM about this fact.

The monitor processes work like server processes. They have several input channels and they are waiting for commands (in a *select* system call) processing only the incoming messages. MM is controlled by GRED (e.g. start, finish, start local monitors, collect trace), PROVE (collect trace), LMs (buffer is full on a local host). An LM is controlled by MM (start, finish, stop processes, send trace, restart processes, clock synchronisation) and the processes (connect, buffer full).

The processes should actively connect to LM. Moreover, instrumentation library functions in the processes recognise if the buffer is full and tell this fact to LM. This solution simplifies the structure of the LM process. It is waiting in a *select* system call and consumes no CPU time and other resources. When there is an input on one of the two connections (socket from MM and pipe from the processes), it wakes up and processes the input command.

The start-up and the termination of GRM is controlled by GRED. The main monitor of GRM has no information where to start the local monitors. GRED provides all the necessary information since it knows the hosts from a configuration file, and directories of binaries and their access method (host name, user account, remote shell program name) are defined in dialogs of GRED or in its startup script. At start-up of the monitor GRED launches MM with a script (on a remote host or locally) passing its listening socket port number as an argument and MM connects to GRED on this given port. GRED sends information about the execution hosts and MM launches an LM on each host. MM performs the first clock synchronisation and after that GRED starts the application.

After the start of the application the processes connect to their local monitor processes and start generating trace events. Their starts and exits are also events put into the trace buffer but monitor processes do no bookkeeping and GRM cannot recognise when the application is finished. However, GRED knows when the application terminates. GRED sends a message to MM after program termination and GRM collects the yet uncollected trace from the local monitors.

When an instrumented application process is started an instrumentation function call is performed first. This instrumentation function is responsible for connection to the monitor, for receiving the shared memory segment (and semaphore) identifiers and for generating the start event of the process. An LM creates a FIFO with predefined name (LM_FIFO) through which processes can send the messages. At start the process sends a connection message to LM (through LM_FIFO). LM sends the identifiers of the shared objects to the process through a temporarily opened new FIFO which is destroyed after the connection. The process now is able to generate events and to put them into the shared trace buffer. When the buffer is filled up to a certain limit, the process recognising this fact sends a notification to LM through LM_FIFO. Trace collection will be then performed as described in Section 4.1.

PROVE and GRM are independent tools and they can be started in an arbitrary order. Both tools are launched within GRED thus, it can give PROVE the necessary information to connect to GRM when both tools are already active. The monitor notifies PROVE when trace collection is finished and PROVE can start reading the trace from the trace file.

4.   MONITORING WITH GRM

GRM supports both event counting and event tracing providing only statistics or full trace of events. The statistics collection and visualisation are included into *Visual*MP to better support the evaluation of long-running programs. Performance evaluation should start with statistics collection and the analysis of the communication and execution time statistics of the program helps to focus on performance bottlenecks in the execution. Thus, instrumentation for trace collection can be focused and the generation of too large trace files can be avoided.

An important goal in the design of the monitor was that no events must be lost if processes terminate abnormally. For this purpose the local monitor provides a trace buffer in the shared memory segment. Thus, at abnormal termination of a process the last generated events can be saved and analysed in PROVE. This solution implies that the processes should have access to the shared memory segment. The local monitor creates this segment before the application is started. It also creates a semaphore to provide exclusive access to the buffer. The instrumentation functions in the application processes are responsible for the generation of events and their placement in the buffer.

Trace is stored in the local file system where MM is executed. If PROVE is executed on the same host, it can read the file directly and work as its previous off-line version (it reads a trace file and then visualises it). However, if PROVE is executed on a different host (e.g. when the application is executed on a remote cluster) trace should be transmitted to PROVE. An obvious solution would be that MM sends trace data directly to PROVE through their socket connection. However, it would impose a great overhead on trace collection. If the network between the hosts of MM and PROVE is slow the transmission of large amount of trace data takes a long time and the application could be suspended for the transmission. Instead, PROVE launches a small reader process (see *Figure 2*a) on the host of MM that reads the file and sends it to PROVE through a socket. Thus, the application can be continued when MM finishes trace collection and the transmission is done during the execution.

GRM always generates a trace file whether visualisation is off-line or on-line, whether PROVE is executed on the same host as MM or not. Its trace format is the same as defined by Tape/PVM because this format was used for monitoring of PVM programs in GRADE for post-mortem visualisation.

The causal order of events can be ensured by two methods. One of them is the use of logical clock while the other method is to compute a global time reference for the local timestamps estimating the clock differences for any moment of execution. We chose the latter method because PROVE originally relied on consistent global timestamps provided by Tape/PVM and a visualisation tool needs not only causal order of events but also precise time values for exact event visualisation. Drifts of the clocks can be eliminated for a short period of execution and the offsets can be determined quickly by the well-known "ping-pong" message exchange. The generated trace can be globally consistent if clock synchronisations are performed regularly and local clock values are adjusted to a consistent global timestamp at each event generation. OCM [[8]] is an example of such a technique that is plausible for on-line monitoring. GRM uses this technique, too. The main monitor records the offsets of the clocks and performs the correction of the clock values of trace events at trace collection.

4.1   Semi-on-line trace collection procedure

When the buffer on a processing element is filled with trace data it should be transferred to other place or processed immediately to make empty space for future data. To easily recognise the influence of the monitor on the application execution and possibly eliminate it in the statistics we choose a simple trace collection scheme. When a buffer is full, the main monitor stops all processes of the application, collects all trace data from each processing element and writes it into a global trace file in the local file system of the MM process. The collection scheme is the following:

1. When the buffer is full (a limit is reached, e.g. 90% of the available space), the process actually recognising this situation notifies the LM process.
2. LM notifies MM through the socket connecting them.
3. MM sends a STOP_PROCESSES command to each LM. An LM receiving such a command requests the semaphore ensuring that no process will write a trace event into the buffer during the collection and all events are fully written out into the buffer). Then it sends a SIGSTP signal to each process to stop their execution and sends a notification back to MM.
4. When all hosts stopped all processes MM collects the trace data from each local host. It sends a COLLECT_TRACE command to one LM which receiving this command will send the trace data to MM through the socket. MM writes trace data into a file. It is repeated for each host.
5. MM finishes the collection by sending a RESTART_PROCESSES command to each LM. The local monitors then send SIGSTRT signal to the processes to restart their execution and release the semaphores of the shared buffer enabling the processes to modify the buffer again.

Since MM collects data from the hosts one after the other in the fourth step and performs no merging on the trace we can only ensure that trace events of individual processes are in time order. The tool processing the trace should sort data itself in a pre-processing phase. We have chosen this method because the original PROVE sorted already the Tape/PVM trace and simplifies greatly the work of the main monitor process.

Stopping all processes before trace collection and restarting them after finishing it, the collection phase can be recognised in the trace (and visualisation). No events are generated in the application during trace collection. The collection phase can be seen in PROVE since no events are generated during this phase (see *Figure 3*). This solution makes possible to eliminate the collection overhead from the statistics.

4.2   An example of monitoring and visualisation

Figure 3 shows an example N-Body Problem simulation. PROVE displays two consecutively collected trace blocks during execution. The white gap in the middle represents the collection time when no events have been generated by the application. The black sections in the process lines indicate the computation and PROVE shows the bad load-balancing in this program. E.g., Slave0 (first line) works much more than the other three slave processes in the second phase (after the white gap in the PROVE window).

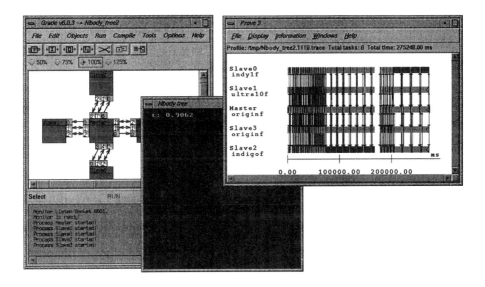

Figure 3. Semi-on-line visualisation in PROVE. Two trace blocks are shown in PROVE

CONCLUSIONS AND FUTURE WORK

GRM is a new monitoring tool of *Visual*MP designed from scratch to fully support the possibilities of the environment and make it more usable for the whole program development cycle. Its key feature is the semi-on-line monitoring that can be used for debugging and performance visualisation of long-running applications.

The monitor processes are themselves simple server processes and their functionality can be easily extended.

Our next task is to implement the collection and visualisation of statistics. PROVE will be extended with new statistics windows to support this monitoring mode. Macrostep-by-macrostep debugging [[3]] is under development and GRM and PROVE will support this mode of the debugger in *Visual*MP. Dynamic instrumentation is designed but not implemented in GRM. We intend to use an existing or create a new automatic performance analysis tool to help the programmer in the performance analysis stage of the parallel program development cycle in *Visual*MP.

References

[1] J. Chassin de Kergommeaux, E. Maillet and J-M. Vincent: "Monitoring Parallel Programs for Performance Tuning in Cluster Environments", In "Parallel Program Development for Cluster Computing: Methodology, Tools and Integrated Environments" book, P.Kacsuk and J.C.Cunha eds, Chapter 6., will be published by Nova Science in 2000.

[2] P. Kacsuk, G. Dózsa, T. Fadgyas, and R. Lovas: "GRADE: a Graphical Programming Environment for Multicomputers", Journal of Computers and Artificial Intelligence, Slovak Academy of Sciences, Vol. 17, No. 5, 1998, pp. 417-427

[3] P. Kacsuk: "Macrostep-by Macrostep Debugging of Message Passing Parallel Programs", PDCS'98, Los Angeles, 1998, pp. 527-531

[4] P. Kacsuk: "Performance Visualization in the GRADE Parallel Programming Environment", accepted for HPCN Asia, Beijing, China, 2000.

[5] T. Ludwig and R. Wismüller: "OMIS 2.0 – A Universal Interface for Monitoring Systems", In M. Bubak, J. Dongarra, and J. Wasniewski, eds., Recent Advances in Parallel Virtual Machine and Message Passing Interface, Proc. 4th European PVM/MPI Users' Group Meeting, volume 1332 of Lecture Notes in Computer Science, pp. 267-276, Krakow, Poland, November 1997. Springer Verlag.

[6] É. Maillet: "Tape/PVM: An Efficient Performance Monitor for PVM Applications. User's guide", LMC-IMAG, Grenoble, France, 1995.
      Available at http://www.apache.imag.fr/software/tape/manual-tape.ps.gz

[7] B.P. Miller, M.D. Callaghan, J.M. Cargille, J.K. Hollingsworth, R.B. Irvin, K.L. Karavanic, K. Kunchithapadam, T. Newhall: "The Paradyn Parallel Performance Measurement Tool", IEEE Computer, November 1995. pp. 37-46.

[8] R. Wismüller, J. Trinitis, and T. Ludwig: "OCM – A Monitoring System for Interoperable Tools", In Proc. 2nd SIGMETRICS Symposium on Parallel and Distributed Tools SPDT'98, pp. 1-9, Welches, OR, USA, August 1998. ACM Press.

QUALITY OF DISTRIBUTED APPLICATIONS

Henryk Krawczyk, Bogdan Wiszniewski
Faculty of ETI, Technical University of Gdańsk, Gdańsk, Poland
{hkrawk,bowisz}@pg.gda.pl

Abstract   A comprehensive evaluation framework that supports assessment of various quality attributes across all phases and products of the software development cycle, enables analysis of relations between design drivers and quality attributes, and provides a measurement toolset for various parallel and distributed software quality characteristics is described.

Keywords: quality assessment, iterative development, software quality improvement

1.   INTRODUCTION

As modern software applications become more reliant on parallel execution and physical distribution of their components, attaining excellence in final product quality gets more challenging to software developers. There are two aspects of concern: *quality of design*, and *quality of conformance*. Quality of design is the degree of excellence to which the product is designed. Quality of conformance is the degree of excellence to which the product conforms to user expectations. In general, software development is *iterative* – evaluations and development/improvement decisions are repeatedly performed until a satisfactory level of quality can be achieved (see Figure 1). Strategies for improvement decisions require substantial support from various frameworks and tool-sets. There are three broad classes of such settlements: software design tools, quality measurement tools and quality assurance tools. Software *design tools* typically support some CASE methodology. Examples include *PARallel Software Engineering (PARSE)* project [3], or *Software Engineering for Parallel Processing (SEPP)* project [2]. Software *quality measurement tools*, such as *Statistica* provide packages for quality checking, process analysis and statistical evaluation, or as *COCOMO*, support cost estimation in software development. Software *quality assurance tools* implement common quality improvement methodolo-

Figure 1   Steps of a distributed application development

gies, for example *Personal Software Process (PSP)* [4] or *Capability Maturity Model (CMM)* [4].

This paper refers to the *Quality Evaluation of Software Applications (QESA)* model, which integrates various aspects of quality across all phases and products of software development [4]. An important feature of QESA is warehousing relevant quality data from past projects in specially defined *Quality Evaluation Document (QED)* archives. The corresponding QESA toolset is particularly useful in the iterative development of parallel and distributed software, as already demonstrated in several commercial application systems for collaborative computing and distributed database management.

2.   QUALITY ANALYSIS METHODOLOGY

Quality evaluation model used by QESA is a tree representing a hierarchy of quality parameters, like the example one shown in Figure 2.

Figure 2   An example quality tree

The tree root corresponds to a general quality assessment, implied by lower level parameters: from the top level *attributes*, through *characteristics* down to measurable *metrics*. Attributes, such as *functionality* or *performance*, are represented by just a few discrete values (grades) from a certain range. Characteristics, such as *complexity* or *execution time*, are represented as functions that describe complex relationships in a multidimensional space of measurable values, while metrics represent points in that space and indicate concrete measured values. A degree to which each measurable characteristic can contribute to a given attribute's grade is determined by a *translation* function. A degree to which values of concrete metrics affect the respective characteristics is also determined by the relevant translation functions. Translation functions, along with attributes, characteristics and metrics can be interactively selected by evaluators from a generic set by using the QESA toolset, in a process known as the model *calibration*. This is similar to the concept of model calibration in COCOMO – the more aspects of the evaluated phase product are taken into account by the evaluator the more accurate estimates can be. This in turn is determined by the ability to collect a sufficiently large set of measured values.

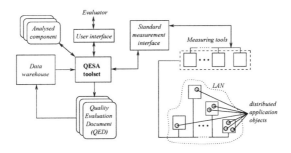

Figure 3   The QESA toolset

General architecture of the QESA toolset is shown in Figure 3. The user (evaluator) can interactively perform experiments for both *measurement* and *evaluation* purposes. Measurement experiments involve selection of appropriate metrics and the usage of specialized tools for measuring concrete values [4] of a given application model as a set of objects located on network nodes. These tools can be either used on-line, via the regular QESA user interface, or run as stand-alone applications. Data collected by them are passed through the specially defined standard measuring interface, for *normalization*, i.e., mapping of the actual (measured) values onto the $< 0, 1 >$ range. Normalized values of metrics are then *composed* into resultant metrics that contribute in some pre-defined way to the characteristics or attributes of the two upper levels of the tree. Details of each particular normalization and composition are recorded as entries in the respective *Quality Evaluation Document (QED)*.

3.   CASE STUDIES AND CONCLUSIONS

The QESA methodology has been used for several industrial distributed OO applications based on the client-server model. We use different *computational environments*, including configuration of individual workstations, as well as the connecting LAN, and utilize various *programming platforms*, including the language (C++, Java), application architecture (CORBA objects), and supporting libraries (processing, communication and API). Based on *iterative development steps* we evaluate applied design methodology and different versions of obtained products.

It shall be noted that the designer and the evaluator are both interested in obtaining a product of a final quality conforming to a certain predefined level. In achieving that, the designer will look for so called design drivers, being a set of alternative aspects of the product design that could be changed to imply the *desired* product quality. At the same time, the evaluator will look for a set of quality attributes that could be assessed to measure the *actual* product quality. Unfortunately, for parallel and distributed software applications this leads often to a non-solvable multi-criterial decision problem. For example, the selection of an object oriented platform, say CORBA, contributes to the flexibility attribute, but at the same time reduces the range of available communication protocols. On the other hand, objects may have a dedicated diagnostic interface and their management is considered more reliable then in other, non-object oriented platforms. In consequence, the drivers' positive impact on dependability, is negative on performance, as management of objects consumes usually a non-negligible portion of the computational power of hardware platforms. Therefore a broad compromise should be found. Our experience with QESA confirms the tendency of modern software systems to require a growing amount of experimentation in their development, as already indicated by Basili et. al [1]. Equally important is the fact that distributed applications require in each case an individual approach. This may imply that in the near future the classic concept of a CASE tool, supporting a specific development methodology commonly believed to be a major vehicle for developing high quality software product of some corresponding class of applications will evolve into less imperative *recommender system*, proposing to the user alternative solutions and using some form of interaction with the user to negotiate a consensus solution.

References

[1] V.R. Basili, F. Shull, and F. Lanubile. Building knowledge through families of experiments. *IEEE TSE*, 25(4):456–473, 1999.

[2] J.C. Cunha, P. Kacsuk, and S. Winter, editors. *Parallel Program Development for Cluster Computing*. Nova Science, 2000. (to appear).

[3] I.E. Jelly and I. Gorton. The PARSE project. In I. Jelly, I. Gorton, and P. Croll, editors, *Software Engineering for Parallel and Distributed Systems*, pages 271–276. Chapman and Hall, London, 1996.

[4] H. Krawczyk and B. Wiszniewski. *Analysis and Testing of Distributed Software Applications*. Research Studies Press, Baldock, Hertfordshire, UK, 1998.

PERFORMANCE TECHNOLOGY FOR COMPLEX PARALLEL AND DISTRIBUTED SYSTEMS

Allen D. Malony, Sameer Shende
Department of Computer and Information Science
University of Oregon, Eugene, OR, USA
{malony,sameer}@cs.uoregon.edu

Abstract   The ability of performance technology to keep pace with the growing complexity of parallel and distributed systems will depend on robust performance frameworks that can at once provide system-specific performance capabilities and support high-level performance problem solving. The TAU system is offered as an example framework that meets these requirements. With a flexible, modular instrumentation and measurement system, and an open performance data and analysis environment, TAU can target a range of complex performance scenarios. Examples are given showing the diversity of TAU application.

Keywords: performance tools, complex systems, instrumentation, measurement, analysis

1.   INTRODUCTION

Modern parallel and distributed computing systems present both a complex execution environment and a complex software environment that target a broad set of applications with a range of requirements and goals, including high-performance, scalability, heterogeneous resource access, component interoperability, and responsive interaction. The execution environment complexity is being fueled by advances in processor technology, shared memory integration, clustering architectures, and high-speed inter-machine communication. At the same time, sophisticated software systems are being developed to manage the execution complexity in a way that makes available the potential power of parallel and distributed platforms to the different application needs.

Fundamental to the development and use of parallel and distributed systems is the ability to observe, analyze, and understand their performance at different levels of system implementation, with different performance data and detail, for different application types, and across alternative system and software environments [5]. However, the growing complexity of parallel and distributed systems challenge the ability of performance technologists to produce tools and methods that are at once robust and ubiquitous. On the one hand, the sophistication of the computing environment demands a tight integration of performance observation (instrumentation and measurement) technology optimized to capture the requisite information about the system under performance access, accuracy, and granularity constraints. Different systems will require different observation capabilities and technology implementations specific to system features. Otherwise restricting technology to only a few performance observation modes severely limits performance problem solving in these complex environments. On the other hand, application development environments present programming abstractions that hide the complexity of the underlying computing system, and are mapped onto layered, hierarchical runtime software optimized for different system platforms. While providing application portability, a programming paradigm also defines an implicit model of performance that is made explicit in a particular system context. System-specific performance data must be mapped to abstract, high-level views appropriate to the performance model. The difficult problem is to provide such a performance abstraction uniformly across the different computing systems where the programming paradigm may be applied. This requires not only a rich set of observation capabilities that can provide consistent relevant performance information, but a high degree of flexibility in how tools are configured and integrated to access and analyze this information. Without this ability, common performance problem solving methodologies and tools that support them will not be available.

In this paper, we propose an approach to performance technology development for complex parallel and distributed systems based on a general complex systems computation model and a modular performance observation and analysis framework. The computation model, discussed in Section 2, defines a hierarchical execution architecture reflecting dominant features of modern systems and the layers of software available. In Section 3, we present the TAU performance framework as an example of a flexible, configurable, and extensible performance tool system for instrumentation, measurement, and analysis. TAU's ability to address complex system performance requirements is demonstrated in Section 4 using examples drawn from MPI, multi-threading, and combined task/data parallelism performance studies. We conclude the paper with an outlook towards open performance technology as a plan for developing next-generation performance tools.

2.   A GENERAL COMPUTATION MODEL

To address the dual goals of performance technology for complex systems – robust performance capabilities and widely available performance problem solving methodologies – we need to contend with problems of system diversity while providing flexibility in tool composition, configuration, and integration. One approach to address these issues is to focus attention on a sub-class of computation models and performance problems as a way to restrict the performance technology requirements. The obvious consequence of this approach is limited tool coverage. Instead, our idea is to define an abstract computation model that captures general architecture and software execution features and can be mapped straightforwardly to existing complex system types. For this model, we can target performance capabilities and create a tool framework that can adapt and be optimized for particular complex system cases.

Our choice of general computation model must reflect real computing environments. The computational model we target was initially proposed by the HPC++ consortium [3]. In this model, a *node* is defined as a physically distinct machine with one or more processors sharing a physical memory system (i.e., a shared memory multiprocessor). A node may link to other nodes via a protocol-based interconnect, ranging from proprietary networks, as found in traditional MPPs, to local- or global-area networks. A *context* is a distinct virtual address space residing within a node. Multiple contexts may exist on a single node. Multiple *threads* of execution, both user and system level, may exist within a context; threads within a context share the same virtual address space.

3.   TAU FRAMEWORK

The computation model above is general enough to apply to many high-performance architectures as well as to different parallel programming paradigms. Particular instances of the model and how it is programmed defines requirements for performance tool technology. For any performance problem, a performance framework to address the problem should incorporate:

- an *instrumentation model* defining how and when performance information is made available;
- a *performance measurement model* defining what performance information is captured and in what form;
- an *execution model* that relates measured events with each other;
- a *data analysis model* specifying how data is to be processed;
- a *presentation model* for performance viewing; and
- an *integration model* describing how performance tool components are configured and integrated.

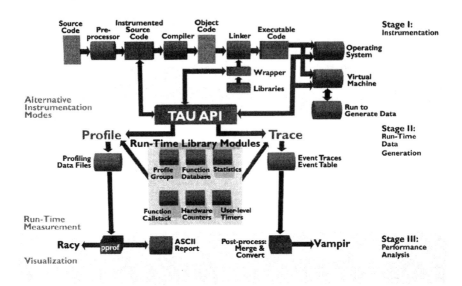

Figure 1   Architecture of TAU

We have developed the TAU performance framework as an integrated toolkit for performance instrumentation, measurement, and analysis for parallel, multithreaded programs that attempts to target the general complex system computation model while allowing flexible customization for system-specific needs.

The TAU performance framework [10] is shown in Figure 1. It is composed of instrumentation, measurement, and visualization phases. TAU supports a flexible instrumentation model that allows the user to insert performance instrumentation calling the TAU measurement API at several levels of program compilation and execution stages. The instrumentation identifies code segments, provides mapping abstractions, and supports multi-threaded and message passing parallel execution models. Instrumentation can be inserted manually, or automatically with a source-to-source translation tool [13]. When the instrumented application is compiled and executed, profiles or event traces are produced. TAU can use wrapper libraries to perform instrumentation when source code is unavailable for instrumentation. Instrumentation can also be inserted at runtime, using the dynamic instrumentation system DynInst [7], or at the virtual machine level, using language supplied interfaces such as the Java Virtual Machine Profiler interface [11].

The instrumentation model interfaces with the measurement model. TAU's measurement model is sub-divided into a high-level performance model that determines how events are processed and a low-level measurement model that determines what system attributes are measured. The measurement captures data for functions, methods, basic blocks, and statement execution. Profiling and tracing are the two measurement choices that TAU provides. The API lets measurement *groups* be defined for organizing and controlling instrumentation. The measurement library also supports the mapping of low-level execution measurements to high-level execution entities (e.g., data parallel statements) so that performance data can be properly assigned. Performance experiments can be composed from different measurement modules, including ones that can measure the wall-clock time, the cpu time, or processor specific activity using non-intrusive hardware performance monitors available on most modern processors; TAU can access both PCL [9] and PAPI [14] portable hardware counter interfaces. Based on the composition of modules, an experiment could easily be configured to measure the profile that shows the inclusive and exclusive counts of secondary data cache misses associated with basic blocks such as routines, or a group of statements. By providing a flexible measurement infrastructure, a user can experiment with different attributes of the system and iteratively refine the performance of a parallel application.

The TAU data analysis and presentation models are open. Although TAU comes with both text-based and graphical tools to visualize the performance data collected in the previous stage, it provides bridges to other third-party tools such as Vampir [8] for more sophisticated analysis and visualization. The performance data format is documented and TAU provides tools that illustrate how this data can be converted to other formats.

An important component of the performance model presented in a tool is how its integration model provides composition and integration of its different components. The modules must provide well defined interfaces that are easy to extend. The nature and extent of co-operation between modules that may be vertically and horizontally integrated in the distinct layers defines the degree of flexibility of the measurement system.

4.   SELECTED SCENARIOS

Our premise is that TAU can provide a robust and widely applicable performance technology framework for complex parallel and distributed systems. This section presents brief selected performance scenarios that demonstrate that TAU can offer effective technology across complex systems types. We begin with an MPI example showing how communication events are instrumented and performance measured and visualized with respect to other application events. We then discuss multi-threaded applications and the techniques we have developed for Java. The main point to highlight is TAU's ability to support different high-level performance problem solving requirements via system specific instrumentation, measurement, and analysis.

4.1   Distributed Systems and MPI

A common approach to enabling instrumentation in libraries is to define a wrapper library that encapsulates the functionality of the underlying library by inserting instrumentation calls before and after calls to the native routines. The MPI Profiling Interface [6] is a good example of this approach. This interface allows a tool developer to interface with MPI calls without modifying the application source code, and in a portable manner that does not require a vendor to supply the proprietary source code of the library implementation. A performance tool can provide an interposition library layer that intercepts calls to the native MPI library by defining routines with the same name (such as *MPI_Send*). These routines can then call the name-shifted native library routines provided by the MPI profiling interface (such as *PMPI_Send*). Wrapped around the call is performance instrumentation. The exposure of routine arguments allows the tool developer to track the size of messages, identify message tags or invoke other native library routines, for example, to track the sender and the size of a received message, within a wild-card receive call.

Requiring that such profiling hooks be provided in the standardized library before an implementation is considered "compliant", forms the basis of an excellent model for developing portable performance profiling tools for the library. TAU and several other tools (e.g., Upshot [1] and Vampir [8]) use the MPI profiling interface for tracing. However, TAU can also utilize a rich set of measurement modules that allow profiles to be captured with various types of performance data, including system and hardware data. In addition, TAU's performance grouping capabilities allows MPI event to be presented with respect to high-level categories such as send and receive types.

4.2   Multi-Threaded Systems and Java

Multi-threaded systems and applications present a more complex environment for performance tools due to the different forms and levels of threading and the greater need for efficient instrumentation. How to determine thread identity, how to store per-thread performance data, and how to provide synchronized and consistent update and access to the data are some of the questions that must be addressed. TAU provides modules that interface with system-specific thread libraries and provide member functions for thread registration, thread identification, and mutual exclusion for locking and unlocking the performance data. This allows the measurement system to work with different thread packages such as pthreads, Windows threads, Java threads, as well as special-purpose thread libraries such as SMARTS [15] and Tulip [2], while maintaining a common measurement model. Because TAU targets a general threading model, it can extend its common thread layer to provide well-defined core functionality for each new thread system.

We chose the Java language to demonstrate TAU's application in multi-thread systems since it utilizes both user-level and system-level threads and involves the additional complexity of virtual machine execution. The Java 2 virtual machine provides event callback hooks in the form of the Java Virtual Machine Profiler Interface (JVMPI) [11]. TAU uses JVMPI for performance instrumentation and measurement. The TAU measurement library is compiled into a dynamic shared object which is loaded in the address space of the virtual machine. An initialization routine specifies a mapping of events that are of interest to the performance system and registers a TAU interface that will be called when the events occur. When an event is triggered, event specific information is passed to the TAU interface routine by the virtual machine. TAU identifies the thread in which the event takes place and uses the Java thread interface to maintain per-thread performance data. TAU classifies all method names and their signatures into higher level profile group names. In Figure 2 we see the profile of per-thread execution for different methods and groups. Notice that some of the threads (0-3) are performing system functions for the JVM while others (4, 5, and 9) are performing user tasks. Profile (as shown) and tracing performance measurements can be made and reported.

4.3   Hybrid Parallel Systems

Increasingly, scalable parallel systems are being designed as clusters of shared memory multi-processors (SMPs), with MPI or some other inter-process communication paradigm used for message passing between SMP nodes, and thread-based shared memory programming used within the SMP. Runtime systems are built to hide the intricacies of efficient communication, presenting a compiler backend or an application programmer with a set of well-defined, portable interfaces. Performance measurement and analysis tools must embed the hierarchical, hybrid execution model of the application within their performance model. Because TAU supports a general parallel computation model, it can configure the measurement system to capture both thread and communication performance information. However, this information must be mapped to the programming model. We have used TAU to investigate task and data parallel execution in the Opus/HPF programming system [4]. Figure 3 shows a Vampir display of TAU traces generated from an application written using HPF for data parallelism and Opus for task parallelism. The HPF compiler produces Fortran 90 data parallel modules which execute on multiple processes. The processes interoperate using the Opus runtime system built on MPI and pthreads. In systems of this type, it is important to be able to see the influence of different software levels. TAU is able to capture performance data at different parts of the Opus/HPF system exposing the bottlenecks within and between levels.

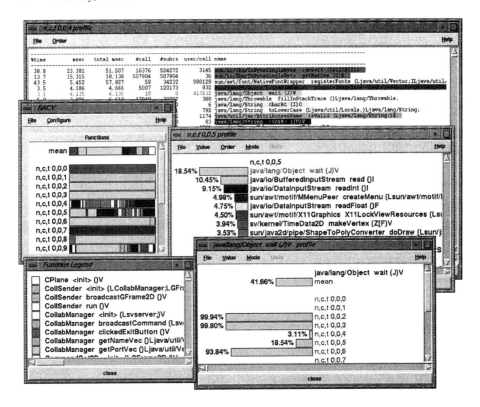

Figure 2   TAU profiles a multi-threaded Java visualization application using JVMPI

5.   CONCLUSIONS

To be at once robust and ubiquitous, TAU attempts to solve performance technology problems at levels where performance analysis system solutions can be configured and integrated to target specific performance problem solving needs. TAU has been developed based on the principle that performance technology should be open, easy to extend, and able to leverage external functionality. The complex system case studies presented here is but a small sample of the range of TAU's potential application [12].

In rapidly evolving parallel and distributed systems, performance technology can ill-afford to stand still. A performance technologist always operates under a set of constraints as well as under a set of expectations. While performance evaluation of a system is directly affected by what constraints the system imposes on performance instrumentation and measurement capabilities, the desire for performance problem solving tools that are common and portable, now and into the future, suggests that performance tools hardened and customized for a particular system platform will be short-lived, with limited utility. Similarly, performance tools designed for constrained parallel execution models

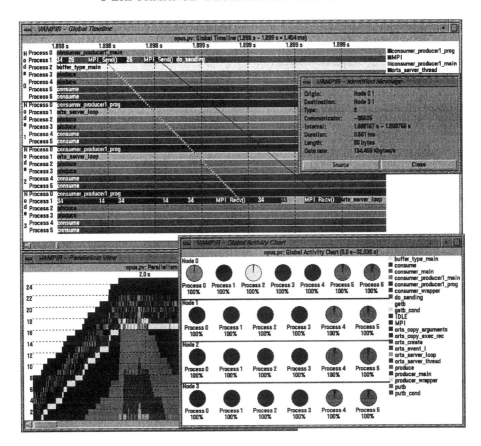

Figure 3   Vampir displays for TAU traces of an Opus/HPF application using MPI and pthread

will likely have little use to more general parallel and distributed computing paradigms. Unless performance technology evolves with system technology, a chasm will remain between the users expectations and the capabilities that performance tools provide. The challenge for the TAU system in the future is to maintain a highly configurable tool architecture while not arbitrarily enforcing constraining technology boundaries.

Acknowledgments

This work was supported in part by the U.S. Department of Energy, DOE2000 grant #DEFC0398ER259986.

References

[1]   Argonne National Laboratory, "The Upshot program visualization system," URL: http://www-fp.mcs.anl.gov/Ïusk/upshot/.

[2] P. Beckman, D. Gannon, "Tulip: A Portable Run-Time System for Object Parallel Systems," Proceedings of the 10th International Parallel Processing Symposium, August 1996.

[3] HPC++ Working Group, "HPC++ White Papers," Technical Report TR 95633, Center for Research on Parallel Computation, 1995.

[4] E. Laure, P. Mehrotra, H. Zima, "Opus: Heterogeneous Computing With Data Parallel Tasks," Parallel Processing Letters, 9(2):275–289, June 1999.

[5] A. Malony, "Tools for Parallel Computing: A Performance Evaluation Perspective," Handbook on Parallel and Distributed Processing, (Eds. J. Blazewicz, K. Ecker, B. Plateau, D. Trystram); Springer, pp. 342–363, 2000.

[6] Message Passing Interface Forum, "MPI: A Message Passing Interface Standard," International Journal of Supercomputer Applications, Special issue on MPI. 8:3/4, 1994.

[7] B. Miller, M. Callaghan, J. Cargille, J. Hollingsworth, R. Irvin, K. Karavanic, K. Kunchithapadam, and T. Newhall. "The Paradyn Parallel Performance Measurement Tools", IEEE Computer, 28(11):37–46, Nov. 1995.

[8] Pallas, "VAMPIR - Visualization and Analysis of MPI Resources," 2000. URL: http://www.pallas.de/pages/vampir.htm.

[9] Research Center Juelich GmbH, "PCL - The Performance Counter Library," URL: http://www.fz-juelich.de/zam/PCL/.

[10] S. Shende, A. Malony, J. Cuny, K. Lindlan, P. Beckman, S. Karmesin, "Portable Profiling and Tracing for Parallel Scientific Applications using C++", Proc. of the SIGMETRICS Symposium on Parallel and Distributed Tools, pp. 134–145, ACM, August 1998.

[11] Sun Microsystems, "Java Virtual Machine Profiler Interface (JVMPI)," URL: http://java.sun.com/products/jdk/1.3/docs/guide/jvmpi/jvmpi.html.

[12] University of Oregon, "Tuning and Analysis Utilities," URL: http://www.cs.uoregon.edu/research/paracomp/tau/.

[13] University of Oregon, "Program Database Toolkit," URL: http://www.cs.uoregon.edu/research/paracomp/pdtoolkit.

[14] University of Tennessee, "PerfAPI - Performance Data Standard and API," URL: http://icl.cs.utk.edu/projects/papi/.

[15] S. Vajracharya, S. Karmesin, P. Beckman, J. Crotinger, A. Malony, S. Shende, R. Oldehoeft, S. Smith, "SMARTS: Exploiting Temporal Locality and Parallelism through Vertical Execution," Los Alamos National Laboratory, Technical Report LA-UR-99-16, 1999.

[16] Sun Microsystems Inc. "The JAVA HotSpot Performance Engine Architecture," Sun Microsystems White Paper, April 1999. http://java.sun.com/products/hotspot/whitepaper.html

EVALUATING PERFORMANCE OF OPENMP AND MPI ON THE SGI ORIGIN 2000 WITH BENCHMARKS OF REALISTIC PROBLEM SIZES

Csaba K. Zoltani[1], Punyam Satya-narayana, Dixie Hisley
Computational and Information Sciences Directorate
High Performance Computing Division
U.S. Army Research Lab
Aberdeen Proving Ground, MD 21005
zoltani@arl.mil

Abstract   Six applications benchmarks, including four NAS codes, provided by H. Jin and J. Wu, previously parallelized using OpenMP, and message-passing-interface (MPI), were run on a 128-processor SGI Origin 2000. Detailed profile data was collected to understand the factors causing imperfect scalability. Our results show that load imbalance and cost of remote accesses are the main factors in limited speed-up of the OpenMP versions, whereas communication costs are the single major factor in the performance of the MPI versions.

Key words: benchmarking, OpenMP, MPI, parallel computing performance

1.   INTRODUCTION

Over the last years, several portable mechanisms for developing parallel programs have been standardized. This set includes relatively low-level libraries like the Message-Passing-Interface (MPI), parallelization directives like OpenMP, and higher level languages including High-Performance Fortran (HPF). Unlike the use of vendor-specific libraries and compiler directives, these libraries and language extensions are supported on a large number of systems. At the same time, Distributed Shared Memory (DSM) systems are emerging as an important class of

---

[1] See acknowledgement. All correspondence should be sent to: zoltani@arl.mil

parallel machines. This includes both the hardware distributed shared memory systems like the SGI Origin 2000 and software distributed shared memory systems like Treadmarks. The main advantage of such systems is that the programmers have the option of programming them using either a shared memory or message passing paradigm or both.

In this paper, we present an experimental study to answer the questions: what are the main obstacles (among factors like communication costs, false sharing, synchronization costs etc.) in achieving scalable performance through each of the paradigms? Though answers have been attempted, the issue remains contentious [3]. We use six benchmark programs, including four NAS codes and two irregular CFD codes. We examine the performance of OpenMP, and MPI versions of these programs on a 128-processor Origin 2000. Besides comparing the scalability of these versions, we use hardware counter-based performance data to understand the difference between the performance of different versions and the reasons for imperfect scalability.

The paper consists of the following. In Section 2, we explain the programming environments and benchmarks used for our experimental study. The results from our experiments are presented and analyzed in Section 3, and conclusions are presented in Section ..

2.   PROGRAMMING ENVIRONMENT

2.1   Origin 2000

The Origin 2000 is a DSM architecture. The machine utilized for this study is part of the U.S. Army Research Laboratory's (ARL) Major Shared Resource Center (MSRC) supercomputing assets. The largest configuration available is comprised of 128 nodes. Each processor has 1 GB of local memory. Each processor is a MIPS R12000 64-bit CPU running at 300 MHz with two 32-KB primary caches and one 8-MB secondary cache. The older R10000 64-bit chips ran at 195 MHz with two 32-KB primary caches and one 4-MB secondary cache.

An interesting aspect of the Origin 2000 system is its capability for reporting detailed profile information to the application programmers. The MIPS R12000 and the older R10000 are two of the very few systems in which the hardware counters are made visible to the end-users of the machine. A small set of events is monitored by the hardware counters, including cache misses, memory coherence operations, floating point operations, and branch mispredictions. Because this monitoring is done in hardware rather than software, it is possible to extract detailed information about the state of the system without affecting the behavior of the program being monitored.

Table 1 Using Event Counts for Performance Problem Identification

performance problem	event count
load imbalance	no. of floating point ops issued per process is not comparable
excessive synchronization	number of store conditionals is high
false sharing	number of store exclusives to a shared block is high
cache unfriendly	L1 and L2 cache misses are high

In our study, profiling data is collected by running the codes with *perfex*, a profiling tool which reports a count for the 32 countable event types, with no modifications to the targeted program and with only a minimal effect on its execution time. We focused on the subset of event counts that are indicative of specific performance inhibitors to scalability. Table 1 shows the performance inhibitors that we examined, and the corresponding event counts that were used to evaluate those potential problems.

2.2   Parallel Programming Environments

For this study, we concentrated on using OpenMP as the mechanism for shared memory programming. The Origin 2000 can also be programmed as a message-passing machine using MPI, which, like OpenMP, is portable across a number of platforms. We used the MipsPro 7.2.1 compiler and compiled the applications with f77 using aggressive optimizations (-O3 flag).

2.3   Benchmarks and Problem Sizes

We have focused our study of OpenMP on four of the NAS Parallel Benchmarks (NPB) which are most relevant to the Army's applications and two additional benchmarks which we call IRREG and LES. The NPB set was developed by the Numerical Aerodynamic Simulation (NAS) program at NASA Ames Research Center for the performance evaluation of parallel computing systems [1]. The NPB mimic the computation and data movement characteristics of large-scale computational fluid dynamics (CFD) applications. In this study, we focused on three simulated application codes (LU, SP, and BT), and one kernel CG.

The assumption is that MPI can give the run with the least amount of computing time requirement. The NAS optimized MPI version of the four kernels tested were then the basis for comparison. In our study, MPI implementations of the benchmarks were obtained from the NPB 2.3 NAS website. The rationale behind the PBN versions given by the working team, is to provide the community with an optimized version of NPB 2.3-serial and a sample OpenMP implementation. The NPB and PBN versions specify three problem sizes for the benchmarks. This paper focuses on the Class B problem sizes, as they are the closest in size to realistic problem sizes, as defined by the applications commonly run at the ARL. Table 2 shows the problem sizes for Class A, Class B, and Class C for each benchmark. A comparison in processing times between Class B and C is given in Figure 5.

Another benchmark we have been focusing on is the Large Eddy Simulation (LES) [4]. LES can be used to characterize turbulent flow, where large length scales signifiy the domain size and small length-scales represent dissipative eddies. Although small scales are modeled due to their isotropic nature, high performance computing resources are required to capture the large energy carrying length scales. In this paper, a vectorized simulation code is optimized and parallelized for Origin 2000 performance. A realistic simulation of flow past a backward-facing step with problem size of 32 x 32 x 32 is used to study scaling behavior. Periodic boundary conditions are applied in the stream-wise and span-wise directions.

Table 2. NPB Problem Sizes (No. of elements)

Benchmark Code	Class A	Class B	Class C
Block Tridiagonal (BT)	64^3	102^3	162^3
LU Solver (LU)	64^3	102^3	162^3
Pentadiagonal Solver	64^3	102^3	162^3
Conjugate Gradient (CG)	12,000	75,000	150,000

The second non-NAS benchmark we have been examining is IRREG [2]. IRREG is abstracted from a computational fluid dynamics application that uses unstructured meshes to model a physical problem. The mesh is represented by nodes, edges that connect two nodes, and faces that connect three or four nodes. For the realistic submarine mesh used in our benchmark runs, the number of nodes, edges, and faces were 92564, 623003, and 504947, respectively.

3.   EXPERIMENTAL RESULTS

In this section, we first present our comparison of the performance of OpenMP and MPI versions of four NAS codes and two irregular CFD codes using OpenMP.

3.1   Comparing OpenMP and MPI Performance

The performance for OpenMP and MPI versions of CG, LU, BT, and SP are shown in Figures 1 and 2. The plots show wall-clock time as a function of the number of processors. In general, two observations can be made from these four plots.

Reasonably good scalability is achieved when up to 64 processors for all of the eight programs (2 versions for each of 4 benchmarks) are used. The speedup starts leveling off for configurations beyond 64 processors, which shows that problem sizes in NAS Class B data sets are not suitable for parallelization on a very   large

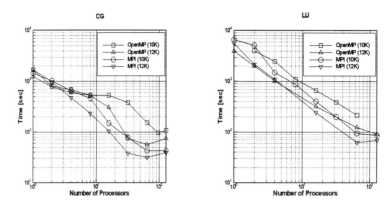

Figure 1. Scalability of OpenMP and MPI Versions of CG and LU

number of processors. For three of the four applications, MPI achieves better performance than the OpenMP versions. The MPI versions are significantly faster for LU and CG, slightly better on large configurations for SP, and slightly slower on BT.

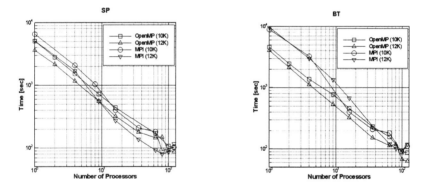

Figure 2. Scalability of OpenMP and MPI Versions of SP and BT

Of this set of benchmarks, using the R10K chip, the poorest speedups are achieved for CG. On 128 processors, the OpenMP version achieves a speedup of 14. A slightly higher speedup of 15 is achieved at the 64-processor configuration. The performance of the MPI version of CG is significantly better on 16, 32, 64, and 128 processors. On both the 64- and 128-processor configurations, the MPI version achieves a speedup of 43. For LU, OpenMP scales reasonably well until 64 processors, achieving a speedup of 32. The MPI version has significantly better speedup again, achieving a factor of 80 on 128 processors. For BT, OpenMP achieves a speedup of nearly 50 on 128 processors. The speedup of the MPI version is only 30. It should be noted that the 1- processor version of MPI performs much worse as compared to the OpenMP sequential version of this code. The results from

MPI and OpenMP are the closest in the case of SP. Speedup of nearly 50 is achieved on 121 processors for both the versions.[2]

We now discuss how profiling data from *perfex* can be used to determine the reasons for imperfect scalability and the differences in performance of OpenMP and MPI versions of the programs. For a shared memory program run on a distributed shared memory architecture, the following factors usually contribute to lower than ideal speedup: load imbalance, which implies that the work in parallelized loops is not evenly distributed among the processors and synchronization costs, which denote the time spent by the processors in coordinating the progress of the computation among themselves. False sharing occurs when two or more processors access different variables that happen to be co-located on the same cache block, with at least one of the accesses being a write. Once the write occurs, the entire cache line is invalidated to other processors. Remote accesses, which means there are frequent references to off-processor data, which are expensive, as compared to references to local data.

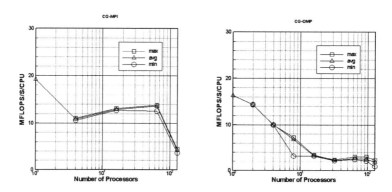

Figure 3. Max, Average, and Min MFlops Across All Procs for OpenMP and MPI for CG

For the message-passing versions, the two common causes of imperfect speedup are communication costs and load imbalance. Since SPMD (Single Program Multiple Data) versions of programs are run and there is no shared memory support, false sharing and synchronization costs do not occur. For each of the eight programs for which we have presented scalability numbers, we analyzed hardware counter data obtained from *perfex*. For all OpenMP programs, the event counts and typical times obtained for synchronization and false sharing were extremely low (less than three seconds), even for the highest number of processors used. In general, a good level of cache friendliness was seen for all programs except CG. Cache friendliness was examined by looking at the average L1 and L2 cache hit rates returned by perfex. L2 cache hits rates were consistently higher than 0.9 for each of the eight programs, and L1 cache hit rates were also greater than 0.9 for all programs

---

[2] This code was executed on 121 processors because it required a square number of processors.

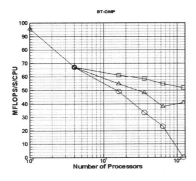
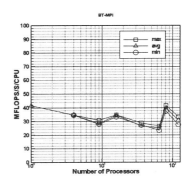

Figure 4. Max, Average, and Min MFlops Across All Procs for OpenMP and MPI for BT

except CG. CG is an irregular code, and, therefore poor L1 locality is achieved. The load imbalance issue was examined by looking at the number of floating point operations performed over different processors in each run. A load balanced program will have very similar numbers for the number of floating point operations performed across all processors. In Figure 3, we show the same data for OpenMP and MPI versions of CG. Detailed data from LU and SP is not presented here, but trends are explained later. In Figure 4, we show the minimum, maximum, and average number of cycles spent on floating point operations across all processors on the OpenMP and MPI versions of BT. The increase in range with increasing number of processors suggests a problem with load balancing.

The difference in the number of floating point operations between different processors explains the limited speedup (50 times on 128 processors) of the OpenMP version of BT. The results are very different from the MPI version of the same code. For the OpenMP version the load is evenly balanced between different processors on all processor configurations. Interestingly, the OpenMP version gives overall better performance than the MPI version of BT. A possible explanation for poor performance of the MPI version is the high communication costs.

The performance of the OpenMP version can be further improved by better work distribution. The program typically has nested loops where the number of iterations across each dimension is 102 (for Class B). The loop-level parallelized OpenMP version achieves parallelism across only a single dimension, so there is no way of using more than 102 processors. Possibly, by using additional directives or by using SPMD-style OpenMP parallelism, the performance of the OpenMP version of BT can be enhanced.

Similar trends are seen from CG. Excellent load balance is demonstrated by the MPI version leading to good performance. Load imbalance can be seen for the OpenMP version, though it is not as severe as in the case of BT. Because of the irregular accesses in this code, the high cost of frequent nonlocal references is likely to be another important factor behind limited speedup. Unfortunately, *perfex* does not provide a mechanism for accurately measuring the number of nonlocal references. Also, remote references can be aggregated in message-passing versions, which is not possible in a shared memory version.

In the case of SP, the OpenMP version achieves good load balance on 100 processors. The number of floating point operations performed by each processor only ranges from 21.21 x 10^6 per second to 18.81 x 10^6 per second. However, on 121 processors, some of the processors do not get any work, for similar reasons as BT. Good load balance for the OpenMP version explains why the performance of the OpenMP and MPI versions is very similar.

With LU, significant load imbalance is observed with OpenMP. On 64 processors, the number of floating point ops performed by each processor ranges from 29.63 x 10^6 to 14.03 x 10^6 per second. The load imbalance for the OpenMP versions explains the difference in the performance of OpenMP and MPI versions.

3.2   Communication Cost Issues

The performance of the benchmark BT under MPI lagged that under OpenMP, (see Figure 2). To understand the issues involved, VAMPIR and VAMPIRTRACE, parallel processing tools from Pallas GmbH, were run. The tools give a breakdown of time spent for different tasks, including MPI, and also identifies load imbalances. Runs were made with 16, 36, and 64 processors. In the latter, 65% of the total processing time was spent on MPI. The MPI runs also showed that load imbalance was present, i.e., only 9 of the processors in the 64 processor case were actually 50% occupied by the application, while in 17 of the processors this figure was less than 25%. Improving MPI processing is feasible, but was not attempted here.

3.3   OpenMP Implementation of Irregular CFD Codes

Both of the non-NAS benchmarks, LES and IRREG, were parallelized using the SPMD style of OpenMP that relies heavily on domain decomposition. While domain decomposition can result in a coarse grain program exhibiting good scalability, it does transfer the responsibility of decomposition from the compiler to the programmer. Once the problem domain is decomposed, the same sequential algorithm is followed but is modified to handle the multiple subdomains. The program is replicated on each thread, but has different extents for the subdomains. Also, data that is local to a subdomain (not shared globally) is specified as private or thread-private. Thread-private is used for subdomain data that need file scope or are used in common blocks. Also, message passing is replaced by shared data that can be read by any thread.

For LES, initialization of the data is parallelized using one parallel region for better data locality among active processors. The main computational kernel is embedded in the time-advancing loop. The time loop is treated sequentially, and the kernel itself is parallelized using another parallel region. In this parallel region, the

32 x 32 x 32 mesh is blocked in the z-direction, and each block is tasked to a different processor.

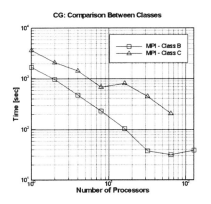
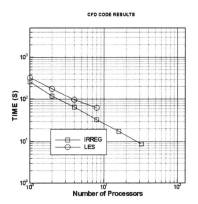

*Figure 5.*Timing for MPI Version of CG for Classes B and C, 12K Chip

Figure 6. Performance of OpenMP of LES and IRREG with the R10K Chip

The IRREG code contains a series of loops that iterate over nodes, edges, and faces. The loops over edges and faces involve indirect accesses to memory locations, which are difficult to analyze and parallelize in a loop-level sense. However, a parallel version of the code can be accomplished by partitioning the nodes among the processors. The edges and faces are assigned to the processor, that owns a majority of the corresponding nodes. The RCB (Recursive Coordinate Bisection) partitioner used in the code does not optimally minimize the number of cut edges (communication effort) but does attempt to reduce the amount of communication and load balance the computational work. The performance of LES and IRREG is shown in Figure 6. A speedup of 5.1 is obtained on eight processors. In LES, the matrix solver, the most expensive module, is made cache-friendly by optimizing it for single CPU efficiency. Inherent data-dependencies contribute to the imperfect scaling observed for eight processors. For IRREG, we measured the speedup on up to 32 processors. The parallel version again scales quite well, getting a factor of 30.0 on 32 processors. The speedup results obtained from our initial attempts to parallelize IRREG using loop-level parallelization resulted in almost no speedups. Data and work distribution using specialized partitioners was extremely important for the parallel performance of this code, which could not be achieved through directives for loop-level parallelism.

4.   CONCLUSIONS

In this paper, we have conducted experiments to study the performance achieved through shared memory (OpenMP implementations) and message-passing (MPI implementations) paradigms for six benchmark programs with realistic problem sizes, run on a 128-processor Origin 2000 with both the older R10K and the newer R12K chips. Moreover, we analyzed hardware profiling data to understand the reasons for imperfect speedups of these codes.

Our experiments lead to several interesting observations. We obtained somewhat better performance from MPI programs, as compared to the OpenMP. The main factor behind limited scalability of the OpenMP versions was load imbalance. Only the outer loops were parallelized, and on large configurations, not all processors could be kept busy. The second most important performance obstacle for OpenMP versions was the cost of remote references. False sharing and synchronization costs were insignificant for the programs in our benchmark set.

The MPI versions demonstrated excellent load balance with parallelism obtained through domain decomposition. The main factor in the limited scalability of MPI versions was communication costs. In our experience in developing parallel versions of two irregular CFD codes, we found that the SPMD style parallelization facility of OpenMP enables easy and efficient parallelization of these applications.

From this study, we can conclude that programmers need to concentrate on achieving good work distribution while optimizing the performance of OpenMP versions, whereas they need to concentrate on improving communication performance while optimizing the performance of MPI versions. Our conclusions are applicable only to the programs that have similar features to the benchmark programs we have studied.

Acknowledgements: The authors wish to express their thanks to Haoqiang Jin and Jerry Wu, for access to the beta version of the updated NAS benchmarks and for generously sharing their experience. Special thanks go to Gagan Agrawal and Lori Pollock of the University of Delaware for their inputs. This work was supported in part by the DoD High Performance Computer Modernization Program.

References

[1]   D. Bailey, T. Harris, W. Saphir, R. vander Wijngaart, A. Woo, and M. Yarrow. "NAS Parallel Benchmarks 2.0". Technical Report, NASA Ames Research Center, NAS-95-020.

[2]   R. Das, D.J. Mavriplis, J. Saltz, S. Gupta, and R. Ponnusamy. "The Design and Implementation of a Parallel Unstructured Euler Solver using Software Primitives". AIAA Journal, 32(3):489-496, March 1994.

[3]   D. S. Nikolopoulos and T. S. Papatheodorou. "A Comparison of MPI, SHMEM and Cache-coherent Shared Address Space Programming Models on the SGI Origin2000". International Conference on Supercomputing, June 1999.

[4]   W. P. Wang. "Coupled Compressible and Incompressible Finite Volume Formulations of the Large Eddy Simulation of Turbulent Flows with and without Heat Transfer". PhD thesis, Iowa State University, 1995.

PERFORMANCE TUNING OF PARALLEL REAL-TIME VOICE COMMUNICATION SOFTWARE

Hermann Hellwagner[1], Klaus Leopold[1], Ralf Schlatterbeck[2], Carsten Weich[2]
[1]*Institute of Information Technology, University Klagenfurt, Austria,*
{hellwagn,klaus}@itec.uni-klu.ac.at
[2]*Frequentis Nachrichtentechnik GmbH, Vienna, Austria,*
{rschlatt,cweich}@frequentis.com

Abstract This paper describes an unconventional way to apply a performance analysis tool for parallel programs (Vampir) to understand and tune the performance of the real-time voice and data communication software running on top of Frequentis' V4 switch. The execution schedule of the strictly time-triggered V4 switching software is computed off-line; analyzing the schedule to identify e.g. performance bottlenecks used to be a complex and time-consuming process. We present our approach to transform the V4 software schedule's information into Vampir trace files and use this tool's facilities to provide a visualization of the schedule. A case study illustrates the benefits of this approach.

Key words: Parallel programming, performance analysis, communication software, real time, fault tolerance

1. INTRODUCTION

Frequentis has for many years provided switching technology for critical voice communication applications. The latest switch generation, called the *V4 switch*, is a parallel, fault-tolerant, real-time voice and data communication system that can, by virtue of modular hardware and appropriate application software, be customized to applications like air traffic control, command and control centers, and wireless network switching systems.

The multi-tasking real-time operating system as well as protocol processing and application software of the V4 switch strictly adhere to a *time-triggered* execution model. Both processing and communication activities of the software components (threads) are *statically* scheduled. However, if a given V4 switch configuration is being overloaded with software modules, the scheduler may compute a sub-optimal schedule only or may even fail to generate a valid schedule. For such cases, the software engineers may provide hints to the scheduler, e.g. priorities of and dependencies among threads. To identify the causes of scheduling problems or to analyze and tune the performance of their software, the engineers until recently had to inspect the scheduler's *text output*; for the case of hundreds of threads in large-scale applications, this clearly is a highly time-consuming and error-prone task.

This paper describes a simple, yet effective way to *visualize* a V4 switch's static software schedule: the V4 schedule is transformed into the trace file format of one of a well-known graphical performance analysis tools for parallel programs (Vampir), and the tool's various display and trace replay facilities are used to inspect the V4 switch's software behavior. A case study given in this paper will illustrate the benefits of this approach.

2.   FREQUENTIS V4 SWITCH TECHNOLOGY

Switch Architecture. The Frequentis V4 switch is a parallel, fault-tolerant, real-time, digital switch for voice and data communication systems. A detailed description of the V4 switch is given in [3], an overview in [4]. Many of the V4 concepts stem from the MARS project at TU Vienna [5].

The core of the V4 architecture is the *V4 ring* which interconnects up to twelve *nodes* using triple-redundant internal communication lines. Each *node* consists of a *carrier board* and up to four *CPU* or *I/O modules*. CPU modules provide processing power to the V4 switch. I/O modules carry interface and driver circuitry and provide connectors for *adapters* to peripheral devices (e.g. microphones) and external communication lines (e.g. ATM).

Software Concepts. The software basis on the V4 switch comprises the operating system, system services like signal processing tasks (e.g. filters, codecs), device drivers, user channel switching, voice and data communication protocol modules, and application software tasks.

V4 software consists of *processes* which comprise a number of *threads* and exchange *messages* with each other. A thread is *periodically executed*; a single invocation is called a *thread instance*. Thread instances have a simple structure: they usually receive some input messages, perform some computation (without blocking), and produce some output messages.

Scheduling Requirements. Threads are the principal active entities in V4 software systems and thus consume processing power. Similarly, messages arriving from communication lines or peripheral devices or being produced by threads, consume V4 ring bandwidth. Packing these computational and communication activities into a valid real-time execution plan under manifold requirements and resource constraints [4], represents a complex task that the V4 off-line scheduler has to solve.

3.   V4 SCHEDULE VISUALIZATION

The basic idea behind the V4 schedule visualization was to transform the V4 scheduler output into the trace format of a well-established graphical performance analysis tool for parallel programs and utilize the tools' various graphs and statistics to understand the V4 schedule.

Vampir [6] was selected as the tool best suited for the V4 schedule visualization, primarily due to its versatility, robustness, and good documentation. (For the eight candidate tools – Jumpshot, Medea, NTV, Pablo, Paragraph, Trace Invader, Vampir, VT [1][2] – and a description of the evaluation process, see [4].)

The V4 off-line scheduler was then extended to generate Vampir trace files [6] and supplementary information. The threads running on the V4 switch represent the active entities in the Vampir trace. The threads can be in states *busy* and *idle* and exchange messages among each other. Threads are numbered contiguously in the trace file. The resulting *timeline* (or *space-time*) *diagram*, which is the most useful diagram for V4 schedule visualization, is easily understood and can display up to several hundred threads. Vampir's select, zoom, and scroll features allow to easily focus in on the threads and the time interval of interest; see Figure 2 for a small example.

4.   CASE STUDY: CALL SETUP SOFTWARE

It is essential that critical voice communication software exhibits good and stable performance. Yet, in a mobile communication system currently under development, it was observed that the *call setup* procedure performed several times worse than expected. The reasons for this adverse behavior were not fully known to the software engineers. One of the first uses of the V4 schedule visualization was therefore to explore the behavior and tune the performance of the call setup procedure in this application.

Call setup is part of the V4 *call control* software. Call control receives call setup messages from the V4 *protocol control* software of a communication link, as shown in Figure 1. Call control then performs a *location lookup* to locate the called partner in the mobile network, asks the so-called router software (not shown) to find a communication interface leading to the partner, and accesses the protocol control software of that interface to actually process the call setup. Programmers have identified the threads and communication links depicted in Figure 1 as potentially time critical for the whole procedure. The call control threads (those within the dotted box) run on the same CPU module, whereas the other threads may reside on different CPUs.

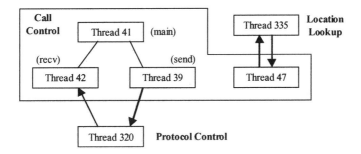

Figure 1 Performance-critical threads in V4 voice call control software

Figure 2 illustrates the scheduled behavior of these threads in a timeline diagram. Notice that the threads execute periodically every 8 ms. The call control threads can communicate via shared memory; hence, no message exchange among them is visible in the diagram. Furthermore, threads 41 and 42 which appear to run "simultaneously" on the same CPU, in fact obey mutual exclusion constraints imposed on them by the scheduler. Finally, notice that the lines depicting the messages in the diagram denote the time intervals when the messages are effectively being transferred on the V4 ring, not when they are being produced or consumed by thread instances; the latter occurs at the end or beginning, respectively, of thread instances only.

A study of the timeline in Figure 2 reveals four sources of inefficiencies in the given call setup procedure:

1. Thread 42 which receives call setup requests from protocol control (thread 320), thread 41 which handles the requests, and thread 39 which finally sends messages back to protocol control, are scheduled just in the wrong order. As a consequence, a request consumed by thread 42 (e.g. at time 5 ms) is processed by the subsequent instance of the main thread 41 (e.g. at time 13 ms) and replied to not earlier than one instance of the sending thread 39 later (e.g. not earlier than at time 19 ms).

2. The messages received by thread 320 from thread 39 (e.g. at time 8.5 ms), apparently arrive too late to be consumed by the current thread instance; their receipt is postponed by 8 ms (e.g. to time 16 ms).
3. The messages sent by thread 320 to thread 42 are scheduled very late (e.g., the message sent at time 11 ms must have been produced by the previous thread instance starting at time 0).
4. Inspecting the message details (which pop up by clicking on a message instance) discloses that one of the messages is slightly too large to fit into a given data channel, requiring a second one which is apparently scheduled subsequent to the first one.

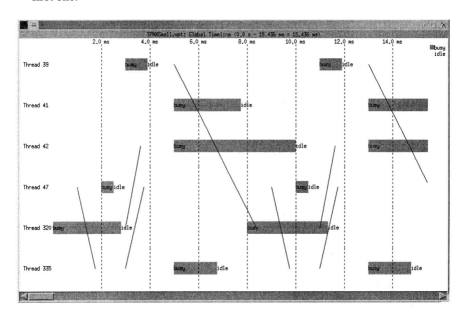

Figure 2 Visualization of V4 voice call control software activities

The study of this visualization enabled the programmers to locate the performance bottlenecks and identify opportunities for software optimizations and devising hints to the scheduler, e.g., by specifying time intervals for the critical threads' invocations (to enforce their execution in the correct order).

References

[1] EU Working Group APART (Automatic Performance Analysis: Resources and Tools). http://www.fz-juelich.de/apart.
[2] S. Browne, J. Dongarra, K. London: *Review of Performance Analysis Tools for MPI Parallel Programs.* 1996. http://www.cs.utk.edu/~browne/perftools-review.
[3] Frequentis Nachrichtentechnik GmbH: *V4 System Description.* 1999.
[4] H. Hellwagner, K. Leopold: *Performance Tuning of Parallel Real-Time Voice Communication Software.* Technical Report TR/ITEC/00/1.02, Institute of Information Technology, University Klagenfurt, May 2000. http://www.itec.uni-klu.ac.at.
[5] H. Kopetz, A. Damm, C. Koza, M. Mulazzani, W. Schwabl, C. Senft, R. Zainlinger: "Distributed Fault-Tolerant Real-Time Systems: The Mars Approach". *IEEE Micro,* Feb. 1989.
[6] Pallas GmbH: VAMPIR 2.0 User's Manual. 1999. http://www.pallas.de.

CLUE — A TOOL FOR CLUSTER EVALUATION

Helmut Hlavacs
Institute for Computer Science and Business Informatics, University of Vienna
hlavacs@ani.univie.ac.at

Dieter F. Kvasnicka
Institute for Physical and Theoretical Chemistry, Vienna University of Technology
dieter.kvasnicka@tuwien.ac.at

Christoph W. Ueberhuber
Institute for Applied and Numerical Mathematics, Vienna University of Technology
christof@uranus.tuwien.ac.at

Abstract   This paper describes the simulation tool CLUE which makes possible the accurate performance assessment and performance prediction of clusters of symmetric multiprocessors (SMPs). Using CLUE, reliable information can be obtained to reach the optimum decision on hardware configurations (processing elements and communication networks) before actually purchasing this hardware.

Keywords: cluster computing, high-performance computing, simulation, parallel computing, execution driven simulation.

1.   INTRODUCTION

In the last few years, clusters of PCs / SMPs have gained significant popularity in the field of HPC due to their favorable price/performance ratio. When purchasing such a cluster, the customer must choose between several alternative configurations. The choice of one particular configuration, however, has a significant influence on the cluster's performance, and it is generally difficult to choose an optimum configuration, as the impact on the customer's software is usually not known in advance.

In this paper, we introduce the simulation and assessment tool CLUE (*clu*ster *e*valuator), which is able to simulate the performance of message passing programs executed on alternative cluster configurations.

The aim of CLUE is to evaluate the performance of parallel software a priori, i. e., before running it on a specific cluster. This way, a potential cluster customer is provided with performance information to aid his decision process. However, CLUE is not intended to guide hardware development in the narrow sense.

2.   RELATED WORK

In the past, several attempts have been made to simulate the performance of parallel programs. N-MAP [2], for example, allows to predict the performance of parallel programs by specifying code fragments only. The PVM Simulator PS [1] follows an approach similar to ours, accepting full PVM programs or program prototypes. Other performance prediction tools are AIMS [7], SPEEDY [6] and DIP [5].

3.   CLUE

CLUE is based on MISS-PVM [4], a library providing an additional layer between PVM and the application program. The simulation is driven by the following input: (i) a configuration file describing the cluster configuration and (ii) a parallel program using PVM for communication, recompiled to call the MISS-PVM API instead of the PVM API. The only source code to be changed is the PVM include file, which must be changed to the MISS-PVM include file.

Simple models have been chosen to describe the cluster hardware in order to keep the model complexity low. Experiments show, however, that the used models are sufficient to obtain accurate simulation results. For instance, the communication time between two processors is modelled by the following parameters: (i) *Send Time*: The time the sender spends in the send call, and (ii) *Transmission Time*: The difference between the send time and the time the message needs to be received by the receiver.

More information about the internal structure of CLUE is given in [3].

4.   NUMERICAL EXPERIMENTS

Up to now, two PC clusters have been examined.

The *Vienna Cluster* was built and operated by the authors. It consists of five dual 350 MHz Pentium II systems ($p = 10$) with 256 MB main memory, 512 KB Level 2 cache and local 4.5 GB hard discs. The nodes are connected via a switched Fast Ethernet network (measured bandwidth: 12.5 MB/s).

The *Aachen Cluster*, a Siemens hpcLine PC cluster, consists of 16 dual processor boards equipped with 400 MHz Pentium II processors ($p = 32$), 512 KB Level 2 cache, 512 MB main memory and local 4 GB hard discs. The nodes communicate either via switched Fast Ethernet or SCI (measured bandwidth: 80 MB/s). The SCI network is configured as a two-dimensional torus.

On both clusters, measurements have been carried out to obtain parameters for the configuration file. As for the Aachen cluster only MPI was available, the parameters for the MPI version of the BLACS were measured, whereas the PVM version was used for simulation.

In order to obtain widely applicable results, three important algorithms have been chosen from the linear algebra package SCALAPACK to be simulated on the two clusters: (i) matrix-matrix multiplication (PBLAS/pdgemm), (ii) Cholesky factorization (SCALAPACK/pdpotrf) and (iii) LU factorization (SCALAPACK/pdgetrf). 2000×2000 matrices were chosen to set up problems of a sizeable computational complexity, the blocking size was set to 100.

In Figs. 1 to 3, the observed and simulated wall clock times are plotted against the processor grid used, where "$N \times M$ Grid" means that $N \times M$ processors were used to compute the task.

5.   CONCLUSION

The diagrams reveal that the accuracy is very good for the Vienna cluster. On the Aachen cluster properties pertinent to floating-point performance are reflected in the simulation results. Thus it may be concluded that CLUE is an accurate tool for evaluating the performance of clusters of SMPs a priori and can thus guide a customer when choosing between several alternative cluster configurations.

References

[1] Aversa, R., Mazzeo, A., Mazzocca, N., Villano, U., *Heterogeneous system performance prediction and analysis using* PS, IEEE Concurrency 6-3 (1998), pp. 20–29.

[2] Ferscha, A., Johnson, J., *Performance prototyping of parallel applications in* N-MAP. In Proceedings of the IEEE Second Int. Conference on Algorithms and Architectures for Parallel Processing, IEEE CS Press, 1996, pp. 84–91.

[3] Hlavacs, H., Kvasnicka, D. F., Ueberhuber, C. W., CLUE—*Cluster Evaluation*. Technical Report AURORA TR 2000-05, Vienna University of Technology (2000). http://www.vcpc.univie.ac.at/aurora/publications.

[4] Kvasnicka, D. F., Ueberhuber, C. W., *Developing architecture adaptive algorithms using simulation with* MISS-PVM *for performance prediction*. In Proceedings of the 1997 International Conference on Supercomputing in Vienna, Austria, ACM Press, New York, 1997, pp. 333–339.

[5] Lamberta J. et al., DIP: *A parallel program development environment*. In Proc. Euro-Par '96, Vol. II, Springer-Verlag, Berlin, 1996, pp. 665–674.

[6] Mohr, W., Malony, A., Shanmugam, K., SPEEDY: *An integrated performance extrapolation tool for* PC++. In Proc. Joint Conf. Performance Tools 95 and MMB 95, Springer-Verlag, Berlin, 1995.

[7] Yan, J., Sarukkai, S., Mehra, P., *Performance measurement, visualization and modeling of parallel and distributed programs using the* AIMS *toolkit*, Software Practice and Experience 25-4 (1995), pp. 429–461.

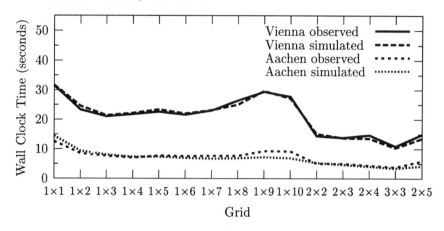

Figure 1   Cholesky factorization of 2000×2000 matrices.

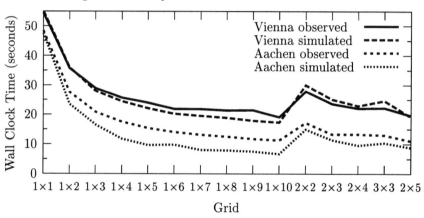

Figure 2   LU factorization of 2000×2000 matrices.

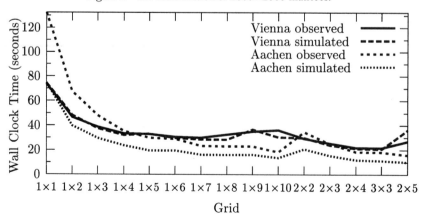

Figure 3   Multiplication of 2000×2000 matrices.

Part II

ALGORITHMS AND LANGUAGES

EFFICIENT RUN TIME OPTIMIZATION WITH STATIC SINGLE ASSIGNMENT

Jason W. Kim and Terrance E. Boult
EECS Dept. Lehigh University
Bethlehem, PA. 18015 USA
{jwk2,tboult}@eecs.lehigh.edu

Abstract   We introduce a novel optimization engine for META4, a new object oriented language currently under development. It uses Static Single Assignment (henceforth SSA) form coupled with certain reasonable, albeit rare language features. The result is a reduction of the optimizer's code footprint and an increase of its "reuse" factor. This engine performs the following optimizations; *Dead Code Elimination* (DCE), *Common Subexpression Elimination* (CSE) and *Constant Propagation* (CP). It performs these optimizations at *both runtime and compile time* with linear complexity time. Also, CP is essentially free, whether the values are really source-code constants or specific values generated at runtime. CP runs along side with the other optimization passes, thus allowing the efficient runtime *specialization* of the code during any point of the program's lifetime.

Keywords: Compiler, Optimization, Run-Time Code Generation, Static Single Assignment, Partial Evaluation

1.   INTRODUCTION

A recurring theme in this work is that powerful expensive analysis and optimization facilities are not *necessary* for generating good code. Rather, by using information ignored by previous work, we have built a facility that produces good code with simple linear time algorithms. This report will focus on the optimization parts of the system. More detailed reports on META4[13, 12] as well as the compiler are under development.

Section 1.1 will introduce the scope of the optimization algorithms presented in this work. Section 2. will dicuss some of the important definitions and concepts related to the META4 programming language and the optimizer used by the algorithms presented herein. The special features of META4 allow for linear (or near-linear) complexity optimization, along with an essentially free run-time constant propagation that is implemented by a simple, compact engine. The code size for the entire optimization engine (without the header and support routines) is less than 250 lines of semi-dense C++ code.

Section 3. will discuss in more detail the background information on the optimization algorithms, which are presented in section 4. (and discussed with more detail in [12]). Sections 5. and 6. end with discussion of related work, lessons learned and future directions.

1.1   Optimization

Optimizations that do not *directly* modify control flow, such as Dead Code Elimination (DCE), Constant Propagation (CP), Common Subexpression Elimination (CSE), and even *Runtime Constant Propagation* (RCP) can be implemented in a two pass algorithm. Each optimization[1] has a prepass algorithm that generates the needed data structures. They share a single postpass algorithm which actually carries out all actions.

Let N be the size of the program[2] and let $h(p)$ be the cost of the hash function for keys of some constant length p. Then, as we will see in 4.6, the prepass is at most $O(h(p)N)$ and the postpass is $O(N)$. If $h(p)$ is a constant, this reduces the complexity to $O(N)$, i.e. linear time.[3]

META4 implements Partial Evaluation (henceforth PE)[8, 10, 14] as CP at execution time. The programmer is able to generate and invoke specialized versions of *any* code segment with specific run time values treated as constants and propagated through (and re-optimized) at *any time* during the lifetime of the program. META4 supports (R)CP as well as unrestricted Run Time Code Generation.

This work will also show that CP, even at runtime does not explicitly require a separate prepass but can run as a part of the other optimizations featured here. The programmer only needs to specify that a particular instance is a *known* value and instruct the optimizer to generate a specialized form of the routine(s) that use this value. To the best of our knowledge, this is the first work that combines these optimizations along with runtime CP that is executed by a single, unified engine in linear (or near linear) time.

2.   META4: LANGUAGE DESIGN AND COMPILER BASICS

Before the actual optimization engine can be discussed in detail, it is first necessary to briefly mention the some of the important attributes of the META4[13] language which actively contribute to the optimization process.

The first definition addresses the issue of storage. A unit of storage in META4 is known as an instance; and is identified by a pair of numbers. The first number identifies a unique instance which correspond to a textual variable name in the source code, and the second specifies the Static Single Assignment[7] index for that instance. The SSA index guarantees that an instance has one unique point of creation. Storage

---

[1] except for (R)CP, which do not require a prepass.

[2] SSA does add additional bulk to the code size. However the bloat is a constant factor because the added code is a simple rewrite of assignments and control-flow joins. In practice, the expansion is a small constant.

[3] Unfortunately, hash functions are very difficult to analyze *exactly*, but experience indicates that a good hash function *can* be considered a constant for most kinds of inputs of fixed size.

or data members of classes do exist in META4, but they are not directly accessible. Rather we introduce a single concept, property that generalizes and expands on data members and member functions.

A property is a behavioral trait of a class that is typed, named, inheritable, specializable, generalizable. It may require arguments, and may also return values. A crude analog would be a virtual member function of a class in C++ or Java.[4] Note that within META4, the *only way* an instance can be accessed from a class is through a property[13]. Furthermore the property is the only mechanism for communicating with an object in META4. Operations that are generally considered as primitives (such as add, subtract etc..) are also properties (of the integer class). The unification of storage and function invocation allows META4 language to separate storage from inheritance. Its definition also specifies the types and data-flow directions of all parameters. In addition a property may be declared as a predictable property which will be described later.

An invocation is an abstract wrapper for the binding of a property with its actual arguments. There are two main types of invocation, a concrete statement which binds arguments to the property being invoked and a metastatement which is a subtype of invocation used for encapsulating control flow change. A nonempty list of properties serves as the "continuation." For example, a "loop" metastatement contains two properties, a "test" continuation and a "body" continuation. The latter is conditionally (re)executed pending the result from the "test". The two subclasses of invocation, metastatement and statement, are combined to form structured control-flow[4] equivalent of the program.

All code segments, a.k.a. implementations, are sequences of invocations. An implementation defines the body of a property. It is an array of invocations that also contains information on the instances used within that implementation. If a property can accept as arguments multiple *types* for the same parameter, then it has more than one implementation. As long as the actual type for that parameter is known at compile time[5], a new implementation can be generated that better meets the argument specifications. This can potentially aid in producing better (*i.e.*, faster executing) code by avoiding dynamic dispatch for invocations as well as through RCP. This also directly supports *polyvariant specialization* and *polyvariant division* [9] as a property can have an implementation that are generated for specific argument *values* as well as specific *types*.

2.1   Synergistic Cooperation Between Programmer, Compiler and the Language

In META4, certain keywords are provided, so that the programmer can inform the compiler of information that would be very useful and difficult to obtain automatically. These are analogous to certain annotations used in various PE engines for the language C[10, 14, 9]. Similar ideas are used here to help the optimizer in improving the code. However, in this work, "annotations" are not added onto an existing language, but

---

[4]The renaming is necessary, as these "properties" in META4 are not strictly equivalent to member functions in other languages such as Java or C++[13].

[5]Whenever that may be.

are an integral part of the programming process that has been designed from ground up to support principled use of Run Time Code Generation (RTCG). This entices the programmer to work with the language and the compiler in producing good code.

The programmer specifies the dataflow to and from a property. Thus the compiler knows exactly which parameters import data to the property (i.e. are *incoming* parameters), which parameters return data (i.e. are *outgoing* parameters), and which parameters do both (i.e. are *in/out* parameters). Also, many "primitive" functions, such as integer operations have predictable results i.e., given the same input, they always produce the same output, and have no side-effects. This predictability can be exploited in numerous optimizations. Many user defined properties are also predictable in the same manner as "primitives," but automatically detecting this is generally difficult. However, in META4, due to the explicit data flow, SSA and careful definition of primitives, guaranteeing the correctness of predictability is easy. It is impossible for a programmer to mark a non-predictable property as predictable. Regardless, when the programmer correctly marks a property as predictable, both the programmer and the compiler benefit from this explicit presence of semantic information. Therefore, we encourage the programmer to specify these as *predictable properties*.

The nature of properties and predictable properties serve to shortcut some of the analysis that a compiler would need to carry out. They play a critical role in optimization as well as during RTCG and PE.

3.   OPTIMIZATION IN META4

Previously reported optimization algorithms [1, 3, 2] operate on intermediate forms of "primitive" operations, and sometimes group optimization algorithms together to form more expensive[6] and more powerful combined optimization [16, 5] that allows them to find and optimize complex structures not amenable to repeated passes of separate optimizations.

The linear complexity algorithms presented here are arguably weaker than the more expensive combined approaches in [16, 5] but make up for it by allowing for the direct manipulation of user defined *properties*, not just "primitives." For purposes of the optimization algorithms presented here, there are no differences between "primitive" *properties* and user defined *properties*. The only difference is that "primitives" have direct machine code form, while user defined properties are usually composed of these "primitives".

These aid compilation in three ways. First, common subexpression elimination can now eliminate common calls to complex user defined properties. Second, the compiler knows exactly which parameters to a property will change, and which will not, that is data-flow is made explicit to both programmer and compiler, and is strongly enforced. Third, SSA adds additional data-flow information to the compiler, i.e. a tighter knowledge of what changes where.

Rather than using a powerful and expensive analysis engine which tries to guess which part is known, specializable, or not known, the knowledge of the programmer is exploited, and by supplying enough tools and fast, simple yet effective analysis

---

[6]*i.e.*, quadratic or $N log(N)$[3] complexity, as opposed to linear

routines, the programmer can specialize (manually or otherwise) during any phase of its life cycle (even at runtime of the program itself) any algorithm that can be specialized. Because of the strong encapsulation and the availability of dataflow information, the development of complex analysis engines engines is made easier. These tools can provide suggested optimizations that the programmer is free to use (or ignore). In addition, the compiler itself is available to the programmer as a class and can be specialized, increasing the efficiency for appropriate tasks.

During the optimization pass (whenever that may be), invocations of *predictable* properties that have all incoming parameters KNOWN can be marked DEAD and once the invocation is activated, all outgoing parameters can be marked KNOWN. This operation can occur at any time during the lifetime of the program. Since values generated at runtime can be marked as *known* and be propagated, this is a valid form of runtime specialization of the program.

In reiteration, the specialization options available are runtime constant propagation and programmer controlled inlining/unrolling of statements/loops[7].

4.   ALGORITHMS AND IMPLEMENTATION

The overall design of the optimization engine in the META4 compiler is extremely simple yet powerful in its capabilities. Each application of the optimization engine is composed of one or two passes. DCE and CSE require a prepass to generate the information required in the second pass.

There is a main driver routine called *traverse*(*impl*, *op*) which traverses through the intermediate representation $impl$.[8] The argument *op* is a routine which processes an invocation. *traverse*() invokes *op* on each invocation in $impl$. The second pass is merely the application of *traverse*() to the implementation $impl$ with a special *op* called *postpass_apply*(). The following sections 4.2, and 4.3 explain the prepass algorithms. The postpass algorithm is explained in section 4.5.

4.1   Helper Routines

In the SSA world, an instance which is created by assignment has a predecessor, which is the right hand argument. e.g. assuming $x_i = y_j$, then the *predecessor*(x_i) is y_j. SSA enforces that x_i contains the exact same value as y_j.

The routine *isdead*(i, *impl*) returns TRUE if the argument i is DEAD within $impl$. A variable v is DEAD if it already has a predecessor and its only use is to construct other variables. If a variable is only used as a copy for another, and it has a predecessor, then the variable need not be created, and the predecessor can be used in its place.

4.2   Dead Code Elimination (DCE)

In this SSA world, *dead code* is any invocation which modifies only non-external variables. These variables also must not be used as incoming parameters to other invocations. *Dead conditional branch elimination* is handled as part of the postpass. As *traverse*() processes each invocation, the special postpass operator *postpass_apply*()

---

[7]The inlining/unrolling algorithms are omitted for space reasons

[8]As defined in 2., the "intermediate form" worked on by the optimizer is the implementation, which is an array of statements and metastatements.

handles any cleanup duties required for metastatements, such as killing off any dead branches and aligning the SSA indices of variables. The actual DCE prepass algorithm is called *prepdce()* and is used as an operator argument to *traverse()*. *prepdce()* actually marks statements LIVE, if they use or modify an argument (e.g. external parameter) to the property that *impl* implements. All statements not marked LIVE will be considered for removal during the postpass.

4.3   Common Subexpression Elimination (CSE)

Assume some predictable property fp and within some implementation $impl$, the set of chronologically ordered list of invocations of fp in $impl$ called S. There exists a subset of S called S_{equiv} with one or more invocations s_k such that for all *incoming* parameters p_n in fp and for all s_a, s_b in $S_{equiv}, nth\_arg(s_a, n)$ equals $nth\_arg(s_b, n)$. Trivially, each invocation in S can be its own S_{equiv}, but the goal here is to partition S into its largest equivalent subsets, given the current state of information available to the compiler. All invocations in S_{equiv} are considered to be *equivalent*. Thus all but the chronologically first invocation s_1, in S_{equiv} can be marked DEAD and the future uses of the outgoing parameters for the rest of the statements in S_{equiv} can be replaced by the respective outgoing arguments of s_1.

When *traverse(generate_S)* below is applied to an implementation *impl*, it generates the set S for each predictable property invoked in *impl*.

```
generate_S(statement s, impl)
   prop = invoked_property(s)
   if prop is a predictable, then  add s to the end of S for prop.
```

Prepcse(), the second prepass for CSE partitions each S generated above into a list of S_{equiv}.

```
prepcse(implementation impl):
   for_each entry S in impl.S_list {
      if (partition(S, list_of_S_equiv))
         for_each entry f in list_of_S_equiv {
            statement base is first invocation in f
            for_each remaining statement s_j in f { mark s_j DEAD
               for_each outgoing parameter arg_i of s_j
                  predecessor(arg_i) = args(base, i) } } }
```

In *prepcse()*, list_of_S_equiv is a hash table containing a list of invocations that partitions a particular S. The hash key used to access list_of_S_equiv is an array of instances[9] comprised of the incoming parameters of the invocation.

The following routine actually partitions S into non intersecting sets of invocations S_{equiv}, and returns TRUE if at least one S_{equiv} has more than one invocation in it. Of course, $h()$ is the hash function for an instance list.

---

[9] Since a pair of numbers denote an instance, an instance_list is also a list of numbers.

```
partition(invocation_idx_list S, list_of_S_equiv)
  integer c = 0;  for_each invocation pi in S {
    hkey = concatenation of all incoming params of pi.
    if hkey is already in list_of_S_equiv then c = c + 1;
    insert pi into the end of list_of_S_equiv[h(hkey)] }
  return S.size() > c;
```

4.4   Breaking the Single Assignment Chain (BSAC)

Prep_bsac() finds all chains of non-useful (*i.e.*, non-overlapping) generation of variables and marks them DEAD and sets the predecessor for the killed variables. (Runtime) Constant propagation will work, even after the SSA chain has been broken, as any SSA chains that had conflicting usage frontiers are NOT broken. The only other requirement is that the meta-level information for all related entities be available when creating a new implementation of a property.

```
prep_bsac(statement s, impl)
  if s is not DEAD or LIVE; then prop = invoked_property(s)
    if is_assignment(prop) and last use of right hand arg of s is s then
      mark s DEAD; mark the left hand argument of s DEAD;
      set left hand argument's predecessor as right hand side of s
```

4.5   The Post Pass Algorithm and the driver

The *postpass_apply*() routine uses the information generated in the prepass and actually carries out the optimization/specialization as needed. The *activate*() call within *postpass_apply*() invokes the property bound to the current statement and updates the StorageTag[10] records of all outgoing parameters. These new known values can then be used as arguments to other properties.

```
postpass_apply(statement s, impl)
  if s is not DEAD or LIVE then prop = invoked_property(s);
    for_each argument instance arg
      if isdead(arg) then replace arg with predecessor(arg)
        if all incoming args are KNOWN and is_predictable(prop)
          activate(s)* and mark s DEAD; mark all outgoing params KNOWN;
```

This next routine is the main driving engine: The argument *op* is any of the routines above that have the correct interface. The job of the *op.pre_process*() and *op.post_process*() is to handle any setup and cleanup required for processing metastatements. Currently, the only operator that has a defined pre_process() and post_process() is *postpass_apply*(). Specifically, it kills any dead branches. Deciding to kill a branch is as simple as considering the number of live invocations in the implementation of that branch. If it is zero, then the branch can be killed. Also, if the test variable for the loop or conditional is KNOWN, than the appropriate branch can be killed.

---

[10]When an instance i is assigned a StorageTag s, this implies that i now has a *value* associated with it. This value does *not necessarily* imply a *physical address*. The name is somewhat misleading but its use is retained for historical reasons.

```
traverse(impl, op) : for each invocation s in impl
  if is_metastatement(s) then op.pre_process(s);
    for_each continuation c in s traverse(c.impl, op)
    op.post_process(s) // kill dead branches
  else  op(s, impl)
```

4.6   Costs of the Passes

Each operator argument to *traverse()* is executed once per invocation. Assuming C is the cost of the operator and N the size of the program, the cost of the optimization is $O(CN)$. C is either 1 in the case of *generate_S()*, or is proportional to the number of *parameters* p to a property, which can be considered a constant. The routine *prepcse()* is executed once per pass, not once per invocation like the other operators. *prepcse()* processes each candidate invocation exactly once, and the total number of candidate invocations is trivially less than N. Therefore its complexity is $O(h(p)N)$ where $h(p)$ is the hash function for the constant length p. It is arguable that for an optimistic view of the hashing cost, $h(p)$ is constant thus reducing the overall complexity to $O(N)$.[11]

5.   RELATED WORK

In [5], Click and Cooper report that that an optimization framework simultaneously combining constant propagation, global value numbering (a form of CSE) and dead code elimination is possible. The cost is quadratic in the size of the program, but this cost is mitigated by the fact that the combined framework can detect and optimize away some program structures undetected in separate, iterated applications of its parts. There is an explicit tradeoff with the optimization engine presented here. While being linear in complexity, the CSE engine presented in section 4.3 is arguably weaker than the *global value numbering* based expression matchers presented in [2] and reworked in [3, 5] since it can not directly detect equivalent compound structures of "primitives." (*e.g.*, two loops that calculate the same value). However, this lack is mitigated by the fact that additional programmer-controlled information is available as *language features* to the compiler. Specifically, it is possible to group certain invocation sets as a user defined "predictable property" which will allow equivalent invocations of the property to be weeded out by the CSE engine; thus encouraging programmers to work with the compiler in generating good code.

Another advantage of this approach is that constant propagation is essentially free. That is, there needn't be a separate pass of the engine for propagating them. All that needs to be done is a certain meta-level instance (that correspond to a real instance) be marked KNOWN at some point during the lifetime of the program, and the next time the postpass is run, the constant propagation proceeds side by side, similar in spirit to what the more complex combined optimization [5, 16, 2, 3] frameworks do. The only requirement here is that along with the actual machine code of the routine being specialized, the meta-level information (specifically the implementation for the property and all other related structures) must be available to the compiler at

---

[11] A more detailed outline of the linearity of these algorithms is in [12].

specialization time. Of course, the *activate*() call would not be made unless ALL parameters are KNOWN at that time.

The need for guessing when to carry out inter-procedural analysis [1, 15] is neatly avoided here as well. The only time inter-procedural analysis is performed is at the beck and call of the programmer, that is when the programmer hints that an invocation is *inlined* at its call site or when there are metastatements within an implementation (metastatements are always "inlined"). This is in keeping with the philosophy espoused here, which is that the programmer can provide necessary hints so that the compiler can do its job efficiently and productively, and these hints are provided as necessary language features explicit in the program, not from an outside analysis facility. However, this does not preclude the future addition of an analysis engine should the need arise.

6.   CONCLUSION

As software increases in size and complexity, it is vitally important that it be organized, designed and produced in a reusable, updatable manner. This inevitably leads to abstractions that negatively impact performance. Yet by allowing the programmer to *remove* such abstraction layers by *specialization* when needed, it is possible to recapture some of the inherent performance lost to the abstraction layers.

Some question the choice to ask the programmer to provide information that drives the optimization, e.g. the predictable tag. For safety, the compiler can verify the user supplied tags such as predictable. Doing so is inexpensive in META4 due to the strong encapsulation via properties as well as the data-flow specification. While verification is cheap, the analysis required to detect potential optimizations is more expensive and not necessary on every invocation of the compiler. As mentioned previously, one can provide a tool that suggests optimizations at the request of the programmer.

Currently missing from META4 but found in other systems like SELF[11] are features like automated runtime profiling. Also, the current lack of certain control-flow related optimizations such as strength reduction and invariant code motion (especially the latter) will have to be addressed in the future. In principle, the metastatement abstraction is powerful enough to encapsulate language level parallel constructs. We hope to extend META4 to handle parallel and distributed computation in the future.

While available literature is filled with separate research efforts regarding specialization [10, 14], optimization [1, 5], runtime code generation [11, 6, 10, 14] and object-oriented programming, there are precious few that explore the intersection of these research areas. Despite the lack of a formal partial evaluation framework, we hypothesize that the combination of the approaches presented in this work (*e.g*, the language features, the RTCG/PE facilities and the efficient optimization engine) is powerful enough for all *principled* uses of specialization and RTCG in an object-oriented development system. Showing evidence to such is ongoing.

References

[1]   Aho, A., Sethi, R., and Ullman, J. *Compilers, Principles, Technques and Tools*. Addison-Wesley, 1986.

[2] Alpern, B., Wegman, M. N., and Zadeck, F. K. Detecting Equality of Variables in Programs. In *15ᵗʰ Annual ACM Symposium on Principles of Programming Languages* (1988), pp. 1–11.

[3] Brandis, M. M. *Optimizing Compilers For Structured Programming Languages.* PhD thesis, ETH Zurich, 1995.

[4] Brandis, M. M., and Mossenbock, H. Single-Pass Generation of Static Single Assignment Form for Structured Languages. *ACM Trans. on Programming Languages and Systems 16*, 6, 1994, 1684–1698.

[5] Click, C., and Cooper, K. D. Combining Analysies, Combining Optimizations. *ACM Trans. on Programming Languages and Systems 17*, 2, 1995, 181–196.

[6] Consel, C., and Noel, F. A General Approach for Runtime Specialization and its Application to C. Tech.Rep., University of Rennes / IRISA, France, 1995.

[7] Cytron, R. K., Ferrante, J., Rosen, B. K., and Wegman, M. N. Efficiently Computing Static Single Assignment Form and the Control Dependence Graph. *ACM Trans. on Programming Languages and Systems 13*, 4 (Oct. 1991), 451–490.

[8] Engler, D. R., Hsieh, W. C., and Kaashoekoek, M. F. 'C: A Lanaguage for High-Level, Effiecient, and Machine-Independent Dynamic Code Generation. In *Proc. of the 23rd Annual ACM Symposium on Principles of Programming Languages (POPL)* (Jan 1996), vol. 23, ACM, Inc.

[9] Grant, B., et al. Annotation Directed Run-Time Specialization in C. In *In Proc. of the ACM SIGPLAN Symposium on Partial Evaluation and Semantics-Based Program Manipulation (PEPM)*, June 1997, pp. 163–178.

[10] Grant, B., et al. An Evaluation of Staged Run-Time Optimzations in DyC. In *Proc. of the ACM SIGPLAN Conference on Programming Language Design and Implementation (PLDI)* (1999), ACM, pp. 293–304.

[11] Hörzle, U. *Adapative Optimization for SELF: Reconciling High Performance with Exploratory Programming.* Ph.D. thesis, Stanford University, Aug. 1994.

[12] Kim, J. W. Efficient Run-Time Optimization Using Static Single Assignment. Tech.Rep. LU-CS-99-12-01, Department of Electrical Engineering and Computer Science. Lehigh University, 1999. Online at http://www.eecs.lehigh.edu/~jwk2/.

[13] Kim, J. W. The META4 Programming Language. Tech. Rep. LU-CS-1999-12-02, Department of Electrical Engineering and Computer Science. Lehigh University, 1999. Online at http://www.eecs.lehigh.edu/~jwk2/.

[14] Marlet, R., Consel, C., and Boinot, P. Efficient Incremental Run-Time Specialization for Free. In *Proc. of the ACM SIGPLAN Conference on Programming Language Design and Implementation (PLDI)* (1999), ACM, pp. 281–292.

[15] Rosen, B. K., Wegman, M. N., and Zadeck, F. K. Global Value Numbers and Redundant Computations. In *Fifteenth Annual ACM Symposium on Principles of Programming Languages* (1988), pp. 12–27.

[16] Wegman, M. N., and Zadeck, F. K. Constant Propagation with Conditional Branches. *ACM Trans. on Programming Languages and Systems 13*, 2 (April 1991), 181–210.

ON CLASSIFICATION HEURISTICS OF PROBABILISTIC SYSTEM-LEVEL FAULT DIAGNOSTIC ALGORITHMS

Tamás Bartha, Endre Selényi
Computer and Automation Research Institute, Hungarian Academy of Sciences
Kende u. 13–17, H-1111 Budapest, Hungary
bartha@sztaki.hu,selenyi@mit.bme.hu

Abstract   System-level fault diagnosis of massively parallel computers requires efficient algorithms, handling a many processing elements in a heterogeneous environment. Probabilistic fault diagnosis is an approach to make the diagnostic problem both easier to solve and more generally applicable. The price to pay for these advantages is that the diagnostic result is no longer guaranteed to be correct and complete in every fault situation. In an earlier paper [2] the authors presented a novel methodology, called *local information diagnosis*, and applied it to create a family of probabilistic diagnostic algorithms. This paper examines the identification of fault-free and faulty units in detail by defining three heuristic methods of fault classification and comparing the diagnostic accuracy provided by these heuristics using measurement results.

Keywords: multiprocessor systems, system-level fault diagnosis, probabilistic algorithms

1.   INTRODUCTION

Massively parallel computing systems are built up of a large amount of functionally identical *processing elements* (PEs). PEs execute the user application in a distributed manner, and cooperate using a communication medium to unify the partial results in complete solution. The probability of an error occurrence during application execution in an massively parallel system is significant due to the large number of components and the long continuous time of operation. Therefore, keeping the delivered system service uninterrupted by tolerating the effects of occurring errors is very important for parallel systems. This aim can be achieved by a fault tolerant architecture. *Automated fault diagnosis* is an integral part of multiprocessor fault tolerance. Its task is to locate the faulty units in the system. Identified faulty units are stopped, and physically or logically excluded from the set of available resources, and the computer is reconfigured to use only the fault-free system devices.

Existing methods for system-level fault diagnosis can be categorized into *deterministic* and *probabilistic* methods. Deterministic diagnosis algorithms guarantee the correct and complete identification of the fault set, provided that certain a priori requirements on the structure of the test arrangement and the behavior of the faulty units are satisfied. These requirements are usually strict and often impractical. The resulting deterministic algorithms are too complex and not efficient enough to handle large systems. Probabilistic diagnostic algorithms only attempt to provide correct diagnosis with *high probability*. This implies that the created diagnostic image can be either *incorrect* (fault-free processors are misdiagnosed as faulty, or vice versa) or *incomplete* (the fault state of certain processors cannot be classified). The benefits of the probabilistic approach are simpler, faster algorithms, and no restrictive assumptions on the test arrangement or on the fault sets.

2.   SYSTEM-LEVEL FAULT DIAGNOSIS

System-level fault diagnosis uses a simplified fault model. The system is built of a set of $u_i \in U$ units $(i = 1, 2, \ldots, n)$, connected by a set of $v_j \in V$ interconnection links $(j = 1, 2, \ldots, m)$. The units and links form a graph $S = (U, V)$. A unit u_i can either be *fault-free* (written as f_i^0) or *faulty* (f_i^1). It may test one or more other fault-free or faulty units. The complete collection of test assignments is a digraph $T = (U, E)$, where $E \subseteq V$ contains the set of $t_{ij} = (u_i, u_j)$ tests between units u_i and u_j. Two sets can be associated with each u_i unit: (1) the set of units tested by u_i, $\Gamma(u_i) = \{u_j | t_{ij} \in E\}$, and (2) the set of testers of u_i, $\Gamma^{-1}(u_i) = \{u_j | t_{ji} \in E\}$. The union of tested and tester units is the set of neighbors $N(u_i) = \Gamma(u_i) \cup \Gamma^{-1}(u_i)$. The set of units, that are reachable from u_i via directed edge sequences consisting of at most k edges are called the k-neighbors: $N_k(u_i)$. The cardinality of these sets are denoted by $\nu(u_i)$ and $\nu_k(u_i)$, respectively. Edges of the T digraph or *testing graph* are labeled by the $a_{ij} \in A$ test results. Tests have a binary (pass/fail) outcome. The A set of test results is called the *syndrome*.

The syndrome can be interpreted according to various test invalidation models. Test invalidation is the effect of the behaviour of a faulty unit on a test result. For example, a faulty tester unit may produce an nondeterministic pass/fail test result, independent on the state of the tested unit. This test invalidation scheme is called the *symmetric invalidation* or PMC model [5]. Other test invalidation schemes are also possible. In *heterogeneous* systems consisting of various functional units, test invalidation will likely be heterogeneous as well. The *generalized test invalidation* scheme provides a unified framework to handle the differences of the invalidation models of system components [6]. The model is described in Table 1. Due to the complete test assumption fault-free units always test other units correctly. Test results of faulty tester unit can have three outcomes: always pass, always fail, or arbitrarily pass/fail independent on the fault state of the tested unit. These results correspond to the constants 0, 1, and X. Nine possible test invalidation models are encompassed by the generalized scheme, denoted by the respective C and D values. For example, symmetric invalidation is referred to as the T_{XX} test invalidation model.

Table 1   Generalized test invalidation

Tester unit	Tested unit	Test result
fault-free	fault-free	pass
fault-free	faulty	fail
faulty	fault-free	$C \in \{\text{pass, fail, or arbitrary}\}$
faulty	faulty	$D \in \{\text{pass, fail, or arbitrary}\}$

The relationship between tester and tested units encapsulated by generalized invalidation can be used to derive *parameterized one-step implication rules*. One-step implications have the form of "fault state a of unit u_i implies the fault state b of unit u_j" (denoted by $f_i^a \rightarrow f_j^b$). An implication rule is affected by three main parameters: (1) the test invalidation of the tester unit, (2) the (hypothesized) fault state of the tester/tested unit, and (3) the actual test outcome. Four types of one-step implication rules exist: tautology, forward implication, backward implication, and contradiction. A contradiction provides a sure implication: it expresses that either the fault-free or the faulty state of a certain unit is *incompatible* with the syndrome: $f_i^a \rightarrow f_i^{\bar{a}}$. The complete set of parameterized one-step implication rules derived from the general test invalidation model can be found in [2].

Two one-step implications can be combined into a two-step implication using the transitive property: if $f_i^a \rightarrow f_j^b$, and $f_j^b \rightarrow f_k^c$ are two valid one-step implications, then they imply $f_i^a \rightarrow f_k^c$. The set of all one-step and multiple-step implications obtained by repeated application of the transitive property is the *transitive closure*. It contains all information that can be extracted from the syndrome. In the following section we describe how the transitive closure can be utilized in the diagnostic procedure.

Local information diagnosis

The transitive closure is obtained using the implication rules derived from the generalized test invalidation model, and so it is the complete source of topology and fault set independent diagnostic information. A diagnostic algorithm based on the transitive closure executes the following steps: first, one-step diagnostic implications are extracted using the parameterized implication rules and the actual syndrome. Then, multiple-step implications are obtained by transitively combining one-step implications. Inference propagation may continue until all possible implication chains are expanded in full length, that is, the transitive closure is created. All units involved in contradictions found in the transitive closure can be surely classified as fault-free or faulty. Finally, other units are diagnosed by a deterministic or probabilistic fault classification method.

There are two main performance bottlenecks in the above outlined procedure. First and foremost, generating the transitive closure of a large inference graph is a computation-intensive task. The underlying idea of *local information diagnosis* (LID) is that a probabilistic algorithm can achieve high probability of diagnostic correctness without expanding the implication chains in full length. Two main types of fault patterns can occur in a massively parallel system: (1) the faults are scattered throughout the system, separated from each other, and (2) the faults are located close to each other forming a group. In most practical cases both situations can be handled using just a portion of the diagnostic information [3]. The other performance bottleneck originates in the classification of those units which are not involved in a contradiction and whose fault state cannot be surely identified. Deterministic algorithms require complex methods for this task, since they must guarantee a correct and complete diagnosis (if only in a restricted set of cases). Probabilistic algorithms do not use the requirements necessary for correct operation of deterministic methods, and therefore can provide good diagnostic performance even beyond the traditional limits.

Along these guidelines we presented in an earlier paper [1] a family of probabilistic diagnostic algorithms based on the local information diagnosis methodology. These simple and efficient algorithms use the *generalized test invalidation* principle making them able to handle a class of heterogeneous systems. Here we outline the mechanism only of the *Limited Multiplication of Inference Matrix* (LMIM) algorithm, the interested reader can find the detailed definition of the other LID methods in [2]. In the initial phase of the LMIM algorithm one-step implications are collected and stored in the $2n \times 2n$ **M** *inference hypermatrix*. The **M** matrix consists of four $n \times n$ binary minor matrices: $\mathbf{M}^{00}$, $\mathbf{M}^{01}$, $\mathbf{M}^{10}$, and $\mathbf{M}^{11}$. The $\mathrm{m}^{xy}[i,j]$ element of the $\mathbf{M}^{xy}$ minor matrix $(x, y \in \{0, 1\})$ equals to 1 if there exists an $f_i^x \rightarrow f_j^y$ one-step implication between units u_i and u_j, otherwise it is 0.

Transitive closure can be computed by the logical closure of the **M** matrix. This is achieved by the repeated application of the $\mathbf{M}^{(k+1)} \leftarrow \mathbf{M}^{(k)} \cdot \mathbf{M}^{(k)}$ iteration until no new implications appear in the matrix. In the LMIM algorithm the **M** matrix is multiplied only a few, constant times. Thus, the matrix will contain only a subset of the diagnostic inferences included in the transitive closure. Nonzero elements in the main diagonal of the $\mathbf{M}^{01}$ and $\mathbf{M}^{10}$ minor matrices signify contradictions. For example, if $m^{01}[i, i]$ equals to 1, then the $f_i^0 \to f_i^1$ implication holds, that is unit u_i is surely faulty. Similarly, all u_j units corresponding to the nonzero $m^{01}[j, j]$ and $m^{10}[j, j]$ elements can be surely classified. For other units a heuristic fault classification rule must be used to determine their fault state. The quality of the employed fault classification heuristic significantly affects diagnostic accuracy. Our previous paper used one of the possible heuristic rules. This paper introduces two additional fault classification heuristics, called *Election* and *Clique*, to the existing *Majority* heuristic described in [1]. The diagnostic performance of the three heuristics are compared using measurement results.

3. FAULT CLASSIFICATION HEURISTICS

The three fault classification heuristics called *Majority*, *Election*, and *Clique* presented in this section are all based on the assumption that the number of faulty units does not exceed the number of fault-free units in the system. However, each heuristic uses this assumption differently.

3.1 Majority heuristic

The idea of Majority heuristics is simple: since only the fault-free units produce reliable test results, only the implications from the fault-free states (stored in the $\mathbf{M}^{00}$ and $\mathbf{M}^{01}$ minor matrices) should be considered. The $f_j^0 \to f_i^0$ and $f_j^0 \to f_i^1$ implications ($j = 1, 2, \ldots, n$) can be interpreted as votes for the fault-free and faulty state of the u_i unit, respectively. The fault classification can be made as a majority decision between the votes for the fault-free/faulty state. The sum of votes, i.e., the sum of $f_j^0 \to f_i^0$ and $f_j^0 \to f_i^1$ implications can be calculated by counting the nonzero elements stored in the ith column of the $\mathbf{M}^{00}$ and $\mathbf{M}^{01}$ matrices (see Figure 1). Comparing the two sums $\Sigma^0[i] = \sum_j m^{01}[j, i]$ and $\Sigma^1[i] = \sum_j m^{00}[j, i]$, the unit is diagnosed as faulty if $\Sigma^0[i] < \Sigma^1[i]$, otherwise it is fault-free.

3.2 Election heuristic

The Election heuristic applies the mechanism of the CFT algorithm [2] to limited inference methods. The idea is to identify the faulty units sequentially one-by-one. Units are ranked according to the likelihood of them being faulty for the purpose of selection, and in each identification step the unit with the highest ranking is diagnosed as faulty. Then, the diagnostic uncertainty is decreased by removing the useless and confusing implications originating in the actually located faulty unit. Naturally, rankings must be recomputed each

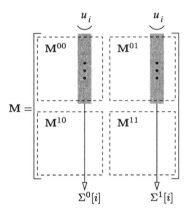

Figure 1   Calculation of the $\Sigma^0[i]$ and $\Sigma^1[i]$ values

---

Election heuristic
{ initialization }
for each $u_i \in U$ **do**
    $LF[i] \leftarrow \Sigma^1[i] - \Sigma^0[i]$
    $NLF[i] \leftarrow \sum_j LF[j], u_j \in \Gamma^{-1}(u_i)$
end for
{ election }
$\Upsilon \leftarrow U, \Phi \leftarrow \emptyset$
while $\exists j, k, m^{01}[j, k] \neq 0$ **do**
    find u_m with:
        maximum $LF[m]$, and
        minimum $NLF[m]$
    $\Phi \leftarrow \Phi \cup u_m$
    $\Upsilon \leftarrow \Upsilon - u_m$
    $\forall u_i \in U, m^{01}[m, i] \leftarrow 0$
    recalculate $LF[i]$ and $NLF[i]$
end while { classification }
$\forall u_i \in \Phi, u_i$ is faulty
$\forall u_j \in \Upsilon, u_j$ is fault-free

Clique heuristic
{ initialization }
for each $u_i \in U$ **do**
    $C^0[i] \leftarrow C^0[i] \cup u_j$, if $m^{00}[i, j] \neq 0$
    $C^1[i] \leftarrow C^1[i] \cup u_j$, if $m^{01}[i, j] \neq 0$
end for
{ clique closure }
for each $u_i \in U$ **do**
    for each $u_j \in C^0[i]$ **do**
        $C^0[i] \leftarrow C^0[i] \cup C^0[j]$
        $C^1[i] \leftarrow C^1[i] \cup C^1[j]$
    end for
end for
{ classification }
find u_m with:
    maximum $|C^0[m]|$, and
    minimum $|C^1[m]|$
$\forall u_i \in C^0[m], u_i$ is fault-free
$\forall u_j \in C^1[m], u_j$ is faulty
other units are unknown

Figure 2   Pseudo code of the Election and Clique heuristics

time the set of diagnostic implications is changed. The procedure is outlined in Figure 2.

The likelihood $LF[i]$ of the faulty state of unit u_i is estimated as $LF[i] = \Sigma^1[i] - \Sigma^0[i]$. For ranking units with identical LF values, the likelihood $NLF[i]$ of the faulty state of units testing u_i is also counted: $NLF[i] = \sum_j LF[j]$ for each $u_j \in \Gamma^{-1}(u_i)$. The units are sorted to find the unit u_m most likely to be faulty with the most reliable testers, i.e., having the maximum $\mathrm{LF}[m]$ and the minimum $\mathrm{NLF}[m]$ values. The u_m unit is then added to the Φ set of faulty units. The unit and its $f_m^0 \to f_i^1$ implications are removed from the $\mathbf{M}$ inference matrix, and the entire selection procedure starts again. When there are no more implications in the $\mathbf{M}^{01}$ minor matrix the remaining units are classified as fault-free.

3.3   Clique heuristic

The Clique heuristic is based on the diagnostic algorithm by Maestrini et al. [4]. The concept is similar to the Majority heuristic: if some fault-free units could be located, then their test results could reliably identify the fault state of other units. However, instead of comparing the feasibility of the fault-free/faulty states individually, the algorithm tries to group the units into two separate cliques. The *friendly* clique $C^0[i]$ of unit u_i contains units with a fault state identical to u_i (they are either all fault-free or faulty), while the *foe* clique $C^1[i]$ groups units with a fault state opposite to u_i (if u_i is fault-free, then they can only be faulty, and vice versa). Obviously, the clique sets of neighbor fault-free units are identical.

Cliques are initialized using the implications in the $\mathbf{M}^{00}$ and $\mathbf{M}^{01}$ minor matrices. Clique membership is then extended using the following two rules: (1) "my friend's friend is my friend", and (2) "my friends foe is my foe". The other two possible rules: (3) "my foe's friend is my foe", and (4) "my foe's foe is my friend" are not used, since they could lead to inconsistent cliques due to faulty units. Then the algorithm searches for the u_m unit with a maximum cardinality $C^0[m]$ set and minimum cardinality $C^1[m]$ set. The units belonging to the $C^0[m]$ set are called the *Fault-Free Core*, they are classified as fault-free. Units in the $C^1[m]$ set are diagnosed as faulty. Since some parts of the system can be separated by faulty units, there can be units neither contained in the $C^1[m]$ set nor in the $C^1[m]$ set. These units get the *unknown* classification, i.e., the Clique heuristic may lead to an *incomplete* diagnostic image.

4.   MEASUREMENT RESULTS

The presented methods were compared using measurement results. For the purpose of measurement they were implemented in a dedicated simulation environment. The measurements examined many characteristics of the algorithms, including the effect of fault set size, fault groups, number of iterations, and system topology on diagnostic accuracy. The simulations were performed on a 2-dimensional toroidal mesh topology containing 12×12 processing elements. Random fault patterns of various size were injected and the system was diagnosed in 512 subsequent simulation rounds. Although several homogeneous and heterogeneous invalidation schemes were involved in the simulation, here we can present only the results for the symmetric (PMC) test invalidation model due to volume constraints.

The effect of the fault set size on diagnosis accuracy is shown in Table 2. The first two columns contain the number of faults injected in the system and the percentage of faulty units. For the Majority and Election heuristics the number of simulation rounds with incorrect diagnosis (**MDR**), and the maximum number of incorrectly classified fault-free (**MGM**), and faulty (**MFM**) units per round are presented. According to the results the Majority heuristic gives a better overall performance than the Election heuristic, although the latter is less prone to misdiagnose a fault-free unit as a faulty unit. The Clique heuristic did not make any diagnostic mistakes, therefore the number of simulation rounds with incomplete diagnosis (**ICR**) and the maximum number of unknown units (**UM**) is given. Clearly, the number of unknown units considerably exceeds the total amount of units misdiagnosed by the other two methods, this is the price of the accurate diagnostic performance of the Clique heuristic.

Table 2   Diagnosis accuracy versus number of faults

Faults		Majority			Election			Clique	
		MDR	**MGM / MFM**		**MDR**	**MGM / MFM**		**ICR**	**UM**
4	(2.7%)	0	0 /	0	0	0 /	0	0	0
16	(11%)	0	0 /	0	0	0 /	0	10	1
36	(25%)	13	1 /	1	106	0 /	2	171	13
72	(50%)	222	5 /	6	463	0 /	8	510	58
96	(66%)	454	6 /	8	507	2 /	12	512	63

The higher degree of inference propagation (increasing the length of implication chains) improves diagnostic performance. Figure 3 presents this effect in the case of randomly injected fault patterns consisting of 36 and 72 faulty units. The number of simulation rounds with incorrect diagnosis is shown in the function of inference propagation iterations. Recall, that the length of implication chains doubles in each iteration, i.e., numbers 1, 2, 3, and 4 correspond to one-, two-, four-, and eight-step implications. The results justify our assumption: in the simulated system for random fault sets subsequent iterations improve diagnostic accuracy less and less.

We also examined the effect of system topology on diagnostic accuracy. Three regular communication topologies were simulated: (a) hexagonal toroidal grid with three connections, (b) 2-dimensional toroidal mesh with four connections, and (c) triangular toroidal grid with six connections. Figure 4 plots the number of simulation rounds with incorrect diagnosis in the function

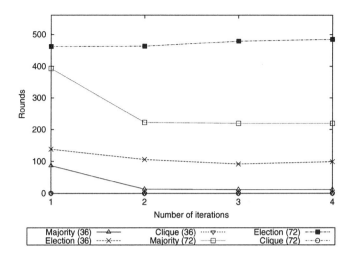

Figure 3   The effect of inference propagation

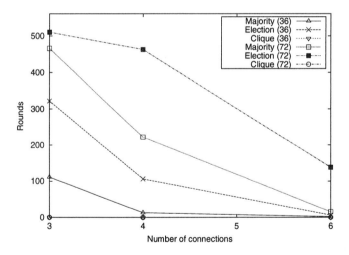

Figure 4   The effect of system topology

of connectivity. Random fault patterns consisting of 36 and 72 faulty units
were injected in the system. As it can be seen, all of the heuristics perform
better regardless of fault set size as the number of connections increases. In
a completely connected system each heuristic would provide a correct and
complete classification.

5.   CONCLUSIONS

This paper described the concept of local information diagnosis, a novel approach to efficient probabilistic system-level diagnosis of massively parallel systems. The LID method uses a generalized test invalidation model to comply with heterogeneous structures and converts the syndrome into a topology and invalidation independent implication set. The paper demonstrated the legitimacy of the limited inference approach: it is possible to achieve high diagnostic accuracy even using only a portion of diagnostic information contained in the transitive closure by evaluating the implication chains in the inference graph only in a limited length.

Three different fault classification heuristics were presented. These heuristics apply ideas of existing successful algorithms in the LID framework. The main characteristics of the heuristics were compared by simulation and measurements. The Majority and Election heuristics have similar diagnostic performance and complexity. They provide a complete diagnostic image, but make a low amount of diagnostic mistakes in the case of large fault sets. The Clique heuristic produces correct diagnosis even for many faulty units, but as a disadvantage the more units remain unknown than are misdiagnosed by the other two methods.

References

[1] T. Bartha and E. Selényi. Efficient algorithms for system-level diagnosis of multiprocessors using local information. In *Proc. of the DAPSYS '96 Workshop on Distributed and Parallel Systems*, pages 183–190, Miskolc, October 1996.

[2] T. Bartha and E. Selényi. Probabilistic system-level fault diagnostic algorithms for multiprocessors. *Parallel Computing*, 22:1807–1821, 1997.

[3] D. Blough, G. Sullivan, and G. Masson. Fault diagnosis for sparsely interconnected multiprocessor systems. In *19th Int. IEEE Symp. on Fault-Tolerant Computing*, pages 62–69. IEEE Computer Society, 1989.

[4] P. Maestrini and P. Santi. Self diagnosis of processor arrays using a comparison model. In *Symposium on Reliable Distributed Systems (SRDS '95)*, pages 218–228, Los Alamitos, Ca., USA, September 1995. IEEE Computer Society Press.

[5] F. Preparata, G. Metze, and R. Chien. On the connection assignment problem of diagnosable systems. *IEEE Trans. Electronic Computers*, EC-16(6):848–854, December 1967.

[6] E. Selényi. *Generalization of System-Level Diagnosis*. D. Sc. thesis, Hungarian Academy of Sciences, Budapest, 1984.

SCALABLE CLASSIFICATION OF LARGE DATA SETS BY PARALLEL GENETIC PROGRAMMING

Gianluigi Folino, Clara Pizzuti, Giandomenico Spezzano
ISI-CNR, c/o DEIS, Univ. della Calabria, 87036 Rende (CS), Italy
{folino,pizzuti,spezzano}@si.deis.unical.it

Abstract   A parallel genetic programming approach to data classification is presented. The method uses cellular automata as a framework to enable a fine-grained parallel implementation of GP through the grid model. Experiments on real datasets from the UCI machine learning repository show good results with respect to C4.5. The generated trees are smaller, they have a misclassification error on the training set comparable, but, more important, they generalise better than C4.5. Furthermore, performance results show a nearly linear speedup.

Keywords: data mining, parallel genetic programming, cellular automata

1.   INTRODUCTION

Data classification is an important *data mining* task [1] that tries to identify common characteristics in a set of objects contained in a database and to categorize them into different *classes*. The classification process builds a model for each class by using the features of a subset of the available data, called *training set*. The models of each class are then applied to determine the class of the remaining data (*test set*) in the database. The most famous technique for data classification is constituted by *decision trees* and C4.5 [4] is the most popular decision tree based classification method. In the last few years several methods to builds accurate decision trees have been proposed. Among them, *genetic programming (GP)* [3] has been demonstrated to be able to classify a database by generating and evolving decision trees. When applied to large datasets, however, GP performance drastically degrades due to the necessity to deal with large populations of trees where each tree is constituted by a high number of nodes. In this paper a parallel cellular genetic programming approach to data classification is presented. The method uses cellular automata as a framework to enable a fine-grained parallel implementation of GP through the grid model. The parallel implementation has been realized on a distributed memory multicomputer Meiko CS-2. Experimental results show good performances with respect to C4.5 and nearly linear speedup.

2.   DATA CLASSIFICATION USING CELLULAR GENETIC PROGRAMMING

Genetic programming is a variation of genetic algorithms in which the evolving individuals are computer programs represented as trees [3]. Genetic programming showed to be a particularly suitable technique to deal with the task of data classification by evolving decision trees. For a detailed description of data classification by means of Genetic Programming see [2]. When the database contains a high number of examples with many features, large decision trees are requested to accurately classify them. A decision tree generator based on genetic programming should then cope with a population of large sized trees. Processing large populations of trees containing many nodes considerably degrades the execution times and requires an enormous amount of memory. Parallel strategies can help to increase the performances of genetic programming and to realize a really scalable data classification package based on it. The models used for the parallel implementation of the genetic programming can be classified in three main groups according to the structure of parallelization: *global, course-grained* or *island model,* and *fine-grained* or *grid model.* The latter model is also called cellular because of its similarity with cellular automata with stochastic transition rules [5]. A *cellular genetic programming algorithm* (CGP) can be designed by associating with each cell of a grid two substates: one contains an individual (tree) and the other its fitness. At the beginning, for each cell, a tree is randomly generated and its fitness is evaluated. Then, at each generation, every tree undergoes one of the genetic operators (reproduction, crossover, mutation) depending on the probability test. If crossover is applied, the mate of the current individual is selected as the neighbour having the best fitness and the offspring is generated. The current string is then replaced by one of the two offspring. The replacement of the original individual can be done in several way. For example, it can be replaced by the best among itself and the offspring or one of the offspring can replace it at random. The CGP algorithm on a 2-dimensional toroidal grid can be described by the pseudo-code shown in figure 1.

```
Let pc, pm be the crossover and mutation probability
for each point i in grid do in parallel
generate a random individual ti
evaluate the fitness of ti
end parallel for
while not MaxNumberOfGeneration do
for each point i in grid do in parallel
 generate a random probability p
  if (p < pc) then
     select the cell j, in the neighborhood of i,
     such that tj has the best fitness
     produce the offspring by crossing ti and tj
     replace ti with one of the offspring
  else
    if (p < pm + pc) then
      mutate the individual
    else
      copy the current individual in the population
    end if
  end if
 end parallel for
end while
```

Figure 1   Pseudo-code of the cellular genetic algorithm.

3.   IMPLEMENTATION AND RESULTS.

The parallel implementation of the CGP algorithm has been realised on a distributed memory multicomputer. We chose this parallel architecture because it is that best matches the rather coarse grain and variable length of genetic programs. Essentially CGP is a data parallel code. We implemented the CGP model using a one-dimensional domain decomposition (in the x direction) of the grid that contains the population in conjunction with the SPMD model. We used the standard tool for genetic programming *sgpc* (ftp.io.com/pub/genetic-programming) to apply the GP algorithm to each cell, suitably modified to meet the requirements of the CGP algorithm. The method has been implemented on a Meiko CS-2 parallel machine with 48 130-Mhz processors and 256 Mbytes of memory per processor. Experiments have been executed on five real databases contained in the UCI Machine Learning Repository (www.ics.uci/mlearn/MLRepository.html), known as STAT-LOG datasets. The maximum depth of the new generated subtrees is 6 for the step of population initialization, 8 for crossover and 2 for mutation. The population size has been set to 1600 elements. In table 1 the results generated by C4.5 with pruning and the CGP method are presented. The results have been obtained by running the algorithm 5 times and the best result with respect to the misclassification

Table 1   Results generated by C4.5 and parallel CGP.

	C4.5			CGP		
Database	Size	Train	Test	Size	Train	Test
Australian	60	4.6	12.1	30	10.43	10.00
Mushroom	30	0.0	0.5	33	0.00	0.04
Satimage	478	8.9	15.5	187	18.71	20.35
Segment	113	6.1	11.5	98	9.41	9.74
Shuttle	34	3.3	3.5	25	3.35	3.45

error on the test set is shown. It is clear from the table that the trees generated by the *CGP* algorithm with respect to C4.5 are smaller, for almost all the dataset, they have a misclassification error on the training set comparable, but, more important, they generalize better than C4.5. The performance results that we have measured with the parallel implementation of the algorithm are very interesting since they give good scalability and show a nearly linear speedup. An intensive study of the applicability of the method on very large databases is under investigation, as well as an analysis to reduce the I/O times and the time needed to fitness evaluation.

References

[1] U.M. Fayyad, G. Piatesky-Shapiro and P. Smith (1996). From Data Mining to Knowledge Discovery: an overview. In U.M. Fayyad & al. (Eds) *Advances in Knowledge Discovery and Data Mining*, pp.1-34, AAAI/MIT Press.

[2] G. Folino, C. Pizzuti and G. Spezzano (1999). A Cellular Genetic Programming Approach to Classification. *Proc. Of the Genetic and Evolutionary Computation Conference GECCO99*, Morgan Kaufmann, pp. 1015-1020, Orlando, Florida.

[3] J. R. Koza (1992). *Genetic Programming: On Programming Computers by Means of Natural Selection and Genetics*, MIT Press.

[4] J. Ross Quinlan (1993). *C4.5 Programs for Machine Learning*. San Mateo, Calif.: Morgan Kaufmann.

[5] T. Toffoli and N. Margolus (1986). *Cellular Automata Machines A New Environment for Modeling*. The MIT Press, Cambridge, Massachusetts.

A NEW HEURISTIC FOR THE PROCESS-PROCESSOR MAPPING PROBLEM

Zoltan Juhász

University of Veszprem, Department of Information Systems, Veszprem, Hungary,
University of Exeter, Department of Computer Science, United Kingdom
juhasz@irt.vein.hu

Stephen J. Turner

University of Exeter, Department of Computer Science, United Kingdom
SJTurner@exeter.ac.uk

Abstract

This paper describes a new heuristic for the n-process p-processor task-assignment problem. The algorithm is based on repeatedly merging pairs of processes in order to reduce the initial n-node task interaction graph to a p-node one and at the same time trying to minimise the overall program execution time. We present the mapping algorithm and analyse its performance by comparing the results with optimal assignments. It is shown that for communication intensive problems running on a homogeneous network of processors, the algorithm produces acceptable suboptimal solutions in polynomial time, with errors less than 10% and typically below 5%.

1.   INTRODUCTION

Processes of a parallel program, when executed on any realistic parallel computer, have to be assigned (mapped) to processors. Normally, the number of processes in a program is larger than the number of processors, hence more than one process might have to be mapped onto a single processor. The way this mapping is performed has a pronounced effect on the execution time and efficiency of the parallel system. It has been shown by Bokhari [1] that the general mapping problem is *NP*-hard. Polynomial solutions exist only for a small set of specific cases, such as mapping arbitrary programs onto a two-processor system [3].

This paper describes a new task-allocation heuristic method we have developed. It is not our primary goal to develop the 'best' mapping heuristic. Our main purpose is to create a low-complexity algorithm that creates acceptable and fast mappings in practical situations.

2.   THE NEW HEURISTIC

We assume a parallel system consisting of n communicating processes and p processors without precedence relations among the processes. We further assume that this system can be described by a task interaction graph, whose nodes represent processes and edges represent communication between them. The weight t_i of node q_i represents the processing cost of the given process and the edge weight c_{ij} represents the cost of communication between processes q_i and q_j. The execution of communication and computation operations is not overlapped.

Processes in the graph are fully connected; however, an edge weight of zero indicates that there is no communication between a pair of tasks. If tasks are mapped onto the same processor, the cost of internal communication is taken to be zero. The time to complete all external communication in the system is the sum of all individual communication costs (this basically represents a system where communication is performed over a shared bus).

The fundamental idea of our method is to start the problem with an initial partition consisting of k, $k = n > p$, number of clusters. Thus in the initial phase, each cluster has one element, i.e., one process. The aim is to reduce the number of clusters by merging pairs of them iteratively until the number of clusters k becomes p. Our method [4] attempts to minimise the overall execution time, not just the communication time using the cost $t_{ij} = \max(t_i + t_j, Q) + C - c_{ij}$, where Q is the maximum of all cluster execution costs of the current partition, $Q = \max_{1 \leq i \leq k}(t_i)$ and C is the sum of all communication costs, $C = \sum_{i=1}^{k-1} \sum_{j=i+1}^{k} c_{ij}$. Hence, two clusters in a partition $\mathcal{P}(k)$ consisting of k subsets are merged if and only if their merge provides the best overall execution time for the new partition $\mathcal{P}(k-1)$. The merge reduces the number of clusters to $k-1$, and then this process is repeated until $k = p$.

The complexity of the algorithm is determined by the number of merge steps and the cost of each merge iteration. The total number of merges performed is $n - p$. As the merge involves an update of the task list and the adjacency matrix, the cost is $O(n)$ and $O(n^2)$, respectively. Thus, the overall complexity of the algorithm is $O(n^3)$.

Begin pseudo-code
  { *Start with n tasks, $k = n$ clusters and p processors* }
  while $(k > p)$ **do**
    $T_{min} \leftarrow \infty$
    for i:=1 **to** $n - 1$ **do**
      for j:=i+1 **to** n **do**
        $t_{ij} \leftarrow \max(t_i + t_j, Q) + C - c_{ij};$ {exec time of partition}
        if $t_{ij} < T_{min}$ **then**
          $T_{min} \leftarrow t_{ij}; i_{min} \leftarrow i; j_{min} \leftarrow j;$
        endif
      end for
    end for
    merge $q_{i_{min}}$ and $q_{j_{min}}$;
      update task list and adjacency matrix to reflect merge;
    k:= k-1;
  end while
End pseudo-code.

3.   RESULTS

It is difficult to evaluate the performance of any task-assignment method since for large values of n it is practically impossible to obtain the optimal mapping and its execution time. For this, we chose to evaluate our algorithm first for small values of n, $(n < 13)$. This enabled us to compare the results with the optimal ones and also to examine the behaviour of the algorithm under different conditions.

In Fig. 1 we can see the results of mapping a process graph with random computation and random communication costs, both with uniform distribution. The ratio of the total computation cost to the total communication cost was varied as $w = \{0.01, 0.025, ..., 1.0, 2.512, ..., 39.811, 100.0\}$. For $w \geq 1.0$ the error is less than 10%. For $w \geq 2.512$ the error becomes less than 3%. It is worth noting that for very small values of w the maximum error is at approximately $p = n/2$. For weights around 1.0, the maximum error peak moves to the minimum value of p – the largest difference between n and p. As we further increase the weight, the maximum error occurs, again, at approximately $n/2$.

4.   CONCLUSIONS

The results indicate that for parallel problems with small overall communication cost the partitioning algorithm does not perform very well. We believe

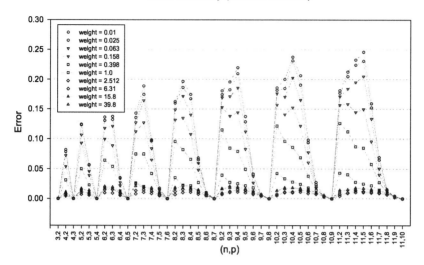

Figure 1   Error figures for systems with random computation and communication costs.

this is not a serious disadvantage. For the practically communication-free case the MULTIFIT bin-packing algorithm [2] would produce good results.

If, however, the algorithm has a communication cost larger than or at least equal to the computation cost, our algorithm produces a mapping that will result in an execution time less than 10% (typically 5%) longer than the optimal time.

There are several remaining problems to investigate. Experiments are currently underway to examine the performance of the heuristic for large values of n and we will be looking at extending the heuristic to work with heterogeneous processor networks and with system topologies that use parallel communication paths.

References

[1] S. H. Bokhari, On the Mapping Problem, *IEEE Trans. Computers*, Vol. c-30, No. 3, March 1981.

[2] E. G. Coffman, Jr., M. R. Garey and D. S. Johnson, An application of bin-packing to multiprocessor scheduling, *SIAM J. Comput.* **7** (1978), 1-17.

[3] H. S. Stone, Multiprocessor scheduling with the aid of network flow algorithms, *IEEE Trans. Software Engrg.* **SE-3**, 1 (Jan. 1977).

[4] Zoltan Juhasz and Stephen J. Turner, *A New Heuristic for the Process-Processor Mapping Problem*, Technical Report 381, Department of Computer Science, University of Exeter, November 1998.

FIFO BUFFERS IN TIE SAUCE

Franck Pommereau
LACL, Universit Paris 12,
61 avenue du Gnral de Gaulle,
94010 Crteil, France
pommereau@univ-paris12.fr

Abstract   This paper introduces a new semantics for FIFO buffers (more usually called *channels*) in a parallel programming language, B(PN)^2. This semantics is given in terms of M-nets, which form an algebra of labelled high-level Petri nets. The proposed approach makes usage of asynchronous link operator, newly introduced in the algebra of M-nets, and repairs some drawbacks of the previous M-net semantics. Channels are now fully expressible within the algebra (it was not the case), they are significantly smaller (in number of places), and they offer several other advantages.

Keywords: Parallel programming, Petri nets, process algebras, FIFO buffers, semantics.

1.   OVERVIEW

B(PN)^2 [6] is a general purpose parallel programming language provided with features like parallel composition, iteration, guarded commands, communications through FIFO buffers or shared variables, procedures [9] and, more recently, real-time extensions with abortable blocks and exceptions [11].

The semantics of B(PN)^2 is traditionally given in terms of Petri nets, using a low-level nets algebra called *Petri Box Calculus* [4, 3] or its high-level version, *M-nets* [5]. These two levels are related by an *unfolding* operation which transforms an M-net in a low-level net having an equivalent behavior. In this paper, we focus on M-net semantics since it is much more compact and intuitive. Using PEP toolkit [8], one may input a B(PN)^2 program and automatically generate its M-net or low-level net semantics in order to simulate its behavior or model-check it against some properties.

The purpose of this paper is to propose a new M-net semantics for channels in

B(PN)^2. This semantics uses asynchronous links capabilities newly introduced in M-nets and Petri Box Calculus [10]. The proposed semantics has three main advantages: it is completely expressible in the algebra of M-nets, its size (in terms of the number of places in the unfolding) is considerably smaller than of the existing semantics and finally, it avoids the "availability defect" of the existing semantics (a message sent to a channel was not immediately available for receiving).

B(PN)^2 is presented in [6] and its M-net semantics is fully developed in [9]. In the following, we focus on the intuition in order to keep the paper compact but as complete as possible.

2.   M-NETS PRIMER

M-nets form a class of labelled high-level Petri nets which were introduced in [5] and are now widely used as a semantic domain for concurrent system specifications, programming languages or protocols [1, 2, 7, 9, 11, 12, 13]. The most interesting features of M-nets, with respect to the other classes of high-level Petri nets, is their full compositionality, thanks to their algebraic structure. As a consequence, an M-net is built out of sub-nets with arbitrary "hand-made" nets as base cases.

A place in an M-net is labelled with its *type* (a set of values) which indicates the tokens that the place may hold. In order to define an algebra of M-nets, each place also has a *status* in $\{e, i, x\}$ which reflects whether it is an *entry*, an *internal* or an *exit* place. An M-net is initially marked by its entry marking, in which entry places hold one token from their type and the other places are unmarked. Then, tokens are expected to flow from the entry places to the exit ones. A transition t is labelled with a triple $\alpha(t).\beta(t).\gamma(t)$ where $\alpha(t)$ contains synchronous communication actions, $\beta(t)$ carries asynchronous links annotations and $\gamma(t)$ is a guard which is a set of conditions for allowing or not the firing of t. Finally, arcs are labelled by multi-sets of values or variables, indicating what they transport on firing.

When a transition t fires, variables in its annotation and on its surrounding arcs are bound to values, with respect to its guard $\gamma(t)$ and the types of its inputs and output places. Transition t is allowed to fire only if such a coherent binding can be found using tokens actually available in its input places. When firing occurs, tokens are consumed and produced coherently with respect to the binding.

M-net algebra provides various operations for control flow and communications setup as described in figure 1. Let us give more details about communications.

Scoping an M-net is the way to perform *synchronous communications* between its transitions. Figure 2 gives an illustration of scoping in a trivial case: in M-net N, transition t_1 carries an action $A(x)$ and t_2 has an $\widehat{A}(y)$; the M-net

$N_1; N_2$	sequence	N_1 runs then N_2 does
$N_1 \| N_2$	parallel composition	N_1 runs concurrently with N_2
$N_1 \,\square\, N_2$	choice	N_1 or N_2 runs but not both
$[N_1 * N_2 * N_3]$	iteration	N_1 runs once (initialization), then N_2 runs zero or more times (loop) and finally N_3 runs once (termination)
$[A : N]$	scoping	sets-up synchronous communications between transitions
N **tie** b	asynchronous links	makes asynchronous links between transitions

Figure 1   Operations on M-nets.

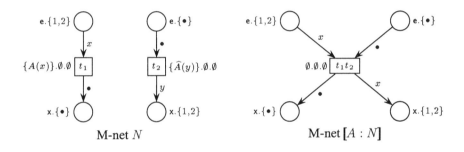

Figure 2   An example of scoping. (x and y have been unified to x.)

resulting from scoping $[A : N]$ has one transition $t_1 t_2$ which is a mix of t_1 and t_2 such that x and y are unified (here to x) in order to allow an actual communication. (x and y may also be constants in which case unification is only possible when $x = y$.) In a more complex M-net, all maching pairs of transitions such as t_1 and t_2 in figure 2 are considered by the scoping. In the general case, annotations α are multi-sets of actions.

Asynchronous links are available through *links* annotations. A transition may *export* an item x on a *link symbol* b thanks to a link $b^+(x)$; such an exported item may be *imported* later with a link $b^-(y)$. (Here again, x and y may be constants or variables.) Figure 3 gives a basic example of an asynchronous communication between two transitions. In a more complex M-net N, there would be also a single place s_b for all the links on b and all the transitions in N with a link $b^+(x)$ (resp. $b^-(y)$) would be attached an arc to (resp. from) s_b. In general, annotations β are multi-sets of links.

In order to give a type to the places added by operator **tie**, each link symbol

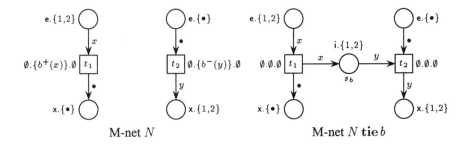

Figure 3   An example of asynchronous link (*b* has type $\{1,2\}$)

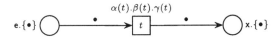

Figure 4   A simple M-net, denoted by $\alpha(t).\beta(t).\gamma(t)$ in this paper.

b is associated a type which becomes the type of any place created by an application of **tie***b*.

Of course, synchronous *and* asynchronous communications are allowed on the same transition. We will see an example of this in the proposed semantics for channels. Notice also that scoping and asynchronous links are commutative (each one with itself), so we use extended notations such as $[\{A, A'\} : N]$ or N **tie** $\{b, b'\}$.

In the following, in order to avoid many figures, $\alpha(t).\beta(t).\gamma(t)$ will denote an M-net with a lonely transition t annotated by $\alpha(t).\beta(t).\gamma(t)$ and having only one input place and one output place, both of type $\{\bullet\}$ (see figure 4).

3.   B(PN)² AND ITS M-NET SEMANTICS

Figure 5 gives a fragment of the syntax of B(PN)², semantics is given compositionally: it exists a function Mnet which gives an M-net for each fragment of a B(PN)² program. The definition of Mnet is recursive on the syntax; base case is either an atomic action, giving an M-net like on figure 4 where t would be labelled in order to implement the action, or a declaration which semantics is given using some special "hand-made" *resource M-nets* (like for channels in the next section).

A B(PN)² program is basically a block which may start with some local declarations (variables, channels or procedures), followed by a command which may contain sub-commands and possibly nested blocks. A variable is named

program	::=	**program** block	(main program)
block	::=	**begin** scope **end**	(block with private declarations)
scope	::=	com	(arbitrary command)
	|	vardecl ; scope	(variable or channel declaration)
	|	procdecl ; scope	(procedure declaration)
vardecl	::=	**var** *ident set*	(variable declaration)
	|	**var** *ident* **chan** k **of** *set*	(channel declaration)

Figure 5   A fragment of the syntax of B(PN)^2 (procdecl and com are not detailed here).

with an identifier *ident* and takes its value from the *set* given in its declaration; a channel is declared similarly but with an additional capacity k, it may be 0 for handshake communication, $k \in N$ for a k-bounded channel or ∞ for an unbounded channel.

The semantics for such a block is obtained from the semantics of its components: we just put in parallel the M-net for the command and the M-net for all the declarations; then we scope on communication actions in order to allow private communications between components. There is an additional *termination net* which is appended to the command M-net with the purpose to terminate the nets for the declarations. Terminating such a net consists in cleaning it for a possible re-usage. The semantics of any declared resource X contains a transition with an action $\widehat{X_t}$ which performs the cleaning, so the termination net just consists in a parallel composition of M-nets such as $\{X_t\}.\emptyset.\emptyset$.

In the next section, we show and discuss the existing semantics for a channel declaration.

4.   EXISTING CHANNELS IN B(PN)^2

Channels for B(PN)^2 were proposed in [6] and reworked in [5] with the M-net semantics depicted in figure 6. There are actually three different semantics, depending on the capacity k of the channel: N_0, N_1 and N_k. Three actions are available for a block which declares a channel C (regardless to its capacity): $\widehat{C!}$ for sending, $\widehat{C?}$ for receiving and $\widehat{C_t}$ for terminating it when the program leaves the block. In order to communicate with the channel, the M-net which implements the program carry actions $C!$ or $C?$. Action C_t can be found in the associated termination net.

In figure 6, transitions are named coherently on M-nets N_0, N_1 and N_k so, excepted when specified, the following description is generic.

The first action on the channel can be performed on transition t_1. For N_0 this means sending (with an action $C!$ in the program) and receiving (action $C?$) on the same transition (it is handshake communication), the guard ensures that the communication is actual; for N_1 and N_k a value is stored in the channel.

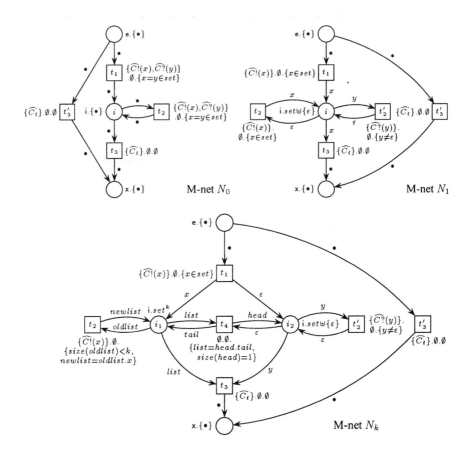

Figure 6 Existing semantics for a channel declaration "**var** C **chan** k **of** *set*". For capacity $k = 0$ (handshake communication) we use the M-net in the top left, for $k = 1$ we use the M-net in the top right and for $k > 1$, including $k = \infty$, the M-net in the bottom.

Transitions t_2 and t'_2 are for sending and receiving. In N_0, both actions are performed on the same transition t_2. For N_1 or N_k, these actions are separated. In N_1 a value $\varepsilon \notin set$ is used to denote an empty channel. Annotations on arcs ensure that one value can be sent to the channel only if place i holds value ε. The guards ensure that only values in *set* are stored in the channel and that ε is never used in a receiving. For N_k, the situation is more complex since the queue that the channel actually stores is encoded into structured tokens which are k-bounded lists. These lists are stored in i_1 whose type set^k contains all sequences of at most k values from *set*, plus an additional ε for the empty sequence. Transition t_2 adds a value at the end of the list. When place i_2 holds an ε, transition t_4 may extract the head of the list in i_1 and store it in i_2. On the other side, transition t'_2 in N_k is like t'_2 in N_1.

Transitions t_3 and t'_3 are for channels termination (whenever they have been used or not).

For N_k, it is easy to see that the mechanism is quite complex since it requires lists manipulations. Unfortunately, k-bounded channels are certainly the most commonly used. . . Moreover, an important drawback in N_k may be pointed out: the program has to wait for the firing of t_4 before to be able to receive a value which yet has been sent to the channel.

Let us conclude the current section with a remark on the size of the unfolded M-nets. As far as places are concerned, the unfolding operation produces one low-level place for each value of the type of each place in the M-net. As a direct consequence, unfolding N_k leads to $1 + |set|^k$ places just for i_1; the other places unfold in either 1 or $1 + |set|$ low-level places. So, we can state that the number of places in the unfolding of N_k is $O(|set|^k)$.

5.   A NEW SEMANTICS FOR CHANNELS

First of all, let us eliminate the case of capacity $k = 0$ (handshake communications): the semantics for this particular case remains the same. Thus we give its expression (for a declared channel C) as follows:

$$(\{\widehat{C_t}\}.\emptyset.\emptyset) \;\square\; [\quad \{\widehat{C!}(x), \widehat{C?}(y)\}.\emptyset.\{x = y \in set\}$$
$$* \;\; \{\widehat{C!}(x), \widehat{C?}(y)\}.\emptyset.\{x = y \in set\}$$
$$* \;\; \{\widehat{C_t}\}.\emptyset.\emptyset \;\;]$$

(As explained before, notations as $\{\widehat{C_t}\}.\emptyset.\emptyset$ stand for an M-net like on figure 4 with label $\{\widehat{C_t}\}.\emptyset.\emptyset$ on its transition.)

For bounded non-zero capacities ($1 \leq k < \infty$), we will use a single M-net, depending on k. In order to avoid explicit lists, the stored values are numbered modulo k and the M-net takes care to remember the numbers for the next value to be sent and, separately, the next to be received.

In order to bound capacity, we use a collection of tokens, one for each possible value in the channel, which are considered as "tickets for sending" or "tickets for receiving". Sending a value to the channel is allowed only with a ticket, if none is available, then sending is impossible. Each sending transforms a "ticket for sending" into a "ticket for receiving" and symmetrically. So, when one action (say sending) is not allowed to fire because of a lack of ticket, it must wait for the other action (here receiving) to convert one of its tickets. This system avoids conflicts since the sending transition consumes "tickets for sending" while the receiving transition does not, and symmetrically. This way, we preserve full concurrency between sendings and receivings.

In the following, we use K for the set $\{0, \ldots, k-1\}$. The M-net for channels uses asynchronous links for data storage and values numbering; the following link symbols are used with the following meaning: *bag* allows the channel to store pairs (v, n) where v is a value and n its number (we can deduce from this that *bag* must have type *set* $\times$ K); then *ns* and *nr* are used to remember the number for the next value to send or receive (both have type K), in the following, we call them the "next counter"; finally *ts* and *tr* store tickets for sending or receiving (also of type K).

The complete semantics for a k-bounded channel C ($1 \leq k < \infty$) is:

$$\mathsf{Mnet}(\textbf{var C chan } k \textbf{ of } set) \;=\; [\,\{I, T\} : core\,] \;\; \textbf{tie} \;\; \{bag, ns, nr, ts, tr\}$$

where I and T are synchronous communication actions used internally. The core of the semantics can be expressed as two concurrent iterations, one for sendings and the other for receivings:

$$core = [\,init * send * terminate\,] \;\; \| \;\; [\,wait_i * receive * wait_t\,]$$

In this M-net, the sending part can be considered as active and the receiving part as passive: M-net $wait_i$ waits for *init* to be executed and similarly, $wait_t$ waits for *terminate*. These waiting M-nets can be simply expressed as: $wait_i = \{\widehat{I}\}.\emptyset.\emptyset$ and $wait_t = \{\widehat{T}\}.\emptyset.\emptyset$.

M-net *init* is composed of a single transition which fires when the first sending occurs.

$$init = \{\widehat{C!}(x), I\} . \{bag^+((x, 0)), \; tr^+(0), \; ts^+(1), \; \ldots, \; ts^+(k-1),$$
$$ns^+(1 \bmod k), \; nr^+(0)\} . \emptyset$$

It stores the sent value, giving it number 0, produces all the tickets and initializes "next counters". It also triggers M-net $wait_i$ thanks to a synchronization on I. (Notation "$ts^+(1), \ldots, ts^+(k-1)$" is void when $k = 1$.)

Notice that there is no need to add a guard such as $x \in set$ because the type of *bag* ensures it must be the case. It is the same with *send* and *receive* whose definitions are:

$$send = \{\widehat{C!}(x)\} . \{ts^-(t), \; tr^+(t), \; ns^-(n), \; ns^+(n+1 \bmod k),$$
$$bag^+((x, n))\} . \emptyset$$
$$receive = \{\widehat{C?}(y)\} . \{tr^-(t), \; ts^+(t), \; nr^-(n), \; nr^+(n+1 \bmod k),$$
$$bag^-((y, n))\} . \emptyset$$

Termination is not done in one single action because we do not know where tickets are and how many tokens place s_{bag} holds (if ever it has some). So, we consider an iteration which triggers $wait_t$ on starting:

$$terminate = [\, \{\widehat{C_t}, T\}.\emptyset.\emptyset$$
$$* \; \emptyset.\{tr^-(t), \; ts^+(t), \; bag^-((y, n))\}.\emptyset$$
$$* \; \{\widehat{C_t'}\}.\{ts^-(0), \; \ldots, \; ts^-(k-1), \; nr^-(r), \; ns^-(s)\}.\emptyset \,]$$

(notation "$ts^-(0), \ldots, ts^-(k-1)$" is reduced to "$ts^-(0)$" when $k = 1$).

The purpose of this iteration is to consume all remaining values in the channel and to convert one ticket for each such value. Iteration may terminate when (and only when) all the values are consumed (and so, all the tickets are converted). It consumes all the "tickets for sending" and the "next counters" while synchronizing with the program on a second termination action $\widehat{C'_t}$.

In order to model unbounded capacity, we do not need anymore to count modulo k, and we can forget the system of tickets (just by removing all the links on ts and tr). Sending is always possible since the capacity is unbounded and receiving is controlled by its "next counter" and the availability of data in bag (actually, "tickets for receiving" were useless from the beginning but it was necessary to manage them coherently with "tickets for recieving").

On termination, in this case, we cannot rely on tickets to know if the channel is empty but we can trust "next counters": we add a guard $r = s$ to the termination of iteration *terminate*, it means that the count of $bag^-(\cdots)$ equals the count of $bag^+(\cdots)$ and so that the channel is empty.

Now, let us consider the size of the unfolding in the k-bounded case. Here no place is directly visible since we only gave expressions but, since control flow operators only produce places with types $\{\bullet\}$, it is enough to focus on places added for asynchronous communications. Places for ns, nr, ts and tr have type K so they all unfold into k low-level places. Place s_{bag} for bag as type $set \times K$ so it unfolds into $|set| \cdot k$ low-level places. So we can state a total of $O((4 + |set|) \cdot k)$ which is a significant improvement with respect to the exponential size in k for the old semantics.

The price to pay for this improvement is having two termination actions instead of only one. In the termination net, a channel C with the old semantics contributed an M-net $\{C_t\}.\emptyset.\emptyset$; for our semantics, we just have to use instead a sequence $(\{C_t\}.\emptyset.\emptyset); (\{C'_t\}.\emptyset.\emptyset)$.

6.   CONCLUDING REMARKS

We can see that the new proposed semantics has several advantages with respect to the old one. First, it is fully expressed in the algebra, with no more "hand-made" M-nets. This application of **tie** tends to show that it is an efficient way to introduce some places with arbitrary types, avoiding to use "hand-made" M-nets.

Moreover, there is no need for complex list management and the program does not have to wait anymore before to receive an actually sent value: it is now immediately available. The new semantics is more homogeneous since exceptions are now for $k = 0$ and $k = \infty$ (instead of $k = 0$ and $k = 1$) which we feel to be exceptions *intrinsically*: a handshake is *not* a buffered communication and an unbounded buffer is certainly not realistic.

Finally, unfolding the M-net for a channel gives now a low-level net with a number of places in $O\left((4 + |set|) \cdot k\right)$ while the old semantics unfolded into $O(|set|^k)$ places. This is a great improvement, especially when considering the model-checking of a B(PN)^2 program with channels.

References

[1] V. Benzaken, N. Hugon, H. Klaudel, and E. Pelz. M-net calculus based semantics for triggers. LNCS 1420, 1998.

[2] E. Best. A memory module specification using composable high-level Petri nets. LNCS 1169, 1996.

[3] E. Best, R. Devillers, and J. Esparza. General refinement and recursion operators for the Petri box calculus. LNCS 665:130–140, 1993.

[4] E. Best, R. Devillers, and J. G. Hall. The box calculus: a new causal algebra with multi-label communication. LNCS 609:21–69, 1992.

[5] E. Best, W. Fraczak, R. Hopkins, H. Klaudel, and E. Pelz. M-nets: An algebra of high-level Petri nets, with an application to the semantics of concurrent programming languages. *Acta Informatica* 35, 1998.

[6] E. Best and R. P. Hopkins. B(PN)^2 — A basic Petri net programming notation. *PARLE'93*, LNCS 694:379–390, 1993.

[7] H. Fleishhack and B. Grahlmann. A Petri net semantics for B(PN)^2 with procedures. *PDSE'97*. IEEE Computer Society, 1997.

[8] B. Grahlmann. The PEP tool. *CAV'97*, LNCS 1254:440–443, 1997.

[9] H. Klaudel. Compositional high-level Petri net semantics of a parallel programming language with procedures. Submitted paper (available on http://www.univ-paris12.fr/~lacl/klaudel/pr.ps.gz).

[10] H. Klaudel and F. Pommereau. Asynchronous links in the PBC and M-nets. *ASIAN'99*, LNCS 1742:190–200, 1999.

[11] H. Klaudel and F. Pommereau. Petri net nemantics of abortion, time-out and exceptions. Technical Report 0021, LACL, Université Paris 12, February 2000.

[12] H. Klaudel and R.-C. Riemann. Refinement-based smantics od parallel procedures. *PDPTA'99*, vol. 4. CSREA Press, 1999.

[13] J. Lilius and E. Pelz. An M-net semantics of B(PN)^2 with procedures. *ISCIS*, vol. 1, 1996.

PARAMETERIZED M-EXPRESSION SEMANTICS OF PARALLEL PROCEDURES

Hanna Klaudel

LACL, Université Paris XII

94010 Créteil, France;

klaudel@univ-paris12.fr

Abstract   A process algebra of parameterized M-expressions is introduced as a syntax for a class of composable high-level Petri nets (called M-nets) and provided in that way with a true concurrency semantics. It is used to give a fully compositional semantics to the parallel specification and programming language B(PN)^2, and in particular to the resources such as variables and procedures. The coherence of this new semantics with the original one is discussed in terms of equivalence of the behavior of associated nets.

Keywords: Process algebra, Petri Nets, Parallel Programming Language, Semantics.

1. INTRODUCTION

The Petri Box Calculus (PBC [2, 1]) is a process algebra with a syntactic domain of Box-expressions and a corresponding semantic domain of Boxes (place/transition Petri nets). It has been introduced with the aim of modeling the semantics of concurrent systems and programming languages. In order to cope with the net size problem, higher level versions of PBC have been considered, and in particular an algebra of M-expressions (high-level equivalent of Box-expressions, [10]) and M-nets (high-level Petri net version of Boxes, [3]) which allow to represent large (possibly infinite) systems in a clear and compact way. The high and low-level domains are related by the operation of unfolding which associates a Box-expression to each M-expression and a Box to each M-net. The same operations are defined in all domains and the high-level operations have been proved coherent with the low-level ones with respect to the unfolding.

B(PN)^2 (*Basic Petri Net Programming Notation*) [5] is a simple and expressive notation which incorporates many of the constructs used in concurrent programming. It is implemented in PEP tool [4] allowing to simulate the modeled system and also to verify its properties via model checking.

Several contributions [5, 3, 12, 7] provide applications of the PBC theory where Box-expressions, M-nets and M-expressions are used as the semantical domain for B(PN)^2. These translations are quite easy for the control flow part of the B(PN)^2 programs, but for the data part (namely variables, channels or procedures) they have always been given through a special encoding, *e.g.*, the Box-expression $D(v, set)$ describing the data box of variable v of type *set*. The following diagram summarizes the existing framework of PBC; each arc represents a mapping from one domain to another; dotted arcs emphasize an unsatisfactory character of some mappings.

Recently, the PBC framework has been enriched by an operation of asynchronous links [8] (N **tie** b where N is an M-net and b an asynchronous communication symbol). This operation produces in N a new place s_b of type $type(b)$ (which plays the role of a buffer) and arcs connecting it with transitions which export or import values to or from s_b. Asynchronous links have been used in order to express and improve B(PN)^2 channels directly in terms of simple M-nets (without considering *ad hoc* resource M-nets) [14].

In this paper we introduce an algebra of *parameterized M-expressions* which are a natural extension of the M-expressions introduced in [10, 9]. This extension follows exactly the same intuition as that defining parameterized M-nets [6] with respect to unparameterized ones [3]. Parameterized M-expressions accept the same operations as parameterized M-nets and the basic case of the algebra corresponds to a simple (see basic M-net $Net(\delta)$ in figure 1) parameterized M-net (contrasting with previous approaches where arbitrary (possibly complex) basic M-nets were considered). We show then, that the remaining B(PN)^2 resources (variable and procedure) can also be expressed directly in the algebra of parameterized M-expressions. This feature emphasizes the full compositionality of the semantics. Moreover, our translation is sound in the sense that the new semantics is equivalent with the previous one in terms of behavior of the associated M-nets.

2.   SYNTAX OF B(PN)^2

B(PN)^2, defined in [5], is a parallel programming language comprising shared memory parallelism, channel communications with arbitrary capacities and allowing the nesting of parallel operators as well as for blocks. The language offers also a standard structuring mechanism by means of procedures; their declaration has the following form:

$$procdecl ::= \mathbf{procedure}\ P(par, \ldots, par)\ block$$

where P is a procedure identifier, and each formal procedure parameter *par* may be specified as a *call-by-value* (if preceded by keywords **value** or **result**) or as a *call-by-reference* one (if preceded by keyword **reference**). When calling a procedure, the values of the **value** arguments are determined and used to initialize the corresponding formal parameters of the procedure. After execution of the procedure body, the values of the **result** parameters are stored in the corresponding result arguments. During execution of the body, every reference to a formal call-by-reference parameter r is treated as an indirect reference to the actual argument v. For example, the atomic action $\langle r = 1 \rangle$ within the procedure body has the immediate effect of the atomic action $\langle v = 1 \rangle$. In other words, r and v are considered to be different names for the same memory location.

3.   HIGH-LEVEL NET ALGEBRA: M-NETS

M-nets [3] form a class of high-level Petri nets provided with a set of operations giving to them an algebraic structure. We use here the parameterized M-nets defined in [6] and their asynchronous links extension from [8]. Like other high-level Petri net models, M-nets carry the usual annotations on places (sets of allowed tokens), arcs (multi-sets of annotations) and transitions (occurrence conditions). In addition, places have a status (entry e, exit x or internal i) used for the compositions of nets. Transitions carry labels which denote communication or hierarchical actions. Communications may be:

- synchronous, similar to CCS ones [13] (*e.g.*, between transitions labelled $\{V(v^i, v^o)\}$ and $\{\widehat{V}(v^i, v^o)\}$, where V symbolizes an access to a program variable v; v^i represents its *input* value and v^o the *output* one);

- asynchronous (*e.g.*, between transitions labelled $\{b^+(k)\}$ and $\{b^-(k)\}$, indicating that a value k is sent by the first transition to a place s_b, considered as a buffer which may carry tokens of type $type(b)$, and is received from s_b by the second);

- or possibly both at the same time.

These communications can be modeled in a compositional way through operations of scoping (for synchronous ones) and asynchronous link (for asynchronous ones).

Hierarchical transitions (labelled, *e.g.*, $\mathcal{X}(a_1, \ldots, a_n)$ where $\mathcal{X}$ is a hierarchical symbol and a_i are variables, values or parameters) indicate a future substitution (refinement) by a parameterized M-net whose arity (number of associated parameters) equals the arity of $\mathcal{X}$; in figures these transitions are denoted by a double-lined border. The basic case of the algebra of M-nets is given by the M-net $Net(\delta)$ represented on the left in figure 1, where δ is a basic parameterized M-expression, introduced latter.

4.   M-NET SEMANTICS OF B(PN)²

The definition of an M-net semantics of $B(PN)^2$ programs is given by a semantic function which associates an M-net with each $B(PN)^2$ program fragment. The main idea in describing a *block* is to juxtapose the nets for its declarations (variables, channels or procedures) and the net for its control flow part followed by a termination net for the declarations, and then to scope over all matching data/command synchronous communication symbols in order to make declarations local to the block. An access to an ordinary program variable v is represented by the action $V(v^i, v^o)$, appearing in the label of a transition t_v in the control flow part of the program, which describes the change of the value of v from its current value v^i to the new value v^o. The value of v is stored in place s_v in the data M-net $N_{Var}(v, set)$ shown in figure 1. It may be updated via synchronization between transitions t_v and t_3 (or t_1). The variable is terminated when transition t_2 (or t_2') fires.

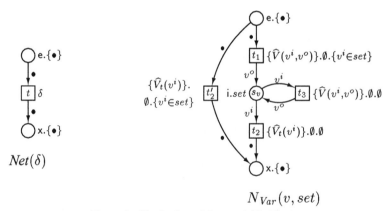

$$N_{Var}(v, set)$$

Figure 1   The basic and data variable M-nets.

The underlying idea of all approaches of an M-net semantics for procedures is to consider a *procedure M-net* devoted to manage all procedure instances. Different values in a fixed set Pid are used in order to distinguish the procedure instances. Call and return of a procedure instance k are distinct actions in the procedure M-net: $\widehat{call}(k)$ and $\widehat{ret}(k)$. They effect the control flow switch from the calling program part to the procedure M-net (respectively the other way round).

In the refinement based semantics, the procedure M-net is obtained by refining *procedure M-net* N_P, see figure 2, which describes in an abstract way the semantics of any procedure. Procedure M-net is initialized at the beginning of the program execution by the occurrence of the silent transition t_i which provides a set Pid of procedure identifiers in place s_p. Transition t represents one execution of a procedure instance. When t becomes engaged, an instance identifier k is taken from place s_p in order to identify the procedure instance which starts. When t completes, k returns in place s_p and becomes again available for possibly another execution of the procedure. Procedure declaration is terminated at block exit by transition t_t which may only occur when all instance identifiers returned to place s_p.

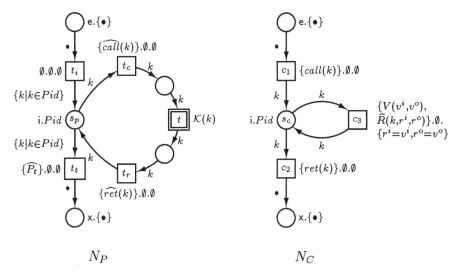

N_P N_C

Figure 2   The procedure and call-return M-nets.

The *call-return M-net* is used to represent each call to a procedure in the control flow M-net of the block which declares the procedure (it can be the block of the procedure it self, in the case of recursive call). An example of such a net, N_C, is depicted in figure 2. It corresponds to the simplest case of a procedure call inside the program body. Transition c_1 performs the call (via a synchronous communication with transition t_c in N_P) and stores its instance identifier in place s_c. A value $k \in Pid$ in the place s_c means that procedure instance k is active. Transition c_3 is used to forward an access to a call-by-reference procedure parameter r to the corresponding global variable v outside of the procedure body. This is performed thanks to synchronizations on V and R. Each occurrence of access transition c_3 consumes and reproduces in place s_c the instance identifier k which effected the change of value of the referenced variable. Finally, transition c_2 represents the return of a specific procedure instance.

A more complex example would be a call-return M-net for a recursive procedure call. In that case, if only one formal call-by-reference parameter r is declared, transition c_3 should be labelled by

$$\{\widehat{R}(k, r^i, r^o), R(k_1, r_1^i, r_1^o)\}.\emptyset.\{r^i = r_1^i, r^o = r_1^o\},$$

where k and k_1 identify two different instances of the procedure, $\widehat{R}(k, r^i, r^o)$ has to synchronize with a transition representing an access to r in the current procedure instance, while $R(k_1, r_1^i, r_1^o)$ has to synchronize with transition c_3 in a call-return M-net corresponding to procedure instance k_1 (which is calling instance k). The general call-return M-net is parameterized and quite complex because it takes into account not only several kinds of procedure parameters, but also the nesting level of each procedure declaration.

5.   PARAMETERIZED M-EXPRESSIONS

Parameterized M-expressions (which we call M-expressions if it does not introduce any confusion) can be viewed as a syntax for parameterized M-nets, and are defined as a natural extension of M-expressions [10, 9] in the same way as parameterized M-nets [6] are an extension of M-nets [3]. This extension allows hierarchical symbols to appear with a list of arguments, and to be refined by M-expressions having the same arity (expressed by a list of formal parameters). The refinement makes an explicit link between the formal parameters of the refining M-expression and the effective arguments coming from the refined M-expression.

We assume a set *Par* of parameters with a mapping *set* giving to each parameter $\psi \in Par$ its type $set(\psi)$. Thus, we consider that each parameterized M-expression E is provided with a list Ψ (possibly empty) of parameters of the form $\mathrm{id}_1, \ldots, \mathrm{id}_n$ where for $i \neq j$: $\mathrm{id}_i \neq \mathrm{id}_j$. A basic parameterized M-expression is $\delta(\Psi)$ where δ is a basic M-expression such that all parameters appearing in δ are present in Ψ. The examples of basic parameterized M-expressions are

$$\mathcal{X}(\mathrm{id}_1, 5).\emptyset(\mathrm{id}_1) \quad \text{or} \quad \{W(\mathrm{id}_2), V(v)\}.\emptyset.\{v = \mathrm{id}_2\}(\mathrm{id}_1, \mathrm{id}_2)$$

where $\mathcal{X}$ is a hierarchical symbol, v is a variable, W and V are synchronous action symbols, and id_1 and id_2 are parameters.

Let $E(\Psi_0)$ and $E_i(\Psi_i)$, for i in a set I, be parameterized M-expressions, and Ψ a list of parameters. Like for M-nets, the control flow operations of the algebra are based on refinement

$$E(\Psi_0)[\mathcal{X}_i \leftarrow E_i(\Psi_i) \mid i \in I]_\Psi$$

where $\Psi_0 \subseteq \Psi$, and Ψ defines the list of parameters of the result. For instance, the parameterized refinement

$$\mathcal{X}(\text{id}_1, 5).\emptyset(\text{id}_1)[\mathcal{X} \leftarrow \{W(\text{id}_2), V(v)\}.\emptyset.\{v{=}\text{id}_2\}(\text{id}_1, \text{id}_2)]_\Psi$$

where $\text{id}_1 \in \Psi$, leads to $\{W(5), V(v)\}.\emptyset.\{v{=}5\}(\Psi)$, where the formal parameters id_1 and id_2 have been replaced by the effective ones, id_1 and 5, respectively. Notice that, we assume that the effective parameters are always compatible with the types of the formal ones; for instance, $5 \in set(\text{id}_2)$.

Let $E'(\Psi')$, $E''(\Psi'')$ and $E'''(\Psi''')$ be parameterized M-expressions and Ψ a list of parameters such that $\Psi' \cup \Psi'' \cup \Psi''' \subseteq \Psi$. The control flow operators of the algebra are the following family, indexed by typed parameter list Ψ:

$E'(\Psi')$;$_\Psi$ $E''(\Psi'')$	sequence	$E'(\Psi') \parallel_\Psi E''(\Psi'')$	parallel
$E'(\Psi') \,\square_\Psi\, E''(\Psi'')$	choice	$[E'(\Psi') * E''(\Psi'') * E'''(\Psi''')]_\Psi$	iteration

and the communication operators (also indexed by Ψ) are as follows, where V is a synchronous and b an asynchronous communication symbol:

$E'(\Psi') \, \mathbf{sy}_\Psi \, V$	synchronization	$E'(\Psi') \, \mathbf{rs}_\Psi \, V$	restriction
$[V : E'(\Psi')]_\Psi$	scoping	$E'(\Psi') \, \mathbf{tie}_\Psi \, b$	asynchronous link.

In the following, we will consider that Ψ contains as few parameters as possible, so the subscripts Ψ will generally be omitted.

6.   PARAMETERIZED M-EXPRESSION SEMANTICS OF DECLARATIONS OF VARIABLES

For each variable v of type set we consider an asynchronous link symbol b_v such that $type(b_v) = set$. The following M-expression corresponds to a declaration of variable v.

$$E_v = \{\widehat{V}_t(v^i)\}.\emptyset.\{v^i \in set\} \quad \square \quad [\quad \{\widehat{V}(v^i, v^o)\}.\{b_v^+(v^o)\}.\{v^i \in set\}$$
$$* \{\widehat{V}(v^i, v^o)\}.\{b_v^+(v^o), b_v^-(v^i)\}.\emptyset$$
$$* \{\widehat{V}_t(v^i)\}.\{b_v^-(v^i)\}.\emptyset \quad] \ \mathbf{tie} \ b_v$$

The left part of the choice corresponds to the situation where variable v is declared but never used in the block. The termination action $\widehat{V}_t(v^i)\}$ is then immediately available.

The right part of the choice represents the case where v is declared and used in the block. The asynchronous link operator $.\mathbf{tie}$ creates a buffer which stores the current value of v. Each access to v is managed by the iteration $[\, I * R * X \,]$ where I is executed once initializing variable v to v^o, R may be executed zero or more times (actually every time a reading or writing of v is required by the control flow part of the program, represented by a synchronous communication label $\{V(v^i, v^o)\}$), and finally X is executed once consuming the value v^i from the buffer and making v unreachable.

7.   PARAMETERIZED M-EXPRESSION SEMANTICS OF DECLARATIONS OF PROCEDURES

We assume that $Pid = \{1, \ldots, n\}$. A declaration of a non-nested procedure P can be described by the following M-expression E_P. It is a scoping (a synchronization followed by a restriction) over a *set* of auxiliary synchronous communication symbols A_k and B_k for $k \in \{1, \ldots, n\}$:

$$E_P = [\, \{A_k, B_k \mid 1 \leq k \leq n\} : [\, \{A_1, \widehat{A_2}\}.\emptyset.\emptyset \; * \; R_1 \; * \; \{B_1, \widehat{B_2}, \widehat{P_t}\}.\emptyset.\emptyset \,] \;\|$$
$$\|_{2 \leq k \leq n} [\, \{A_k, \widehat{A}_{(k+1) \bmod n}\}.\emptyset.\emptyset \; * \; R_k \; * \; \{B_k, \widehat{B}_{(k+1) \bmod n}\}.\emptyset.\emptyset \,] \;\;]$$

with $set(\mathrm{id}) = Pid$ and for all $k \in \{1, \ldots, n\}$:

$$R_k = \{\widehat{call_P}(k)\}.\emptyset.\emptyset \; ; \; \mathcal{K}(k).\emptyset[\mathcal{K} \leftarrow E_{\mathcal{K}}(\mathrm{id})] \; ; \; \{\widehat{ret_P}(k)\}.\emptyset.\emptyset$$

where $E_{\mathcal{K}}(\mathrm{id})$ is a parameterized M-expression describing the body of P. The behavior of the M-net associated to E_P corresponds to that of the M-net N_P illustrated in figure 2. In particular, one may observe that a single silent action $(\emptyset.\emptyset.\emptyset)$ is executed first allowing $|Pid|$ different instances of P to be executed concurrently, and to be terminated by a single execution of a termination action $(\{\widehat{P_t}\}.\emptyset.\emptyset)$, exactly as in N_P.

The general case corresponds to a declaration of a procedure P_j in the scope of procedures P_i for $i \in \{1, \ldots, j-1\}$. We get

$$E_{P_j}(\mathrm{id}_1, \ldots, \mathrm{id}_{j-1}) =$$
$$[\{A_k, B_k \mid 1 \leq k \leq n\} : [\, \{A_1, \widehat{A_2}\}.\emptyset.\emptyset \; * \; R_1 \; * \; \{B_1, \widehat{B_2}, \widehat{P_{j_t}}\}.\emptyset.\emptyset \,] \;\|$$
$$\|_{2 \leq k \leq n} [\, \{A_k, \widehat{A}_{(k+1) \bmod n}\}.\emptyset.\emptyset \; * \; R_k \; * \; \{B_k, \widehat{B}_{(k+1) \bmod n}\}.\emptyset.\emptyset \,]\,]$$

where for all $i \in \{1, \ldots, j\}$: $set(\mathrm{id}_i) = Pid$, and for all $k \in \{1, \ldots, n\}$:

$$R_k(\mathrm{id}_1, \ldots, \mathrm{id}_{j-1}) = \{\widehat{call_{P_j}}(k)\}.\emptyset.\emptyset \; ;$$
$$\mathcal{K}(\mathrm{id}_1, \ldots, \mathrm{id}_{j-1}, k).\emptyset[\mathcal{K} \leftarrow E_{\mathcal{K}}(\mathrm{id}_1, \ldots, \mathrm{id}_j)] \; ; \; \{\widehat{ret_{P_j}}(k)\}.\emptyset.\emptyset$$

where, as above, $E_{\mathcal{K}}(\mathrm{id}_1, \ldots, \mathrm{id}_j)$ is a parameterized M-expression for the body of P_j.

8.   PARAMETERIZED M-EXPRESSION SEMANTICS OF PROCEDURE CALLS

The following M-expression describes a non-nested call $P(v)$ to a procedure P declared with a formal reference parameter r. Let b be an asynchronous link symbol with $type(b) = Pid$. A parameterized M-expression semantics of a procedure call is

$$E_C = [\quad \{call_P(k)\}.\{b^+(k) \mid k \in Pid\}.\emptyset$$
$$* \{V(v^i, v^o), \widehat{R}(k, r^i, r^o)\}.\{b^-(k), b^+(k)\}.\{v^i = r^i, v^o = r^o\}$$
$$* \{ret_P(k)\}.\{b^-(k) \mid k \in Pid\}.\emptyset \quad] \textbf{ tie } b$$

Notice that the above case corresponds to the situation illustrated by M-net N_C in figure 2. One can check that the M-net associated to E_C behaves as N_C does.

A more general case arises when we consider the k-th call to procedure P_j occurring in the body of a procedure P_i with $i \in \{1, \ldots, j\}$. Moreover, we assume that P_j is declared with a reference parameter r_j, P_i with a reference parameter r_i, and that the call is $P_j(r_i)$. Extension taking into account an arbitrary number of reference, value or result parameters are easy to obtain.

$$E_C(\text{id}_1, \ldots, \text{id}_j) =$$
$$[\quad \{call_{P_j}(k)\}.\{b^+(k) \mid k \in Pid\}.\emptyset$$
$$* \{R_i(\text{id}_i, r_i^i, r_i^o), \widehat{R_j}(k, r_j^i, r_j^o)\}.\{b^-(k), b^+(k)\}.\{r_i^i = r_j^i, r_i^o = r_j^o\}$$
$$* \{ret_{P_j}(k)\}.\{b^-(k) \mid k \in Pid\}.\emptyset \quad] \textbf{ tie } b$$

9.   CONCLUSION

In this paper, a new process algebra is defined by introducing a syntactic domain of parameterized M-expressions for the existing semantic domain of parameterized M-nets. The specific feature of the algebra is that it is provided with a true concurrency semantics in terms of high-level composable Petri nets.

The flexibility and the expressiveness of the algebra is illustrated by giving a semantics to a simple but powerful, specification and parallel programming language $B(PN)^2$. This approach simplifies the existing semantics of $B(PN)^2$ improving the results from [10]. In particular, parameterized M-expressions for declarations of variables and procedures, as well as for procedure calls, are presented. Moreover, this translation is sound which means that, for each fragment of $B(PN)^2$ program, the behavior of the M-net obtained from the parameterized M-expression associated to it is equivalent to the behavior of the M-net directly associated to it in the previous approach.

Thus, $B(PN)^2$ has got a fully compositional semantics in terms of parameterized M-expressions and the corresponding M-net, Box-expression and Box semantics (as well as various kinds of underlying Petri net semantics) may directly be obtained thanks to the coherence properties in the PBC theory.

We think that our approach allowing to express systems in a simple process algebraic style can be beneficial for a number of computer scientists, not always familiar with Petri nets, by offering an easy way to take advantage of the use of this model of concurrency and of its associated tools.

Acknowledgments
I am very grateful to Elisabeth Pelz for encouragement and to Franck Pommereau for his comments and help with LaTeX.

References

[1] E. Best, R. Devillers, and J. Esparza. General Refinement and Recursion for the Box Calculus. *STACS'93, LNCS* 655, Springer, 1993.

[2] E. Best, R. Devillers, and J.G. Hall. The Box Calculus: a New Causal Algebra with Multi-Label Communication. *APN'92, LNCS* 609, 1992.

[3] E. Best, W. Frączak, R.P. Hopkins, H. Klaudel, and E. Pelz. M-nets: an Algebra of High-level Petri Nets, with an Application to the Semantics of Concurrent Programming Languages. *Acta Informatica* 35:1998.

[4] B. Grahlmann, and E. Best. PEP – More than a Petri Net Tool. *TACAS, LNCS* 1055, Springer, 1996.

[5] E. Best and R.P. Hopkins. $B(PN)^2$ – a Basic Petri Net Programming Notation. *PARLE '93, LNCS* 694, Springer, 1993.

[6] R. Devillers, H. Klaudel, and R.-C. Riemann. General Parameterised Refinement and Recursion for the M-net Calculus. To appear in *Theoretical Computer Science*.

[7] H. Fleischhack and B. Grahlmann. A Petri Net Semantics for $B(PN)^2$ with Procedures. *PDSE'97*, IEEE Computer Society, Boston, Ma., 1997.

[8] H. Klaudel and F. Pommereau. Asynchronous Links in the PBC and M-nets. *ASIAN'99, LNCS* 1742, Springer, 1999.

[9] H. Klaudel, E. Pelz, and R.-C. Riemann. Relating M-expressions and M-nets. *DAPSYS'98*, Report Nr. TR-120, University of Vienna, 1998.

[10] H. Klaudel and R.-C. Riemann. High Level Expressions and their SOS Semantics. *CONCUR'97, LNCS* 1243, Springer, 1997.

[11] H. Klaudel and R.-C. Riemann. Refinement-based Semantics of Parallel Procedures. *PDPTA'99*, Vol. 4, CSREA Press, 1999.

[12] J. Lilius and E. Pelz. An M-net Semantics for $B(PN)^2$ with Procedures. *ISCIS*, Volume I, Middle East Technical University, 1996.

[13] R. Milner *Communication and Concurrency*. Prentice Hall, 1989.

[14] F. Pommereau. FIFO Buffers in **tie** sauce. DAPSYS'2000, this volume, 2000.

Part III
ARCHITECTURES

A NOVEL EXECUTION MODEL FOR LOGFLOW ON A HYBRID MULTITHREADED ARCHITECTURE[1]

Zsolt Németh
MTA SZTAKI Computer and Automation Research Institute
H-1518 Budapest, P.O.Box 63.
zsnemeth@sztaki.hu

Abstract   A new, hybrid multithreaded architectural platform offers the possibility to create an efficient (reduced) Prolog abstract machine. To meet the requirements of the abstract machine, a novel abstract execution model is necessary. From an existing dataflow based abstract execution model a new one was created in three major steps. In this paper these design considerations are presented.

Key words: parallel execution model, dataflow, Prolog abstract machine

1.   INTRODUCTION

The execution of Prolog (logic) programs usually involves three levels of abstraction. There is an abstract execution model directly related to the Prolog program that tells how source code should be understood. In a classical sense this model can be the depth-first traversal of the search tree but there are various sequential and parallel models as well [[5]][[6]]. Unfortunately, there are no architectures that can execute the program according to the model directly, therefore, an abstract machine level is introduced between the execution model and the physical machine level. Prolog programs are compiled into abstract machine code (like WAM [[12]] and other machines [[6]]), then the abstract code is interpreted by the abstract machine thus reaching the physical level. In this paper a new abstract execution model and principles of a new abstract machine are introduced.

[1] The work presented in this paper was supported by the National Science Research Fund OTKA T022106

The goal of current investigation is finding an efficient way of executing (restricted) Prolog programs on a kind of hybrid dataflow-von Neumann multithreaded architecture. The Logflow distributed Prolog system can be considered as the starting point of the project, where the abstract execution model is the so called logicflow based on dataflow principles [[5]], whereas the abstract machine is the Distributed Data Driven Prolog Abstract Machine (3DPAM) [[7]]. 3DPAM makes an attempt to realise a dataflow execution on top of von Neumann architectures, where all the dataflow features are implemented by software means with considerable overhead.

The aim of multithreading is solving fundamental problems of distributed processing like latency due to remote memory access and synchronisation [[2]]. A multithreaded architecture supports the presence of multiple threads of control and whenever one of them starts idling due to latency, an extremely fast context switch occurs that lets another thread run. A number of multithreaded architectures belong to the group of hybrid dataflow-von Neumann types that can support fast sequential execution and dataflow scheduling among the sequential threads [[10]].

The target architecture of the current implementation is the Kyushu University Multimedia Processor on Datarol (KUMP/D) [[11]]. KUMP/D is a successor of multithreaded Datarol [[1]] and Datarol-II [[8]] machines. It extracts fine-grain threads from a dataflow graph, and executes these threads by means of a program-counter-based pipeline equipped with high-speed registers similar to that of the conventional RISC processors. The FMD (Fine-grain Message Driven Mechanism) is a revised version of the Datarol-II execution mechanism where a number of function instances are created during program execution. Such an instance has a shared program code and a private environment. The code is split into threads, i.e. code blocks, which are executed without any interruption until the termination point. The Fine-grain Message Driven Processor (FMP) is an implementation of the FMD mechanism which assists fine-grain message passing, thread synchronisation, remote memory access and instance frame management.

According to many similarities, a hybrid multithreaded architecture seems to be an ideal platform to implement a logicflow based parallel Prolog system. Two key features can be exploited. The multithreaded property allows a new data layout with possible remote references where a novel way of variable handling [[9]] can be implemented. On the other hand, hybrid feature makes opportunity representing nodes and realising dataflow in a complete new and more efficient form. In this paper the latter issue is in focus and a new abstract execution model is defined.

2.   THE LOGICFLOW MODEL AND THE 3DPAM

The logicflow model is a higher abstraction to the dataflow principles [[5]]. Prolog programs are transformed into a Dataflow Search Graph (DSG), where nodes represent specific Prolog activities and they are groups of simple dataflow nodes. As a consequence, DSG nodes can have inner state and one token is always enough to make a node fire.

A clause is represented by a so called Unify-And ring. The Unify node (A in *Figure 6*) represents the head and the unification, And nodes (B) stand for the body goals and prepare the call. Alternative clauses are connected by Or nodes (C). Finally, group of consecutive facts are depicted by Unit nodes (D).

The solution realised by 3DPAM is very close to the abstract execution model. Token streams are separated by token colours. Nodes must have different states for different token streams, which is realised by different kinds of context tables. This solution can be characterised as if there were just one instance of each type of nodes and the actual behaviour of a node is determined by the token colour and the appropriate context information. Obviously, on a single PE there are multiple token streams, but at a time just one token and one node can be active. The remaining passive tokens are waiting in queues. Thus, tokens are necessary for physically storing and conveying information.

The solution drafted above has some disadvantageous consequences. The existence of context tables restricts the distribution of work in the processor space. Every token stream must return to its originating node in order to maintain the state of the node consistent. This problem appears evidently in two cases. First, in a Unify-And ring subgraphs connected to the And nodes are intended to work in a pipeline parallel way. However, every solution stream must go back to the processing element (PE) where And nodes (and their context table) can be found. Obviously, this form of execution concentrates the work around the given PE. Second, in a cascade of Or nodes the solution stream must go through every step of the cascade up to its root. The only reason is that in each stage the colour of the tokens must be replaced, because Or nodes in the cascade are represented by different records of the (possibly same) context table that can be addressed by the colour. In this case maintaining the consistency of the context tables is an overhead.

Furthermore, at the beginning of the execution thread the passive token information is moved to engine registers (active information) and at the end of the thread they are stored in tokens again. It represents a considerable overhead with respect to the short execution sequences of nodes.

3. THE NEW EXECUTION PRINCIPLES - EXPLOITATION OF HYBRID PROPERTY

3DPAM is nearly a straight mapping of the abstract execution model to the abstract machine. The handling of tokens and realising the dataflow features can be considered as an overhead on architectures, where they are not supported in native mode. While 3DPAM is close to the abstract execution model, the new

Multithreaded Prolog Abstract Machine (MPAM) tries to be close to the physical machine model. MPAM should represent a more efficient realisation of the token based execution yet, by maintaining the semantics.

The key idea is that the underlying architecture is a hybrid dataflow - von Neumann one, i.e. it can support both program counter based sequential execution and dataflow scheduling. More precisely, the Datarol execution model distinguishes the short term and long term execution. Short term execution means sequential processing whereas long term execution is dataflow based scheduling of the sequential threads. At the end the next thread is scheduled on dataflow principles. In other words it is a kind of macro dataflow model, too.

A program consists of simultaneously existing function instances. A function instance has its own context and shared code. Note, that the function instance and the thread are not the same: a function instance may consist of multiple threads that belong to the same context. A thread is terminated whenever a synchronisation or remote memory access causes latency. At this point a fast context switch allows the processor to go on eliminating idle cycles; it is the essence of multithreading.

The first question with respect to the previous sections is how MPAM represents nodes and tokens. MPAM creates physically and logically independent instances of nodes. Each node is represented by a frame, where its own context is stored, furthermore it also has registers for token information. There is a thread (or more threads) attached to the frame. In such a way a node is represented as a function instance: the function code is realised by the threads whereas arguments and local variables of the function are kept in the frame.

In case of 3DPAM, an active node can generate a token that will activate another node. At the thread switch the active node stores the state of computation to token and context fields whereas the node to be activated loads token information. In the MPAM model a running function instance can activate (call) another function. It can pass arguments just like in case of procedure call of other programming models. When the new instance is ready to run, the scheduler may select it for execution. However, at this point, the caller instance remains as it is, its content is not stored in a token. The new instance can proceed without load operations, because all the necessary data are available as arguments. A passive instance is waiting for some results. When the specified results are ready, it can be awaken on dataflow principles, where no load instructions are necessary: the state is the same as it was before, the results are local variables.

In this section the basic principles of a new Prolog abstract machine were set in order to exploit the hybrid feature of the underlying architecture, i.e. by matching all the macro dataflow features in the execution model to their architectural counterpart. Nevertheless, it needs redefinition in the abstract execution model. At this point it would be a trivial solution representing DSG nodes as function instances. However, further modifications in the execution model can result an even more efficient abstract machine.

4. REDEFINITION OF THE ABSTRACT EXECUTION MODEL

In this section Abstract State Machines [[3]] (ASMs, formerly known as evolving algebras [[4]]) will be used for describing the semantics. Without going into details, ASMs are able to describe systems at an arbitrary level of abstraction, give formal definitions and prove semantical equivalence, correctness. Although, it has strict mathematical foundations, it can be treated as a kind of pseudo code for compact and readable formal definitions. In the following subsections this notation is used for demonstrating the working behaviour of different nodes. The ASM fragments are for illustration only and they are not precise definitions, since they are simplified and several (less relevant) features are omitted.

4.1 Node instances

In DSG scheme, due to its pipeline behaviour, streams form a central concept. Streams are maintained (and different streams are separated) by a colouring scheme and, as it was shown, at abstract machine level the context tables represent some restrictions. However, the separation of streams could be defined in another way at abstract execution level. Every node (except for the Unit) has a request.out port and a reply.in port. For an outgoing single token on request.out port, there is a token stream on the reply.in port as an answer (this is a consequence of the all-solution property of Unit nodes.) Since a node can emit multiple tokens, it can receive multiple token streams. Obviously, if it could be guaranteed, that a node emits only one request token, there are no multiple reply streams and thus, they need not be separated.

The key is in the Unify-And ring where And nodes prepare calls to predicates, i.e. they emit tokens towards Or, Unify or Unit nodes. If for each token in the stream a new instance of And node is created, the called node beneath it will receive a single request token. The Unify node merges the answer streams from the last And nodes within the ring. They belong, however, to the same stream representing the answer to the single request token of the Unify node.

```
if node(loc(t))=AND & type(t)=SUCC                                    (1)
then
    instream(stream(loc(t),child(loc(t)),colour(t)),t):=false         (2)
    loc(t):=next(loc(t))                                              (3)
    type(t):=SUB                                                     (4)
    if stream(next(loc(t)),loc(t),colour(t))=undef                   (5)
    then
            extend STREAM by s with
            stream(next(loc(t)),loc(t),colour(t)):=s
            instream(s,t):=true
            endextend
    else
            instream(stream(next(loc(t)),loc(t),colour(t)),t):=true
    endif
```

Figure 1. AND node handling an incoming SUCC token.

Figure 1 depicts a part of the ASM definition of the And node in logicflow model. If the location of token t is an And node and type of t is SUCC (1), then t is taken from the incoming stream (2), moved its location to the next And node in ring (3) and its type is set to SUB (4). The rest (5) is maintaining the outgoing token stream.

Figure 2 is another part of the definition, where the incoming token is a SUB (1). Line (2) shows that the context information assigned to the current location (a counter in this specific example) is indexed (separated) by the colour of the token. From line (3) the token is taken from the incoming stream, then it is moved to the child node as a DO token.

```
if node(loc(t))=AND & type(t)=SUB                                    (1)
then
    counter(loc(t),colour(t)):=counter(loc(t),colour(t))++            (2)
    instream(stream(loc(t),prev(loc(t)),colour(t)),t):=false          (3)
    loc(t):=child(loc(t))
    type(t):=DO
```
Figure 2. AND node handling a SUB token.

Figure 3 shows the semantics of the modified model. After performing the same initial steps, not a new stream but a new node is created (1), its relation to the current node is set, then the token is moved to the newly generated node.

```
if node(loc(t))=AND & type(t)=SUCC
then
    instream(stream(loc(t),child(loc(t))),t):=false
    type(t):=SUB
    extend NODE by n with                                            (1)
    type(n):=AND
    prev(n):=loc(t)
    loc(t):=n
    endextend
```
Figure 3. The modified AND node handling a SUCC token.

The contrast can be seen on Figure 4, where there is no need to maintain the counter of incoming tokens, since it is 1. In other nodes there can be some context information, but they need not be separated by colours, because all tokens at the given node (one request and some replies) belong to the same colour.

```
if node(loc(t))=AND & type(t)=SUB
then
    loc(t):=child(loc(t))
    type(t):=DO
```
Figure 4. The modified AND node handling a SUB token.

Without going into details, it must be mentioned that there is different definition for the last And nodes within a Unify-And ring and other And nodes. Last And nodes do not create new nodes but send SUB tokens toward the Unify node in the ring. Furthermore, due to the lack of streams in the Unify-And ring, there are no need for terminating FAIL tokens. However, another kind of synchronisation is introduced between And nodes and the Unify node in order to keep track of the number of active tokens in the ring.

Although a formal proof is not presented here, intuitively can be claimed that the novel approach, where streams are split into tokens by introducing new nodes ensures, that there is only one incoming token and only one answer stream to each node. They belong to the same context. As a consequence, there is no need for token colours.

4.2   Optimised return

Figure 5 shows the ASM code for an Or node that receives a SUCC token. It replaces the colour to the saved one (2) and passes the token to the parent node (3). The rest (4) is maintaining the answer streams.

As it can be seen here, Or nodes do nothing in this case except replacing the colour. If the token colouring scheme can be eliminated, according to previous section, there is no need to propagate solutions through the cascade of Or nodes, they can reach their root in one step.

```
if node(loc(t))=OR & type(t)=SUCC                                        (1)
then
  colour(t):=colour(loc(t),colour(t))                                    (2)
  loc(t):=parent(loc(t))                                                 (3)
  if instream(stream(loct(t),child1(loc(t)),colour(loc(t)),t)=true       (4)
  then
      instream(stream(loct(t),child1(loc(t)),colour(loc(t)),t):=false
  else
      instream(stream(loct(t),child2(loc(t)),colour(loc(t)),t):=false
  endif
  if stream(parent(loc(t)),loc(t),colour(loc(t),colour(t)))=undef
  then
      extend STREAM by s with
      stream(parent(loc(t)),loc(t),colour(loc(t),colour(t))):=s
      instream(stream(parent(loct(t)),loc(t),saved_colour),t):=true
      endextend
  else
      instream(stream(parent(loct(t)),loc(t),saved_colour),t):=true
  endif
```

Figure 5. Essence of an Or node handling successful results.

This change affects the semantics of Unit and Unify nodes that can be connected to the cascade of Or nodes. The key idea is that the parent function of nodes (parent: NODE→NODE) is augmented with a second one (e.g. ancestor: NODE→NODE) that points to the root of the Or-cascade. In case of success, replies are sent to the ancestor instead of the parent.

4.3   Definition of aggregate nodes

As it was set forth in Section 3, the goal is to create an execution model, where nodes can be mapped to function instances. Although, it is possible at the present stage, increased granularity would reduce the cost related to instance (frame) management and data transfer between frames. The granularity can be increased by grouping together DSG nodes, resulting aggregate nodes.

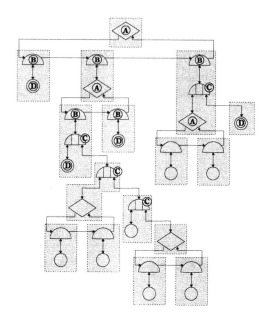

Figure 6. Structure of a DSG and an ADSG graph.

In order to introduce possible groups of DSG nodes, let us examine first the structure of a DSG graph. In [[5]] the connection rules of different DSG nodes are described informally, whereas a more formal approach is presented here. The DSG graph can be depicted as a string, i.e. a sentence where words correspond to nodes. The word 'unit' represents the unit node. The 'unify (And_1) (And_2) ... (And_n)' structure represents a Unify-And ring with n And nodes, where each And_i expression stands for the subgraph below the given And node in form 'and Subgraph'. 'or (Left Right)' denotes an Or node where Left and Right expressions are for the left and right subgraphs, respectively. From these elementary expressions complex sentences can be constructed. The sentences that describe valid DSG graphs form a language. The language is described as a (N, T, P, S) tuple, where N is the set of grammar symbols: N={Query, And, Unify, Or, Or1}, T is the set of terminal symbols (words and symbols of the language): T={unit, unify, and, or, (,)}, S is the sentence symbol: S=Query and P is the set of rewrite rules:

1. Query → unit | Unify | Or
2. And → (and Unify) | (and Or) | (and unit)
3. Unify → unify And*
4. Or → or(Unify Or) | or(Unify Unify) | or(unit Unify) | or(Unify unit) | or(unit Or1)
5. Or1 → or(Unify Or) | or(Unify Unify) | or(Unify unit)

The rules specify the possible connections among nodes. From this structure the aggregate nodes will be derived in a constructive way. First the boundaries of an aggregate node are defined. Obviously, a unit node represents the end of an aggregate node. Similarly, the right branch of an Or structure must be the beginning of an aggregate node. According to Rules 4 and 5, they can be: or, unify and unit nodes. The following points are taken into consideration at specifying the borders of an aggregate node:

1. An aggregate node must not contain two DSG nodes of the same type. An aggregate node is an instance that holds the context. Obviously, the same context cannot be used by two or more nodes.
2. Each aggregate node should contain a unit or unify node. These nodes contain the unification which is the essential driving force of execution and represents a task of bigger complexity. In such a way there are no pure fine-grained control nodes like in DSG model.
3. The data transfer between aggregate nodes should be minimised whenever possible.
4. And nodes are preparing the arguments for a call, i.e. emitting a Do token. Thus, they are strongly related to the nodes below them and therefore, it should be kept together with them. This issue increases locality and decreases data transfer. It is entirely orthogonal to the 3DPAM model, where the Unify-And ring was kept on the same PE and tokens were scheduled below the And node.
5. Aggregate nodes should be of nearly equal size and complexity.

As a consequence of points 3 and 4, Unify nodes are always terminating, whereas And nodes are always starting an aggregate node. The only aggregate node that starts with a unit node is the unit itself. Tracing the rules of DSG grammar from the And, Unify and Or nonterminal symbols up to the point when a unit or unify terminals are encountered yields the following possible combinations of DSG nodes within an aggregate node: unit, unify, and-unify, and-unit, and-or-unify, and-or-unit, or-unify, or-unit. All these types can be seen in *Figure 6* as grey rectangles. Hence the unit of execution is an ADSG node, they are represented as frames at abstract machine level.

5.   CONCLUSION

In this paper the existing logicflow model for parallel Prolog processing and its abstract machine, 3DPAM was described and analysed. A novel, hybrid multithreaded hardware platform was introduced and it was discussed, how its hybrid property can be exploited by a new, Multithreaded Prolog Abstract Machine. According to these needs, the logicflow model has been redefined yielding a new execution model. The redefinition has taken three major, consecutive steps. The introduction of node instances is a way to separate different token streams that allows to eliminate the token colouring scheme. In the absence of token colours, results form alternative branches can be handled in a more efficient way, skipping several nodes of control. Finally, simple DSG nodes can be grouped together yielding aggregate ADSG nodes. It should be noticed that the changes can be considered as a different representation of the same information. There are no semantical changes but in this way there is an execution model that can be mapped onto the abstract machine layer easily. Due to the space limitations, the main steps of this redesign were outlined here.

The transition from the abstract execution model to the abstract machine involves the redefinition of abstract instruction set (not presented in this paper), where instructions may have different meaning according to the given environment. The abstract machine can be executed on the hybrid multithreaded architecture effectively, since it was the starting point for the redesign.

Currently the correctness of redesign is being investigated. The ASM notation is a good framework to compare semantics of different approaches and show their equivalence or difference. It is also able to specify compilation schemes [[3]]. The ASM description of the logicflow model has been completed whereas the new model is being described by this method.

References

[1]   M. Amamiya, R. Taniguchi: Datarol: A Massively Parallel Architecture for Functional Language. Proc. Second IEEE Symposium on Parallel and Distributed Processing, 1990, 726-735

[2]   Arvind and R.A. Ianucci: Two fundamental issues in multiprocessing. Proc. DFVLR Conf. 1987 on Parallel Processing in Science and engineering, Bonn-Bad Godesberg, 1987.

[3]   E. Börger: High Level System Design and Analysis using Abstract State Machines. ASM Workshop, Magdeburg, 21-22 September, 1998.

[4]   Yu. Gurevich: Evolving Algebras 1993: Lipari Guide. In: Specification and Validation Methods, Ed. E. Börger, Oxford University Press, 1995. pp 9-36.

[5]   P. Kacsuk: Execution Models for a Massively Parallel Prolog Implementation. Journal of Computers and Artificial Intelligence, Vol. 17, No. 4. Slovak Academy of Sciences, 1998 (part 1) and Vol. 18, No. 2., 1999 (part 2)

[6]   P. Kacsuk, M.J.Wise: Implementations of Distributed Prolog. Wiley, 1992.

[7]   P. Kacsuk: Distributed Data Driven Prolog Abstract Machine. In: P. Kacsuk, M.J. Wise: Implementations of Distributed Prolog. Wiley, 1992.

[8]   T. Kawano, S. Kusakabe, R. Taniguchi, M. Amamiya: Fine-grain multi-thread processor architecture for massively parallel processing. Proc. First IEEE Symp. High Performance Computer Architecture, 1995.

[9]   Zs. Németh, P. Kacsuk: Analysis and Improvement of the Variable Binding Scheme in LOGFLOW. Parallelism and Implementation of Logic and Constraint Programming. Nova Science Publishers, 1999.

[10]   D. Sima, T. Fountain, P. Kacsuk: Advanced Computer Architectures. Addison Wesley, 1997.

[11]   H.Tomiyasu, T. Kawano, R. Taniguchi, M. Amamiya: KUMP/D: the Kyushu University Multi-media Processor. Proceedings of the Computer Architectures for Machine Perception, CAMP'95. pp 367-374.

[12]   D.H.D. Warren: An Abstract Prolog Instruction Set. SRI Technical Note 309. October 1983

THE NOP PARALLEL PROGRAMMING MODEL

Lajos Schrettner
Department of Computer Science, University of Szeged, Szeged, Hungary
schrettner@inf.u-szeged.hu

Abstract   The proposed node processing (NOP) parallel programming model has a single data structure that makes random memory accesses unnecessary. This radical approach has both advantages and disadvantages, but it is argued that it is worth considering as a viable alternative method of memory management in the context of parallel processing. The model has both imperative and declarative features. Its simple imperative transformations can be efficiently implemented, while larger programs can be constructed in a declarative style. The paper defines the components of the model and describes an implementation that is sequential, but immediately translates into a shared memory parallel implementation. A high level notation is introduced and used to present examples.

Keywords: Parallel programming, programming models, high level languages, portability, architecture independence.

1.   INTRODUCTION

Parallel programming has not become widespread because there are no general purpose models [1][2][3]. A programming model has to be convenient to use for problem solving and has to allow efficient implementation(s). A few proposed parallel programming models and architectures are extensions of the successful sequential von Neumann model and architecture, while others are based on new ideas [4]–[8]. An ideal general purpose parallel architecture is extensible and hides the architectural details from programmers. If these requirements are satisfied, portable parallel programs can be written, opening the way to widespread use of parallel programming.

Partly supported by the Hungarian Science Research Fund (OTKA), Grant No. F022514

If we study existing parallel models, we can observe that random memory access causes implementation difficulties in distributed and even in shared memory environments. A more regulated, more predictable flow of data would be advantageous. Further, imperative style of programming is preferable if we want performance, declarative style is better at ensuring sound design and program correctness. The NOP model achieves regulated data flow by avoiding variables, using implicit references exclusively. The NOP model has operations that are commands in the imperative sense; it also has sequential, conditional and parallel composition operations. On the other hand, a NOP program is a mutually recursive equation set, in this sense it is functional. The equation set determines the control structure of the imperative program, which is then executed to map the input to the final result. Using equations, programmers extend the transformation set of the model.

These design choices are believed to produce a unique, radical, but satisfying model.

2.   THE NOP MODEL

2.1   Data

The only data structure in the NOP model is the *node*. A node is a memory cell which is capable of holding a *value*. Apart from the value, a node can have an arbitrary number of *subnodes*, each of which is a node like itself. The subnodes form a bidirectional ring. If a node has at least one subnode, then one of them is the *active* or *selected* subnode. The active subnode has a special role in certain transformations. In general, a node is the root of a tree of nodes with its subnodes being its immediate descendants. Only the root node and its active subnode are directly accessible. Values stored in node cells can be *atoms* or nodes. Atoms are indivisible entities, they have no builtin properties other than they are different from each other. There is an atom called null.

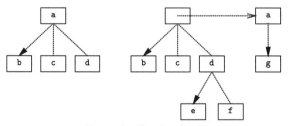

Figure 1   Graphs of nodes

In textual representation, atoms are denoted by character strings (null, 123, 5z), a node with value V and subnodes N, O and P is denoted by $V(N\ O\ P)$. The active subnode is always the first in the subnode list. For example, a(b() c() d()) has value a and subnodes b(), c() and d(). The node a(g())(b() c() d(e() f())) has value a(g()) (a node) and subnodes b(), c() and d(e() f()). In graphical representation (see Figure 1), node cells are depicted as rectangles. The subnodes are placed in order below the node and are connected to it, the active subnode being indicated by a filled arrowhead.

Table 1 Primitive transformations

Description	Mnemonic	Definition		Cost
No operation	skip	$\{\texttt{skip}, N\} = N$		1
Set value	'V'	$\{'V', W(\ldots)\} = V(\ldots)$		$1 + |V|$
Exchange values	exch	$\{\texttt{exch}, V(W(\ldots)\ \ldots)\} = W(V(\ldots)\ \ldots)$		1
Copy up	cup	$\{\texttt{cup}, V(W(\ldots)\ \ldots)\} = W(W(\ldots)\ \ldots))$		$1 + |W|$
Copy down	cdn	$\{\texttt{cdn}, V(W(\ldots)\ \ldots)\} = V(V(\ldots)\ \ldots))$		$1 + |V|$
Select left	left	$\{\texttt{left}, V(N\ \ldots\ O\ P)\} = V(P\ N\ \ldots\ O)$		1
Select right	right	$\{\texttt{right}, V(N\ O\ \ldots\ P)\} = V(O\ \ldots\ P\ N)$		1
Insert subnode	insert	$\{\texttt{insert}, V(N\ \ldots\ O)\} = V(\texttt{null}()\ N\ \ldots\ O)$		1
Delete subnode	delete	$\{\texttt{delete}, V(N\ O\ \ldots\ P)\} = V(O\ \ldots\ P)$		1
Node to value	split	$\{\texttt{split}, N\} = N()$		1
Value to node	replace	$\{\texttt{replace}, N(\ldots)\} = N$	N is a node	1
		$\{\texttt{replace}, A(\ldots)\} = A()$	A is an atom	1

Table 2 Compound transformations

Description	Notations	Definition	Cost
sequence	seq(X Y) X;Y [X Y...]	$\{\texttt{seq(X Y)}, N\} =$ $\{Y, \{X, N\}\}$	$1 + C(X, N) +$ $C(Y, \{X, N\})$
conditional	equ(X Y) X?Y	$\{\texttt{equ(X Y)}, N\} = \{X, N\}$ if $N = V(V(\ldots)\ \ldots)$ $\{\texttt{equ(X Y)}, N\} = \{Y, N\}$ otherwise	$1 + |V| + C(X, N)$ $< 1 + |V| + C(Y, N)$
parallel	all(X) @X	$\{\texttt{all(X)}, V(N_1\ \ldots\ N_k)\} =$ $V(\{X, N_1\}\ \ldots\ \{X, N_k\})$	$k + C(X, N_1) +$ $\cdots + C(X, N_k)$

2.2   Transformations

Operations in the model (called *transformations*) work on an implicit node passed to them. There are primitive transformations that work with nodes in elementary ways (Table 1). Direct access is allowed only to the root of the node tree and to its active subnode. Other subnodes are accessible only after suitable preparations, effectively a "walk" (compound transformation) is needed to bring the desired node into position. This may seem to be inconvenient and inefficient, but these "walks" can be made convenient by hiding them into suitably defined transformations. Also, experiments with a simulator written for the model suggest that the inefficiencies are tolerable. There are three builtin compound transformations (Table 2), these take primitive transformations as parameters. The `equ` transformation uses its first parameter to transform the (implicit) node if the value of that node equals the value of the node's active subnode. Otherwise, it uses the second one. `seq` is self-explanatory, `all` is discussed below. In the definition column, $\{X, N\}$ denotes the result of transformation X applied to node N. The cost column is discussed in the implementation section.

The most important feature of the model is how it handles parallelism with the `all` transformation. Its parameter is a transformation which is applied to all subnodes of the node. The advantage of this parallel operation is that it is initiated on disjoint data sets, so the resulting "processes" can work independently. The parallel operation terminates when all subnodes have been transformed. To initiate parallel processing, the program first has to create independent groups of data (subnodes of a node). The need to rearrange data admittedly costs programmer effort and computing resources, but this is offset by the ease of scheduling the independent "processes" that result from the initiation of the `all` transformation.

2.3   Programs

A NOP program is a potentially infinite (compound) transformation. Infinite transformations occur when iteration is needed to express an algorithm and are defined finitely using recursive equations. For example, assume we are given a node of the form $A(A_1() \ A_2() \ \dots \ A_k())$, where A and A_i are atoms and we are required to construct a transformation that makes active a subnode whose value is the same as that of the node (assuming that there is such a subnode). Then `locate : equ( skip seq( right locate))` specifies how this task could be done. So a program in the NOP model is a set of mutually recursive transformation definitions, where each definition introduces a unique transformation name. It is possible to define the denotational semantics of NOP programs by extending the $\{X, N\}$ notation for arbitrary finite and infinite transformations. The denotation of a transformation is a function that maps nodes to nodes. To define the semantics of a high level language, it only has to specify which transformation a program in that language stands for.

As an example, assume we represent binary digits with the atoms 0 and 1, binary numbers with nodes that contain binary digits in their subnodes. For example, the number 5 is represented by `null( 1 0 1)`. Further, suppose we have a transformation called `add` that adds two numbers, more precisely $\{\text{add}, V(B_1() \ B_2() \ N \ \dots)\} = B(N \ \dots)$, where B_1, B_2, B are binary numbers and B represents the sum of B_1 and B_2. We would like to have a transformation `add4` that adds 4 numbers, ie. $\{\text{add4}, V(B_1() \ B_2() \ B_3() \ B_4())\}$

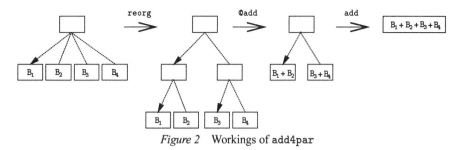

Figure 2   Workings of add4par

$= B()$, where B is the desired sum. A straightforward sequential solution might be as defined by add4seq below. We might do better, however, if we add two pairs of numbers in parallel and then add the results to form the final answer as defined by add4par (Figure 2). For parallel additon to be possible, we first have to reorganise the four numbers into two pairs. Reorganising transformations lie at the heart of NOP programs because of the way the all transformation works.

```
add4seq : [ add addnext addnext]
addnext : [ insert exch add]
add4par : [ reorg @add add]          // reorg omitted
```

Completeness of the model can easily be shown by constructing a NOP transformation that simulates a universal one-tape Turing Machine. The construction is relatively straightforward. Regarding efficiency, the NOP model may seem to be as weak as a Turing Machine because the focus of computation can only be shifted gradually from one place to another. In fact the NOP model offers the same efficiency as a logarithmic-cost RAM [4]. RAM behaviour can be simulated in the NOP model by representing global memory with a suitable node structure (essentially, a binary tree) and RAM operations with equivalent transformation sequences. Any RAM algorithm that uses W address bits to access its data can be simulated by a NOP program that runs at most W times slower.

Before execution, NOP programs can be optimised, making them easier to parallelise and therefore run faster. This is achieved for example by recognising that the equation $\text{seq}(\text{all}(X)\ \text{all}(Y)) = \text{all}(\text{seq}(X\ Y))$ holds for any transformations X and Y. This means that all transformations can be migrated upwards in the transformation tree representing the program, this way making its granularity coarser. Coarse granularity programs are easier to execute in parallel using dynamic load balancing techniques [9]–[12]. Calculating the cost of the two sides, it is seen that the right hand side form can also be faster.

3.   IMPLEMENTATION

In this section a NOP simulator written in C is described. The memory of the simulator is partitioned into four *segments*, each for storing one of the following: *nodes, program, execution stacks, execution units*. The node segment is used to store node cells while the program is running. The management of this segment is very simple because all cells are of the same size, allocation/deallocation requests are served from the list of free/allocated node cells. The program is most conveniently represented as a tree whose internal nodes are labelled with compound NOP transformations (seq, equ, all), its leaves are labelled with primitive transformations. It may be necessary to introduce loops when recursive definitions are used. An execution unit contains state information about a sequential thread of control. These are created at the start of the program and later when an all transformation is executed. One stack per execution unit is needed to handle seq transformations.

3.1   Data and Execution

Nodes are represented by a structure that contains four fields: pointer to left neighbour, value, pointer to active subnode and pointer to right neighbour. If the value of the node is itself a node, then the value field is a pointer to that node, otherwise it is an internal code identifying an atom.

Execution units are structures containing the following four fields: execution stack, pointer to node to be transformed, pointer to parent execution unit, number of active child execution units. During processing, execution units are arranged into a tree. The root of this tree is the first execution unit created to execute the whole program. Descendants of an execution unit are created when an all transformation is executed. At any given instant, only the execution units at the leaves are active, the rest are passive waiting for their children to terminate. Execution units are initialised by setting their node pointer to the node to be transformed and pushing the address of the transformation they have to execute onto their stack. As execution units are completely independent, in a parallel computer they can be scheduled by using simple greedy algorithms. There is no resource contention, no danger of deadlock.

3.2   Cost of Transformations

Primitive transformations (Table 1) can be separated into two groups, members of one group have constant cost, these transformations require only a few pointer assignments to execute. The other group contains transformations whose cost depends on the size of the node tree they have to operate on. The size of a particular value V (denoted $|V|$) tells us how many node cells are allocated for it. It is defined by $|A| = 0$ where A is an atom and $|V(N_1 \ \dots \ N_k)| = 1 + |V| + |N_1| + \dots + |N_k|$ for nodes. The cost of members of the second group reflects that they have to copy whole node trees from one place to another. In Table 2, $C(\mathsf{X}, N)$ denotes the cost of transforming node N with transformation X. equ has to compare two values, so its cost depends on the size of those values. all has to create as many execution units as there are subnodes, this is reflected in its cost. Finally, "cost" does not mean running time on parallel computers, but amount of work to be done.

3.3   Multiprocessor Implementation

The simulator immediately translates into an SM-MIMD implementation. Critical sections found in the node cell allocation/deallocation routines, execution unit handling routines and stack handling procedures can be dealt with using semaphores. It is obvious that there are ample opportunities to move data into private memory: each processor can be given a copy of the program, can have its own execution stack and some execution units can be stored privately. Given a node cell, it is very simple to determine which cells are going to be used next (value and active subnode); given an execution unit, it is easy to find out which units come into play soon. Equally importantly, there is no cache coherence problem because there can only exist cells used exclusively by one execution unit.

The DM-MIMD architecture is ideal regarding extensibility, the main direction of research currently undertaken is the implementation of the NOP model on it. The predictable data flow pattern helps us in determining exactly the data to send if communication becomes necessary, this way communication can be kept to an absolute minimum. Plans include the use of diffusion load balancing techniques for work distribution [9]–[12].

4.   HIGH LEVEL PROGRAMMING

The built-in transformations of the model are the "machine language" on which higher level languages can be based. Any such high level language provides facilities for programmers to define transformations. The most natural way to do this is by extending the functional notation defined for NOP programs earlier. Program execution has two (possibly overlapping) phases: the functional program is executed to result in a structure containing only NOP transformations, which are then executed by the NOP executor. The notation introduced here is called the NOP programming language.

4.1   Parameterised Transformations

Parameterised transformations are general patterns from which concrete instances are created by replacing formal arguments with actual ones. The use of a transformation name with different number of arguments is allowed, as long as every name/arity combination occurs only once. Note that compound NOP transformations can be regarded as parameterised transformations (seq/2, equ/2, all/1). Other parameterised transformations:

```
const( NODE) : [ NODE replace]              // output is always NODE
seta( V)    : [ exch V exch]   // set value of active subnode to V
dor( X)     : [ right X left]          // do X with right neighbour
insert( V)  : [ insert seta(V)] // create new subnode with value V
cequ( V Y N) : [ V Y ? N] // if active subnode = V, do Y, else do N
```

There are constructs similar to the CASE statement of imperative languages. They exhibit the same pattern, namely the node has to be prepared for a test, then after the decision has been made, the node has to be brought back to its initial state before transforming further (doequ/4).

```
doequ( BEFORE AFTER SUCCEED FAIL) :
   [ BEFORE [ AFTER SUCCEED] ? [ AFTER FAIL]]
case( V MATCH NOMATCH)             : // check value of node
   doequ( insert( V) delete MATCH NOMATCH)
casea( V MATCH NOMATCH)           : // check active subnode
   doequ( [ exch insert( V)] [ delete exch] MATCH NOMATCH)
```

Parameters can also be introduced to be used in place of transformation names, this way the "called" transformation is told what other transformation to use but it is free to pass parameters on its own.

```
while( Test BODY)     : Test( [BODY *] skip)
   // * stands for the left side of the equation
repeat( BODY Test)    : [ BODY Test( skip *)]
and( TestA TestB Y N) : TestA( TestB( Y N) N)
or( TestA TestB Y N)  : TestA( Y TestB( Y N))
```

A few simple but useful transformations that will be used subsequently:

```
push     : [ insert exch right]
exchdel  : [ exch delete]
expand   : [ split insert exch @replace]
contract : [ @split exch replace]
```

Recall that all/1 works by transforming all subnodes of a node with the same transformation. It is often desirable to use different transformations on different subnodes, so we define all/2 that transforms the active subnode with its first, the rest of the subnodes with its second parameter.

```
all( ACTIVE REST)  : keepval( xall( ACTIVE REST))
xall( ACTIVE REST) :
   [ @expand seta( 'A') @case( 'A' @ACTIVE @REST) @contract]
keepval( X)        : [ expand exch @X exch contract]
sub( X)            : all( X skip)
```

all/2 and sub/1 can be defined in the same fashion with more parameters as well. An implementation may provide some or all of these transformations as builtin for efficiency.

4.2   Programming Patterns

The goal of *enumeration* is that each subnode value is brought up to the root node. A general way to solve the problem is similar to that of used in xall/2. Bringing a value from the active subnode to the node can be done either by an exchange transformation (enummove) or by a copy (enumcopy).

```
enumpre        : [ @[ expand 'ENUM'] insert]     // preparation
enumfin        : [ delete @contract]             // cleanup
enumnext( MODE) : [ right nullequ( enumfin [ sub( MODE) exch])]
nullequ( Y N)  : cequ( 'null' Y N)
enummove       : enumnext( exch)
enumcopy       : enumnext( cup)
```

It is useful to define a transformation (pc/2) that mimicks the behaviour of a bufferless *producer-consumer* pair. This is achieved by using a node with two subnodes, one of them belongs to the producer, while the other one to the consumer. A producer transformation is used to produce the next value which must be put into the left subnode, then the value is moved into the right subnode, which is then transformed by the consumer transformation. The producer signals the end of item stream with the atom null. With this separation of functionalities, a high degree of flexibility is achieved.

```
pcpre( PPRE CPRE):                              // preparation
    [ expand insert right sub( PPRE CPRE)]
pcfin( PFIN CFIN):                              // cleanup
    [ sub( PFIN CFIN) dor( [ sub( split) exchdel]) exch contract]
pcxfer              :[ exch dor( exch)]         // item transfer
pc( P C)            :[ sub( P) while( notnull [ pcxfer sub( P C)])]
notnull( Y N)       :nullequ( N Y)
```

Reorganisation of data may be needed when we prepare for using the all transformation. This takes place by creating a node with two subnodes, the original node on the left and a new one on the right. A producer transformation extracts the data from the original node and a consumer transformation inserts them into a new structure. This mechanism is captured by greorg below. Very frequently, the producer transformation is enumeration, so it is convenient to define the specialised forms mreorg and creorg.

```
greorg( PPRE CPRE P C PFIN CFIN) :
    [ pcpre( PPRE CPRE) pc( P C) pcfin( PFIN CFIN)]
mreorg( CPRE C) : greorg( enumpre CPRE enummove C skip skip)
creorg( CPRE C) : greorg( enumpre CPRE enumcopy C skip skip)
```

There are a number of problems that can be solved by applying the *divide-and-conquer* method and it is very easy to define a parameterised NOP transformation that serves as a basis for such algorithms. It has four parameters, Test to decide whether the problem at hand can be solved directly or has to be decomposed, ATOMIC to solve a subproblem without decomposition. DIVIDE accepts a suitable node and transforms it into one whose subnodes represent subproblems. Conversely, CONQUER expects subsolutions to be present as subnodes and combines them into a node representing a single subsolution.

```
dc( Test ATOMIC DIVIDE CONQUER):Test( ATOMIC [ DIVIDE @* CONQUER])
```

5.   EXAMPLE APPLICATION - QUICK SORT

qsort/1 uses the divide-and-conquer approach. The atomicity test is the binary selector ifleaf/2 (omitted) which selects its first argument (skip) if there is nothing to be sorted, the second argument otherwise. If there is at least one item, qsplit/1 is used to select one as a pivot element and arrange the rest into two groups. The two groups are sorted, then qmerge/0 is used to construct a node with subnodes containing the pivot element and the members of the two sorted groups in the appropriate order. Both qsplit/1 and qmerge/0 use a producer-consumer pair and enumeration. The algorithm exhibits both fine grained parallelism (by using `pc/2`) and coarse grained parallelism (by sorting two groups of items in parallel using `dc/4`). How much of this potential parallelism is realised, depends on the runtime scheduling of the independent "processes".

```
qsort( CMP)   : dc( ifleaf skip qsplit( CMP) qmerge)
qsplit( CMP) : [
   mreorg(
      const( 'newelem( pivot( gt le))')  // preparation for consumer
      casea( 'pivot'
         exch                            // first item becomes pivot
         qsplace( CMP)                    // others placed relative to pivot
      ) )
      replace contract]                                         // tidy up
qsplace( CMP) : [
      exch                        // exch pivot and new item
      CMP( @dor( qsp) @qsp)            // LESS to the right
      exch]                       // pivot back into position
qsp        : [ exch sub( push)]  // push to end of subnode list
qmerge     : [
      dor( qsp)                   // pivot to end of LESS queue
      sub( enumpre)         // prepare to enum greater items
      pc( enummove push)     // move them to end of queue
      right contract]                                  // tidy up
```

References

[1] L. G. Valiant: A Bridging Model for Parallel Computation, Comm. ACM, Vol. 33, No. 8, pp. 103–111, August 1990

[2] B. M. Maggs, L. Matheson, R. E. Tarjan: Models of Parallel Computation: A Survey and Synthesis, Proc. 28th Hawaii Intl. Conf. on Sys. Sci. (HICSS), Vol. 2, pp. 61–70, 1995

[3] J. B. Dennis: Machines and Models for Parallel Computing, International Journal of Parallel Programming, 22(1), pp. 47–77, February 1994

[4] R. M. Karp, V. Ramachandran: Parallel Algorithms for Shared-Memory Machines, in Handbook of Theoretical Computer Science, Vol. A, Ch. 17, pp. 869–942, Elsevier, 1990.

[5] E. Bal, J. G. Steiner, A. S. Tannenbaum: Programming Languages for Distributed Computing Systems, ACM Comp. Surv., Vol. 21, No. 3, pp. 261–322, ACM Press, Sept 1989

[6] D. Gelernter, N. Carriero: Applications Experience with Linda, in Proc. PPEALS 1998, SIGPLAN Not. (ACM) Vol. 23, No. 9, pp. 173–187, September 1988

[7] B. K. Szymanski (ed.): Parallel Functional Languages and Compilers, ACM Press Frontier Series, ACM Press, 1991

[8] S. Gregory: Parallel Logic Programming in PARLOG, Addison-Wesley, 1987

[9] M. H. Willebeck-Lemair, A. P. Reeves: Strategies for Dynamic Load Balancing on Highly Parallel Computers, Trans. on Par. and Distr. Sys., Vol. 4, No. 9, pp. 979–993, Sept 1993

[10] F. W. Burton, M. M. Huntbach: Virtual Tree Machines, IEEE Trans. on Computers, Vol. C-33, No. 3, pp. 278–280, March 1984

[11] L. Schrettner, I. E. Jelly: A Test Environment for Investigation of Dynamic Load Balancing in Transputer Networks, Transputer Applications and Systems '93, Vol. 36, pp. 284–295, IOS Press, 1993

[12] A. Corradi, L. Leonardi, F. Zambonelli: Diffusive Load-Balancing Policies for Dynamic Applications, IEEE Concurrency, 7(1), January 1999

THREAD MANAGEMENT MECHANISMS OF CEFOS

Makoto Shimosaki, Hideo Taniguchi, Makoto Amamiya
Graduate School of Information Science and Electrical Engneering,
Kyushu University, Fukuoka, JAPAN
{simosaki,tani}@csce.kyushu-u.ac.jp, amamiya@is.kyushu-u.ac.jp

Abstract   This paper describes thread management mechanisms of an operating system for communication-execution fusion, CEFOS (Communication-Execution Fusion Operating System). CEFOS is based on a fine-grain multithreading approach. Once a thread begins to run, it never stops until it is completed, and the maximam run time of a thread is 1 msec. A basic policy of thread management is to realize light-weight threads and fairness of executions. And we suggest the DRD(Display Requests and Data) function which takes small overhead in executions cooperation of processes and OS kernel. The basic mechanisms of thread management, scheduling, preemption, time-slice and synchronizing are described.

Keywords: fine-grain multithread, light-weight thread, fairness, systemcall, upcall

1.   INTRODUCTION

Recently hardware technologies are advancing towards at higher speeds and larger scales. For example, optical-fiber transmission-line technology is now at the level of Giga-bits/sec speed. Giga-bits of memory on a chip and higher clock speeds are under development. So, in the near future, distributed and parallel systems using these high performance hardwares will be constructed.

But it is a problem that software technologies including processor architectures can not make use of high performance of advanced hardwares. So, new software and architecture technology that achieves high performance for internal executions and communications needs to be developed.

Considering these hardware and software trends, we have planned and are pursuing the FUCE (FUsion of Communication and Execution) project. The main objective is to develop a new architecture that fuses communications and computations. The FUCE project is developing a new processor architecture and kernel software on it. We named the processor, FUCE processor, and the kernel software, CEFOS [1].

Both the FUCE processor and CEFOS are designed with the fine-grain multithreading approach. The importance and feasiblity of fine-grain multithreading technique are attracting interest to parallel computer research field. For instance, the MTA machine has been commercialized[3] and the HTMT project is on going with the goal of Petaflops machine[4]. The idea of the FUCE machine emerged from our multithreading architecture and language research[5,6]. Fine-grain multithreading promises high performance in fusing of communications and internal executions. Both of them are controlled by a unified thread execution mechanisms.

In CEFOS, we realize the fusion of communications and internal executions in execution time and function interfaces. We define internal executions as below. First, it is performed in a single computer. Second, it doesn't communicate to threads of the other computers. Last, it is based on executions of data. And we define communications as sending or receiving of data among threads of more than one computer. And we suggest DRD function which enables good cooperation of between executions of process and operating system (OS) kernel. This is a good point of CEFOS. For example, BeOS which is a multithreaded microkernel OS takes a large overhead of upcalls in switching threads. Because it is a microkernel OS. But CEFOS takes a small overhead in switching threads.

And, we aim at fusing communications and internal executions using Distributed Shared Memory (DSM) and Remote Procedure Call (RPC). We will make the environment that RPC is used as well as local calls. As first step, we designed thread management mechanism.

2. SCALE OF THE SYSTEM AND DESIGN METHOD OF THREADS

Our system is constructed connecting some computers with fast network. Software consists of jobs, processes and threads. Figure 1 illustrate these summary. There are 4 of basic design. First, there are some jobs in a system. Second, jobs consist of several processes , and provide services. Third, processes consist of hundreds of threads, and they are executed in one computer. In other words, threads which composes one process are executed in one computer. And there are user processes which are executed in user mode, and kernel processes which are executed in kernel mode. And last, threads never stop until it is completed. And maximum run time is 1 msec.

We design threads based on 2 policies. One is to realize threads light-weight. We attempt to reduce switching threads and to performs switching threads in higher speeds. The other is to realize fairness of executions. We realize fairness of executions not only among processes but also among threads. So we fairly realize each service which a job provides.

3. THREAD MANAGEMENT MECHANISMS

3.1 Cooperation between processes and OS kernel

In realizing the environment which multiple threads run in one process, it is very important to cooperate effectively between executions of processes and OS kernel.

There are two methods to manage threads of user processes [2]. First one is to manage by OS kernel(kernel level way). The other one is to manage by library(user level way). Kernel level way is realized in many OS. And it can realize higher the working ratio of processors and fairness of executions for processes, and distribute processes. But it is a problem that there are a lot of mode changings between kernel and user in switching threads. In the user level way, thread management mechanism of each process manages threads of the process. Therefore, among threads in one process, there is no need to change modes in switching

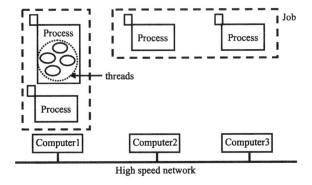

Figure 1   System summary

threads. So executions are done in high speeds. But OS doesn't manage threads, so priority inversion among threads often happens. And it is difficult to distribute executions in multiple processors and to realize fairness of executions. Therefore, [2] deals with these problems by cooperating tightly between executions of processes and OS kernel.

In traditional OS, there are two ways to cooperate between executions of processes and OS kernel. First is systemcall and the other is upcall. Systemcall notifies the requests of processes to OS kernel using SVC instruction or trap instruction. Then OS kernel performs executions based on these notifications. Upcall calls specific executions in the processes. Both of these two ways takes large overheads in the executions.

Therefore, we suggest Display Requests and Data (DRD) function. DRD has 4 peculiarities. First, processes and OS kernel share common memory area(CA). Second, processes and OS kernel display execution requests and data of execution state as information which processes and OS kernel mutually need. Third, Processes and OS kernel cooperate using displayed information. And last, When necessary, processes call OS kernel, and OS kernel calls processes.

DRD function enables cooperation between executions of processes and OS kernel with small overhead. In DRD function, processes and OS kernel behave as below. (4) is performed only when necessary.

(1) Processes display contents of execution requests to OS kernel and internal information of the processes which OS kernel needs. And they are displayed at CA.

(2) OS kernel displays contents of matters and information inside of the OS kernel. And they are displayed at CA.

(3) On the proper occasion, processes and OS kernel perform executions using displayed information at CA.

(4) When size of CA is shortage or in the case of urgency, processes can call OS kernel by systemcall and OS kernel can call processes by upcall.

As described above, our basic way to cooperate between executions of processes and OS kernel is not traditional notification but display. In other words, not sender but receiver has a initiative of executions. In this case, sender means process in (1) and OS kernel in (2). And receiver means process and OS kernel in (3). Therefore, receiver does not need to interrupt executions when it receives the request. In traditional way, sender has a initiative of executions, so receiver must take large overhead to interrupt the execution when it receives the request. But in DRD function, receiver doesn't interrupt the execution and takes small overhead. And this DRD function can minimize mutual call. For example, it is possible that calls from processes to OS kernel are called only when there is no thread which can run in that process.

In CEFOS, we realize the integrated way of kernel level way and user level way using DRD function, and resolve problems both of ways. This integrated way has 2 peculiarities. One is integrated systemcall. The other is cooperate of schedulers. Integrated systemcall reduces the calls from threads of user processes to OS kernel. As cooperation among schedulers, thread schedulers in the process display highest priority of the threads to process scheduler in the OS kernel. And process scheduler in the OS kernel displays control transition requests to thread schedulers in the processes. These are for preemption function which shorten the priority inversion period of the threads. Details of these are later.

3.2   Basic mechanism and function specification

In CEFOS, there are kernel processes which share programs with OS kernel and user processes which don't share programs with OS kernel. We define processes mean both of kernel processes and user processes.

Figure 2 illustrates relation of processes and threads. Basic mechanism and function specification of thread management are as below.

(1) A process has one virtual storage space, and it is the unit of resource operation. And it has process priority.

(2) Sequential run time of a process is limited and a process is time-sliced when necessary.

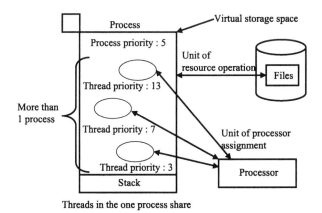

Figure 2   Basic mechanism of process and threads

(3) Execution order of processes is controlled based on process priority. Processes are preempted when necessary.

(4) There is more than one thread in a process. The thread is a unit of processor assignment and has thread priority. Each of the thread in the same process doesn't have its own stack. Threads in the smae process share a stack among them.

(5) Sequential run time of a thread is not limited. Threads are basically not time-sliced. Once a thread begins to run, it never stops until it is completed. But if a process is time-sliced, it is possible for the threads of the process to be interrupted the execution.

(6) Execution order of threads is controlled based on thread priority among threads of processes which have equal priority. If priority inversion among threads happens, executions for resolving priority inversion is performed after completing thread execution which is running at that time. In this way, executions for resolving priority inversion is performed not immediately but after completing thread execution which is running at that time. We named this function semi-preemption.

(5) reduces switching threads. (4) and reduction of mode changings by using integrated systemcalls, we attempt to execute switching threads in high speeds. So we aim at realizing light-weight thread. And we also aim at realizing the fair execution using advantages of (2) ,(3) and (6). Semi-preemption function of (6) reduces switching threads.

3.3   Thread scheduling mechanism

basic mechanism .   Figure 3 illustrates the basic mechanism of scheduling. And explanation of the basic mechanism is below.

(1) There are two styles in completion of thread executions. One is the style to call thread scheduler in completion. The other is the style to call lump of systemcalls in completion.

(2) Thread scheduler is called from completion executions or lump of systemcalls. It selects the thread having the highest priority in the threads which can run. Then selected thread begins to run. And as a cooperation of schedulers, thread scheduler displays priority of the thread which has highest priority in the threads in RUN state or READY state. And if thread scheduler is requested to transit control from OS kernel, it calls lump of systemcalls and prompt to transit control to OS kernel.

(3) In the case that lump of systemcalls is received requests to call OS kernel from completion executions, it accumulates systemcalls requests and calls thread scheduler. And when defined number of systemcalls requests are accumulated, lump of systemcalls calls OS kernel caller to request integrated systemcall. And in the case that lump of systemcalls is prompted from thread scheduler to transit control to OS kernel, it calls OS kernel caller as an integrated systemcall which consists of accumulated systemcalls.

(4) Process scheduler is called in the end of kernel executions for each systemcall or interruption executions. It select and run the process which has the highest priority in the processes which can run. And process scheduler gets information of highest thread priority in other processes from each thread scheduler. And when necessary, it displays a request to transit control.

Time-slice mechanism . Process scheduler measures sequential run time of a process using timer interruption. If sequential run time exceeds defined time (time-slice interval), process scheduler robs of the processor from the process running at that time. And process scheduler re-schedules processes. We define sequential run time is the time which subtract time of READY state from running time. Running time is the time from beginning of the RUN state to beginning of the next WAIT state. And it is not cleared to zero if processor is robbed by preemption in RUN state.

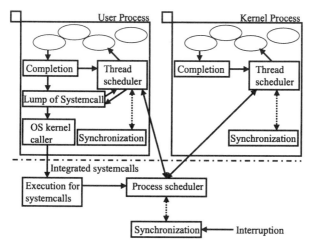

Figure 3   Basic mechanism of scheduling

Preemption mechanism .   Process scheduler senses priority inversion in process executions based on process priority. And it immediately execute preemption.

Figure 4 illustrates semi-preemption mechanism which is for threads of the processes having equall process priority. Explanation is below.

(1) Thread scheduler of each process displays to OS kernel the highest thread priority in the threads of RUN state or READY state.

(2) If there are more than two processes which can run and has the highest priority, process scheduler selects the process as below. First, the threads which have the highest priority in each process are selected. Second, in the threads selected in first, the thread which has the highest priority is selected. Third, process scheduler selects the process which has the thread selected in second. Then process scheduler requests control transition to the thread scheduler of the process which the thread is running at that time.

(3) The thread scheduler which is displayed control transition request transits control to OS kernel in thread switching.

As described above, in semi-preemption function, process scheduler in the OS kernel and thread schedulers in the processes cooperate. In this case, the longest interval of priority inversion is time-slice interval or maximum run time of one thread. Maximum run time of one thread is shorter than time-slice interval. And maximum run time is 1 msec. So the average interval of priority inversion is 500 usec.

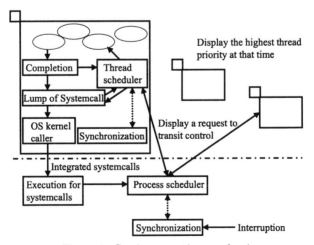

Figure 4   Semi-preemption mechanism

3.4   Synchronizing mechanism

Synchronizing mechanism are as below. We manage synchronization using synchronizing management table. (1) and (2) are for threads in the same process. (3) and (4) are for threads among other processes.

(1) There are two kind of entries in synchronizing management table. One is for the threads of the same process. The other is for threads of the other processes. And we attempt to protect thread executions of the same process from the thread executions of the other processes.

(2) Entries for threads of the same process are shared among threads of the same process in user's space. So, this method can avoid mode changings and can reduce execution time for synchronizing.

(3) Entries for threads of the other processes are shared among processes in user's space. So, this method can avoid mode changings and can reduce execution time for synchronizing.

(4) OS kernel notifies occasion of synchronizing by communicating among computers. So threads do not need to be conscious of threads in other computers.

Figure 5 illustrates synchronizing mechanism. Synchronizing management table consists of two tables. One is for threads in the same process. The other is for threads for threads in the other processes. And a pair of both entries composes synchronizing entry for one thread.

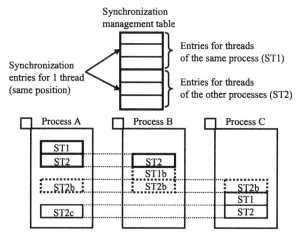

Figure 5   Synchronizing mechanism

4. CONCLUSION

This paper describes thread management mechanism of CEFOS aiming at the fusion of communications and internal executions. In CEFOS, fine-grain multithreading are the basic units of processor assignment.

Basic policy of thread management is to realize light-weight threads and fairness of executions. For former, we attempt to reduce switching threads and to perform switching threads in higher speeds. And for latter, we attempt to realize time-slice, preemption and semi-preemption function. And we suggested Display Requests and Data function for executions cooperation of processes and OS kernel.

We will design the mechanism for the fusion of communications and internal executions, based on DSM and RPC. We will implement these mechanism and evaluate some performance in the future work.

Acknowledgments

We thank Shigeru Kusakabe, Takuya Tanabayashi and Hiroshi Nakayama for their work to design our thread management mechanisms. This project is a part of "research project on architecture for new generation multimedia information technology" sonsored by TAO (Telecommunications Advancement Organization of Japan).

References

[1] Shigeru K. , Hiroshi T. , Kazuaki M. , Hideo T. , Makoto A. : " Parallel and Distributed Operating System CEFOS (Communication-Execution Fusion OS " , IPSJ ISG Notes , Vol.99 , No.251 , pp.25-32 1999 .

[2] Thomas E. A. , Brian N. B. , Edward D. L. , and Henry M. L. , "Scheduler Activations : Effective kernel Support for the User-Level Management of Parallelism , " Proc. of the 13th ACM Symp. on OS Principles , pp-95-109 1991 .

[3] G. Alverson , et al "Tera Hardware-Software Cooperation" , Proc. Supercomputing, San Jose , 1997.

[4] G. Gao , et al "Hybrid Technology Multithreaded Architecture" Proc. The Sixth Sympposium on The Frontiers of Massively Parallel Computation, Annalolis , pp.98-105 , 1996.

[5] M. Amamiya , et al "Datarol : A Parallel Machine Architecture for Fine-Grain Multithreading" , Proc. Third Working Conference on Massively Parallel Programming Models , London , 1997.

[6] M. Amamiya , et al "Co-Processor Design for Fine-grain Message Handling in KUMP/D" , Proc. European Conference on Parallel Processing , Passau , pp.779-788 , 1997.

THE PARALLEL VIDEO SERVER SESAME-KB

Klaus Breidler, Harald Kosch, László Böszörményi

Department of Information Technology,
University Klagenfurt, Austria
{kbreidle,harald,laszlo}@itec.uni-klu.ac.at

Abstract   This paper presents the parallel video server SESAME-KB, by the means of its architectural design, striping, scheduling, caching and admission policy. Furthermore we compare our prototype to approaches which influenced our realization.

Keywords: Parallel Video Server, Parallel Systems and Communication.

1.   INTRODUCTION

Video servers become more and more popular. A better performance of the involved hardware components, especially the increasing performance of the networks support this trend. In the meantime, several parallel video servers are available [1]. Some are commercial (e.g. the Tiger product from Microsoft Research [2]), some are objects of research (e.g. the ELVIRA - Experimental VIdeo serveR for ATM [4]).

In this paper we present our parallel video server SESAME-KB, developed in collaboration with the lab of Parallel Computing in Lyon (ENS Lyon) [6]. We compare our approach to the just mentioned products Tiger and ELVIRA, and the StonyBrook Video Server [3] which influenced our design.

2.   THE SESAME-KB PARALLEL VIDEO SERVER

The parallel SESAME-KB video server runs on the top of a LINUX PC-cluster interconnected by a Fast Ethernet Switched Network. The basis for the video server application is the Parallel Multithreaded Machine (PM^2) [5] platform which uses Lightweight Remote Procedure Calls for communication between the nodes.

Server model.   Fig. 1 describes the logical view of of the parallel video server we developed. This model consists of the following main parts (fig. 1):

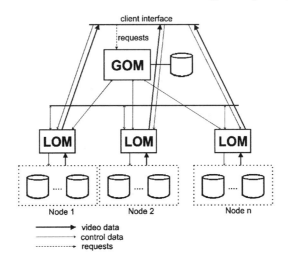

Figure 1   Architecture of the parallel video server

The Global Object Manager (GOM): The Global Object Manager is responsible that the whole server functions. It administrates the traffic of data inside the server. Thus, it requires to have a global view of the server state, i.e. how many resources are occupied by accepted queries, which nodes perform the query, the location of the data (which node, which disk), etc. The main function is the delegation of the accepted query to one of the available Local Object Managers. Furthermore, it is responsible for the admission control, i.e. to accept or reject a query request dependent on the available resources and the administration of the caches of each node.

The Local Object Managers (LOM): The Local Object Managers are located on each node in the parallel video server architecture. A node represents a separate computer. One of the LOMs is chosen to be the master-LOM and the GOM delegates the whole query to this particular LOM. It is then responsible for performing the query, i.e. collecting all necessary parts of the requested sequence and sending back the result to the client if the query is done.

Communication inside the server: A way for saving resources and to gain performance inside the server is the use of threads and Lightweight Remote Procedure Calls in the Parallel Multithreaded Machine (PM^2) environment. Both, control and video data are sent using this environment.

Client interface: To be able to serve video data, the parallel video server has to be able to receive queries from the client. It is the GOM's task to receive and treat the query for performing the admission control and selecting the according master-LOM for executing the query.

Nodes: Each node in the parallel environment is an individual computer which has its own hard disk(s), main memory and CPU. Only the call of the master-LOM makes them working in a coordinated way.

Client-Server communication.   A client-server protocol is presented using TCP and UDP. TCP covers the first part of the protocol until the UDP connection is set up. For the actual delivery of the video data, UDP is used. In order to achieve real-time delivery of the video data, a cyclic scheduling mechanism dividing the time into I/O cycles is implemented. Every cycle, the same amount of data is sent to the client.

To be able to reuse already queried video data and to increase the efficiency, a caching mechanism was implemented. For that, it is necessary to have a global view of the caches being located on each node in the parallel environment in order to reuse data when a new query is accepted. It has to be mentioned that there is no cache replacement strategy implemented so far which means that the cache will be full after having processed a certain amount of queries.

Finally, an admission control based on the available resources and existing video data segments in the cache is presented. A query can only be accepted if there is enough space in one of the I/O cycles on the nodes and if there is enough memory buffer available.

3.   COMPARISON TO RELATED APPROACHES

Implementing a parallel video server requires much more features to be added so that it functions correctly than a serial video server. First of all, video data has to be striped over the nodes involved. Certain algorithms for finding the video data again have to be implemented. In the case of the Tiger video server [2], this is not necessary, because this server is a video-on-demand server which means that every requested video is read from its very beginning. In the ELVIRA video server [4], this case described before only represents an exception since it is possible to query video segments being located inside the video clip.

If there are several nodes involved, mechanisms to cope with nodes that completely fail have to be considered. The Tiger video server mirrors the data over the other nodes. In the ELVIRA project, such a situation was not taken into consideration.

Nevertheless, the architecture of the ELVIRA video server and the execution steps a query has to pass are very similar in the parallel video server SESAME-KB. First of all, both video servers are parallel video servers, i.e. they run on several nodes. A central component in the ELVIRA server receives the queries and does the admission control. Compared to the SESAME-KB video server, the GOM has the same function.

If a query is accepted by the admission control, ELVIRA's work is to choose one of the nodes involved to execute the query. Also this concept is equal to that of the SESAME-KB video server.

Finally, all the other nodes for collecting the video segments not being located on the local node are contacted. The master-LOM's task is exactly the same as described before.

As in the SESAME-KB video server, TCP and UDP are used by the ELIVRA video server for communication and delivery of video data. Note that no caching mechanism can be found in the ELVIRA video server.

Furthermore, no query scheduling mechanism is mentioned for the Norwegian video server. To perform query scheduling on each node of the parallel video server SESAME-KB, some ideas have been taken from the Stony Brook Video Server (SBVS) [3]. There, an I/O cycle time is defined so that the requested amount of data is sent to the client every I/O cycle. This I/O cycle time is also one of the basics for the admission control. In the parallel video server SESAME-KB, this model of a predefined I/O cycle time is adapted on each node involved.

References

[1] Jack Y. B. Lee: Parallel Video Servers: A Tutorial. IEEE MultiMedia 5(2): 20-28 (1998)

[2] Bolosky W.J. et al., "The Tiger Video Fileserver", In: Proceedings of the Sixth International Workshop on Network and Operating System Support for Digital Audio and Video, IEEE Computer Society, Zushi, Japan, April, 1996.

[3] Chiueh T., Venkatramani C., Vernick M., "Design and Implementation of the Stony Brook Video Server", in: Software – Practice and Experience, 27(2): pp 139-154 (1997).

[4] Sandstå O., Langørgen S., Midstraum R., "Video Server on an ATM Connected Cluster of Workstations", in: Proceedings of the XVII International Conference of the Chilean Computer Science Society, SCCC'97, pp. 207-217, Valparaiso, Chile, Nov. 1997.

[5] Benot Planquelle, Jean-Franois Mhaut, and Nathalie Revol. "Multi-cluster approach with PM2", in: Intl Conf. on Parallel and Distributed Processing Techniques and Applications (PDPTA'99), vol. 2, pages 779-785, Las Vegas, NV, June 1999.

[6] Ahmed Mostefaoui: "The Design of a High Performance Video Server for Managing TV Archives", in Proceedings of the Int. ADBIS Conf. 1997, pp. 331-338, Electronic Proc. Springer Verlag, St. Petersburg, Russia.

THE POOR MAN'S SUPERCOMPUTER

F. Csikor, Z. Fodor, P. Hegedüs, S. D. Katz, A. Piróth
Institute for Theoretical Physics,
Eötvös University, Pázmány P. sétány 1/A, 1117 Budapest, Hungary
{csikor,fodor,hegedus,katz,piroth}@pitt.edu

V. K. Horváth
Department of Physics, University of Pittsburgh, Pittsburgh, PA 15260, USA
vhorvath@pitt.edu

Abstract   The goal of the Poor Man's Supercomputer (PMS) project is to construct a cost effective, scalable, fast parallel computer to perform numerical calculations of physical problems that can be implemented on a lattice with nearest neighbour interactions. Our first implementation of PMS was tested by Lattice Gauge Theory simulations. We obtained 3\$/Mflop price-to-sustained performance ratio for double precision operations.

Our PMS project started in 1998 and here we report our recent results achieved with our first PMS machine (PMS1). The nodes in a PMS machine are almost complete PC's since they have excellent cost/performance ratios and they can easily be upgraded. Special PMS communication plug-in boards are installed in each node providing fast communication channels. These communication cards are only used during calculations, the task management is done by a very cheap Token Ring network.

The PMS1 consists of 32 PC's arranged in a three-dimensional, rack mounted, $2 \times 4 \times 4$ mesh. The rack contains four trays and each of them holds eight nodes in two rows (see Fig. 1.1(a)). Each node is powered by its own standard PC power supply located at the bottom of the rack. A node consists of a 100MHz motherboard a 450MHz AMD K6-II processor, 128Mbyte SDRAM, 10Mbit Ethernet card. Each node boots Linux from its own (2.1 Gbyte) harddrive. The price of one node was approximately \$350. The additional cost for the communication cards (see later) is \$40 for each node.

The basic idea behind the hardware is that the PMS communication channels (PMS CH) provide direct connections for each node to its nearest neighbours

Figure 1   a, The PMS1 rack and the trays. b, Nodes connected by flat cables in one direction.

(NN). The PMS CH handles both polled port (PP I/O) operations and direct memory access (DMA) between two selected nodes. The PMS architecture does not define the bus used for the PMS CH. In the PMS1 we have used the simplest ISA bus (see Fig. 1(b)). Implementation of the PMS CH for faster buses is under development. The ISA implementation of the PMS CH includes two plug-in boards, the PMS CPU card and the PMS Relay card. The CPU card contains the main circuits needed for transmitting data, while the Relay card contains the connectors for the flat cables connecting the adjacent nodes and some additional circuits. As a result only the PMS CPU card has to be changed if different bus is used for data transmission. The CPU and RELAY cards are connected together with a short flat cable.

In PMS1 the speed of communication through these cards –limited essentially by the ISA bus speed– is 2 Mbyte/sec, which is greater than the speed of the Token Ring by a factor of two. Furthermore to build up our communication practically no time is needed, while the build-up of the Ethernet connection is rather slow. An important advantage of using the PMS cards is that in principle N/2 pair of nodes may communicate simultaneousiy in a machine which includes N nodes. Altogether we get two orders of magnitude better performance. Note that the system is scalable. One can build machines with larger number of nodes and the total inter-node communication performance will be proportional to the number of nodes.

A main computer controls the whole cluster through the Token Ring network. The machine works in Single Process Multiple Data (SPMD) mode: all nodes execute the same program, while the data may differ on the individual nodes. Some simple Linux scripts are used to copy the executable program code and the data to and from the nodes and to start the program execution. Writing applications for the PMS1 and a single PC is almost identical. One only has to keep in mind the 3-dimensional mesh structure of the machine; no further deep understanding of how the communication works is required. On application level the programmers need to know only few functions like pms_open(), pms_close(), pms_send(), and pms_recv(). These functions are provided in a C library and are supported by low level device drivers written for Linux. Priority issues are handled at the high level.

To test the performance the PMS1 we used lattice gauge theory simulations with double precision variables. Two types of theories were studied. a.) Pure SU(3) gauge theory was studied with the simplest Wilson action. Overrelaxation and heatbath updating algorithms were used for the link variables. b.) We studied the bosonic sector of the minimal supersymmetric extension of the standard model (MSSM). The most CPU time consuming parts were written in assembly language in both cases [2].

These two theories provided about the same performance results for the PMS1. The MSSM results for communication are actually somewhat better. Since it is much more straightforward to compare our SU(3) results than those of the MSSM simulations with the results of the literature, in the following paragraphs we discuss the SU(3) case, too.

For small lattice sizes the most economical way to use our 32 PC cluster is to put independent lattices on the different nodes. The maximum lattice size in the SU(3) theory for 128 Mbyte memory is $\sim 20^4$, or for finite temperature systems $6 \cdot 32^3$. One thermalizes such a system on a single node, then distributes the configuration to the other nodes and continues the updating on all nodes. The sustained performance of the PMS1 is 152Mflop/node (4.9Gflop total) in this case.

Increasing the volume of the simulated system one can divide the lattice between 2 nodes (the $2 \times 4 \times 4$ topology has 2 nodes in one of the directions). For even larger lattices one can use 4 nodes (4 in one direction), 8 nodes (2×4 in two directions) 16 nodes (4×4 in two directions) or 32 nodes ($2 \times 4 \times 4$ in three directions). Again, the most economical way to perform the simulations is to prepare one thermalized configuration and put it on other nodes (this method obviously can not be used for the $2 \times 4 \times 4$ topology, because in this case the whole machine with 32 nodes is just one lattice).

In order to compare our machine with other existing (and proposed) parallel systems used in lattice gauge theory, we use the plot similar to [3]. As it can be seen in Fig. 2, PMS1 is perhaps the best existing machine as far as price/sustained performance (P/P) is concerned. It is particularly important to emphasize that the presented performance 3$/Mflop with ≈ 4.9Gflop total performance of PMS1 is calculated for double precision operations (while some of the performances of the machines on the plot are given for single precision operations).

The PMS1, similarly to other workstation farms has a moderate maximum sustained performance as compared to Teraflop-scale machines (CP-PACS [4] or QCDSP [5]). However, PMS1 has outstanding P/P ratio The reason for this is twofold. a. Machines with 100Mbit fast Ethernet (e.g. Indiana) are inexpensive, but communication is slow, resulting in a high P/P ratio. b. Machines with faster networking (e.g. Alice [6] and Altacluster) give higher performance. However, this is balanced in the P/P ratio by the higher cost of the network. The essential feature of PMS architecture is that the speed of the communication (depending on the size of the machine) is comparable to that of Myrinet. However, the price for such a communication is as low as ≈40$/node, which is more than an order of magnitude less than the cost of Myrinet.

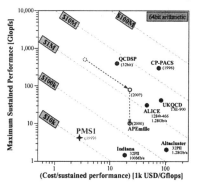

Figure 2 Sustained performance of different machines used in lattice gauge theory as a function of price/performance.

We have presented a description of the status of PMS project. The existing 32-node machine (PMS1) has outstanding price/sustained performance ratio. We plan to increase the number of connected nodes. The use of PCI bus instead of ISA will give an order of magnitude faster communication, which will increase the potential of such a machine. Questions should be sent to pms@labor. elte.hu. This work was supported by Hungarian Science Foundation Grants under Contract Nos. OTKA-T22929-T29803-F17310-M28413/FKFP- 0128/ 1997.

References

[1] Comput. Phys. Commun. 57 (1989) 285; A. Bartonoli et al., Nucl. Phys. B (Proc. Supl.) 60A (1998) 237; http://chimera.roma1.infn.it/ape.html; F. Aglietti et al., Nucl. Instrum. Meth. A389 (1997) 56.

[2] for details see F. Csikor et al., in preparation.

[3] N. Christ, hep-lat/9912009.

[4] Y. Iwasaki, Nucl. Phys. (Proc. Suppl.) 60A (1998) 246; S. Aoki et al., hep-lat/9903001;

[5] D. Chen et al., Nucl. Phys. B (Proc. Suppl.) 73 (1999) 898;

[6] N. Eicker et al., hep-lat/9909146.

AN IMPROVEMENT TECHNIQUE FOR HYBRID PROTOCOL FOR SOFTWARE DISTRIBUTED SHARED MEMORY

Sung-Woo Lee and Kee-Young Yoo
Department of Computer Engineering, Kyungpook University, Korea
swlee@purple.knu.ac.kr, yook@bh.knu.ac.kr

Abstract   Recently, many different protocols have been proposed for software Distributed Shared Memory (DSM) that provides a shared-memory programming model on distributed memory hardware. This paper identifies two problems that deteriorate the performance of a hybrid protocol, an adaptive invalidate/update protocol, and then proposes an improved hybrid protocol to solve these problems. At the point of synchronization, the proposed protocol applies an update protocol not only to the processors previously accessing the page, as in the existing protocol, but also to all processors if the number of processors previously accessing the page is more than a given parameter value. The proposed protocol was implemented in CVM, a software DSM system, and evaluated on eight Sun-ultra1 workstations.

Key words: Distributed Shared Memory, DSM, Shared Memory Programming.

1.   INTRODUCTION

Software distributed shared memory systems (DSM) provide programmers with the illusion of shared memory on top of message-passing hardware [2]. These systems provide a low-cost alternative for shared-memory computing, since they can be built using standard workstations and operating systems. Though many different protocols have been proposed for implementing software DSM [1,4,9], the relative performance of these protocols is application-dependent, that is, the memory access patterns of the application determine which protocol will exhibit a good performance. Accordingly, the ideal situation would be if a system could be built with multiple protocols so that the system could select the appropriate protocol based on the access patterns it observes in the specific application [1,6,9,10,11].

The lazy hybrid (LH) protocol [5,6], an adaptive invalidate/update protocol, is a lazy protocol similar to the lazy release consistency (LRC) [5] invalidate protocol, however, instead of invalidating the modified pages at the time of synchronization, it rather updates some of the pages. The decision on applying an update protocol to a page depends on whether the target processor has accessed the page.

This paper describes two problems that deteriorate the performance of the LH protocol and then presents an improvement technique to cope with these problems.

2. BACKGROUND

This paper is focused on page-based software DSM systems that use multiple-writer protocol and lazy release consistency protocol, such as TreadMarks [4] and CVM[7].

To address the problem of false sharing, i.e. concurrent access to unrelated items in the same page, all of the protocols described in this paper are *multiple-writer* protocols. In a multiple-writer protocol two or more processors can simultaneously modify their local copies of the same shared page. The concurrent modifications are then merged at synchronization points in accordance with the definition of the Release Consistency (RC) [3].

These modifications are summarized as *diffs*. Shared pages are initially write-protected, causing a protection violation to occur when a page is modified. DSM software makes a copy of the page (a *twin*), and removes the write protection so that further modifications to the page can occur without DSM intervention. The differences between the twin and a later copy of the page can then be used to create a *diff*, a run-length encoded record of the modifications made to the page.

The LRC [5] algorithm, one of the possible RC implementations, delays the propagation of shared memory modifications by processor p to processor q until q executes an acquire corresponding to a release by p. The LRC algorithm divides the program execution into intervals and computes a vector timestamp for each interval. This vector describes a happen-before-1 partial order between intervals of different processors. On an acquire operation, the last releaser can determine the set of *write notices* that the acquiring processor needs to receive, i.e. the set of *notices* that precede the current acquire operation in the partial order. A *write notice* is an indication that a page has been modified within a particular interval, yet it does not contain the actual modifications. Upon receiving the *notices* piggybacked on a lock grant message, the acquirer then causes the corresponding page to be invalidated. Access to an invalidated page causes a page fault. Thereafter, the faulting processor must retrieve and apply to the page, all the *diffs* that were created during intervals that preceded the faulting interval in the partial order.

3.   LAZY HYBRID PROTOCOL AND ITS LIMITA-TIONS

3.1   Lazy Hybrid (LH) Protocol

LH [6], an adaptive invalidate/update protocol, is a lazy protocol similar to the LRC using invalidate protocol, however, instead of invalidating the modified pages, it updates some of the pages at the time of an acquire. Each processor uses copysets [5] to track the accesses to pages by other processors. At the point of synchronization, the copyset is used to determine whether a given *diff* should be sent to a remote location. For each *write notice* to be sent, if the releasing processor has a *diff* corresponding to the *write notice* and the acquiring processor is in the local copyset of that page, the *diff* is then appended to the lock grant message.

On arrival at a barrier, each processor creates a list describing the local *write notices* that may not have been seen by other processors. A list for processors p_j at processor p_i consists of processors p_i's notion of all the local *write notices* that have not been seen by p_j. p_i then sends an update message to p_j containing all the *diffs* corresponding to the *write notices* in this list.

3.2   Limitation of LH protocol

After executing several applications using the LH protocol and tracing their behavior, two problems were identified that limit the performance improvement of the LH protocol. First, at the lock synchronization, a releasing processor's copyset is unable to reflect the access pattern that an acquiring processor has generated within the recent interval. Since LRC only requires that the acquiring processor knows (or receives) the events of the memory updates (or *notices*) that precede the current acquire operation in the partial order, the releasing processor cannot know the recent events of the acquire processor. Therefore, the LH protocol can lose an opportunity to apply an update protocol. For example, within the latest interval, an acquiring processor p accesses page x, which they had not previously accessed. The releasing processor q will only send *notices* of page x to p in spite of having *diffs*. p will not then receive those *diffs* at a later synchronization with q or other processors, as p has already seen the *notices* of that interval.

This copyset incorrectness is exhibited in lock-based applications. Although each processor's copysets of a page become the same when the processors arrive at a barrier, it takes a long time to remove discrepancy between each processor's copysets in lock-based applications. In addition, as more processors are included in a system, the degree of discrepancy is increased.

The second problem with the LH protocol relates to the discontinuation effect of *diff* propagation. For example, in Figure 1, except for processor p_3, all the other processors have accessed page x before the barrier synchronization. Therefore, page x's copysets of all the processors are the same as in the figure. At this point, after processor p_1 acquires a lock and causes a write fault (wf_i), p_1 grants the lock to p_2. This grant-message includes the *diff* of page x because x's copyset of p_1 includes p_2. However, the grant message sent to p_3 by p_2 does not include the *diff* because x's copyset of p_2 does not include p_3, as a result, p_4 cannot receive the *diff*. Even though p_4 synchronizes with p_1 after that time, p_4 cannot receive the *diff* corresponding to wf_i by the hybrid protocol.

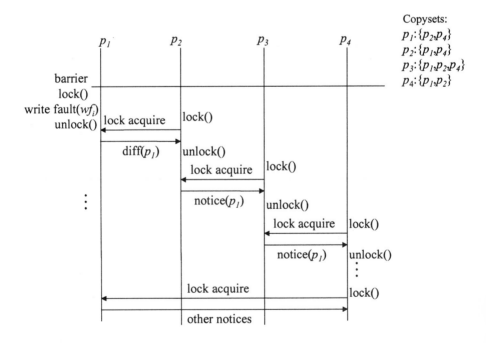

Figure 1. Example of *diff* discontinuation.

4.   PROPOSED IMPROVED TECHNIQUE FOR LAZY HYBRID PROTOCOL

To address the above two problems with LH, an improvement technique is proposed. The resulting improved hybrid protocol (ILH), which modifies LH using the proposed technique, is very similar to LH except for one thing. In the proposed protocol, when a processor sends a lock grant message, the protocol appends the *diff* to the message if the number of processors in the local copyset of that page is more than a given parameter α, as well as when the local copyset includes the processor to receive the message. Here, the parameter α is positive and not more than the number of total processors. The advantages of our protocol are as follows:

(1) Although processor q is not included in the local copyset of processor p, q may have already accessed that page because of the copyset incorrectness.
(2) Although q has not accessed that page, there is a very high possibility that q will access the page in the future, since α processors or more have already accessed the page.
(3) Although q does not access the page to the end, q can still send the *diffs* to other processors at a later synchronization. Accordingly, the adverse effect of *diff* propagation discontinuation is decreased.

If the *diffs* delivered make a good hit, that is, if a processor receiving the *diffs* accesses that page, the number of remote *diff* requests caused by page faults is reduced, thereby improving the total execution time.

Here, variations of parameter α will affect the application's performance. Section 6 includes a discussion on the effect of different values of α based on experimental results, thereby providing an empirical method of determining a performance-efficient α.

5.   IMPLEMENTATION AND EVALUATION

The two protocols, LH and ILH, as described in the previous section, were implemented in the CVM DSM system. The experimental environment consisted of eight SUN utral_1 workstations running Solaris 5.6, connected by a 100M bps fast Ethernet. Six applications were used in this study: TSP from the CVM package, Raytrace, Barnes, Water_squared, Water-Spatial, and Cholesky from Splash-2 [8]. All applications only used lock synchronizations or a combination of lock and barrier synchronizations.

A performance comparison was made of the programs in the application suite using the LH, ILH, and lazy invalidate (LI) protocols. The LI protocol is an LRC using invalidate protocol included in the CVM package. We used 6 as the α value for ILH. Figure 2 shows the normalized execution times for the six applications for each of the three protocols. Table II shows the important performance elements. Total_Msg is the number of messages sent. Data is the amount of data sent, in kilobytes. Diff_Request is the number of messages sent to remote processors to request *diffs*, thereby directly affecting the cost of the page fault. Finally, Diff_Created is the number of *diffs* created in the system.

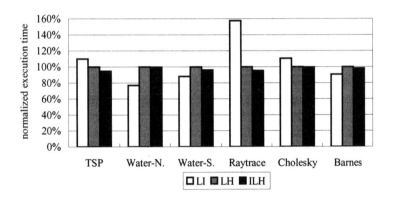

Figure 2. Eight-processor normalized execution times for LI, LH, and ILH.

Table 1. LH and NLH Statistics

Program	Protocol	Run time(s)	Total_ messages	Data(Kbyte)	Remote_ diff_ request	Diffs_created
TSP	LH	22.89	2806	6119	1263	3200
	ILH	21.67	2632	6100	891	3203
Water-Nsquare	LH	17.01	3831	18917	2080	2301
	ILH	16.99	3758	19110	2050	2304
Water-Spatial	LH	25.86	4910	26860	3623	2742
	ILH	24.86	4895	26888	3457	2743
Raytrace	LH	104.72	89470	46919	6936	68871
	ILH	99.69	86815	46787	5025	68856
Cholesky	LH	95.85	23870	117706	5824	22234
	ILH	95.55	23677	117380	5756	22076
Barnes	LH	54.82	88514.55	45156	9366.15	43908
	ILH	53.84	85482.19	45369	6590.46	45057.05

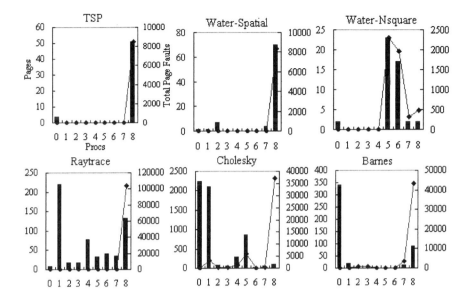

Figure 3. Access pattern analysis.

To explain the performance of each program, the access patterns to shared memory were traced. Figure 3 shows the distribution of the pages based on the number of processors that accessed them. The bar graphs of Figure 3 represent the number of pages that had the same access count (AC), where the AC of a page means the number of processors that accessed that page, and the line graphs represent the total number of page faults related to those pages.

TSP: Since TSP uses a central queue that is the greater part of the shared memory used by the program, most of the pages were accessed by all processors, as shown in Figure 3. Therefore, since ILH can apply an update protocol to most pages faster than LH, ILH could reduce the Diff_Request by about 29% compared with LH. In addition, since ILH does not send any unnecessary *diffs* by the update protocol, ILH did not increase the Data and Diff_Created . Consequently, ILH performed approximately 5% better than LH.

Water-Nsquared: Considering Water-Nsqaured's access pattern, the number of pages whose AC is more than α and the sum of the page faults of those pages are significantly less than the other programs. Therefore, ILH only reduced the Diff_Request slightly compared with LH and did not perform better than LH.

Water-Spatial: While the access pattern of this program allows the ILH to substantially reduce the Diff_Request compared with LH, the Diff_Request is only reduced by 5%. The reason for this is that the number of barrier syn-chronizations is far higher than the lock synchronizations. Nevertheless, since the update protocol derived by ILH has a high hit ratio, ILH performs approximately 4% better than LH.

Raytrace: In this program, pages whose AC is more than α are allocated to a distributed queue. Though their portion of the total number of pages is not very large, compared with Water-Spatial or TSP, the sum of the page faults to those pages constitutes a major portion of the total page faults. Con-sequently, ILH reduces the Diff_Reqeust by 28% compared with LH, and in-creases the Data and Diff_Created by only a small amount. Therefore, ILH performs approximately 5% better than LH.

Cholesky: Though this program also uses a distributed queue whose pages have an AC value higher than α, the actual number of those pages is very small relative to the total number of pages. Therefore, in spite of the lock-based application, ILH did not improve the performance compared to LH.

Barnes: This program's access pattern allowed ILH to reduce the Diff_Request by about 30% compared with LH. However, since too many *diffs* are sent at the lock synchronization, the synchronization delay is in-creased. This effect deepened load imbalance and resulted in an ILH per-formance that is only about 2% better than LH.

6.   DETERMINING PARAMETER α

In the previous section, 6 was used as the value of α in the proposed pro-tocol. Accordingly, to identify an optimal value of α, the ILH protocol was evaluated using different α values, ranging from 4 to 7, with the same appli-cation suite. As a result, we determined that when $\alpha=6$, all applications ex-cept for TSP performed better than at other values. Figures 4 and 5 show the results yielded by Raytrace with different α values. In Figure 5, as the value of α decreases, the Diff_Request dropps dramatically and the Total_Msg de-creases marginally. Nevertheless, as shown in Figure 4, this protocol exhib-ited the best performance when $\alpha=6$, as with a smaller α value, the lock syn-chronization delays increased. This increase in the delays then offset the ad-vantages caused by decreasing the Diff_Request, thereby resulting in a worse overall execution time.

All applications except for TSP showed the same results with that of Ray-trace. TSP showed an adverse result, and performed better with a smaller α value. The reason for this is that since the hit ratio of *diffs* delivered by this dynamic update protocol is already up to 100%, there is no possible incre-ment in the number of *diffs* created (Diff_created) or the total amount of data sent. In addition, the increment of the lock synchronization delay is only slight, since the number of total shared pages is smaller than in other applications, therefore, the total number of *diffs* sent by the proposed protocol is only small.

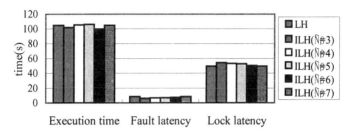

Figure 4. Comparison of execution times with different α values.

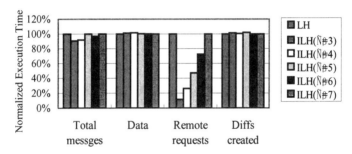

Figure 5. Comparison of important elements with different α values

7.   CONCLUSION

This paper described two problems that deteriorate the performance of the LH protocol and presented an improvement technique to cope with those problems. Based on results using eight workstations, when compared with the LH protocol, the proposed protocol, ILH (α=6), improved the total execution times of four application programs by 2-5%. For these four applications, the ILH protocol reduced the number of remote *diff* request messages up to a maximum of approximately 30%.

Although the proposed protocol for a hybrid protocol adapts well to the access pattern for shared pages, the protocol still exhibits the same flaw inherent from the original hybrid protocol, that is, the increment of lock or barrier synchronization. In both the proposed protocol and the hybrid protocol, to avoid an increase in the number of messages, update information is piggybacked onto a synchronization message. Therefore, the current authors are now developing a mechanism for a hybrid protocol (including the proposed protocol) that restricts the amount of update information piggybacked onto a synchronization message and then sends the rest of the update information through other messages.

References

[1] J. B. Carter, J. K. Bennett and W. Zwaenepoel, "Implementation and Performance of Munin," *Proc. the 13th ACM Symposium on Operating Systems Principles*, pp. 152-164, Oct. 1991.

[2] K. Li and P. Hudak, "Memory coherence in shared virtual memory systems," *ACM Transaction of Computer Systems* 7(4), 321-359, Nov 1989.

[3] K. Gharachooloo, D. Lenoski, J. Laudon, P. Gibbons, A. Gupta and J. Hennessy, "Memory consistency and event ordering in scalable shared-memory multiprocessors," *Proceedings of the 17th Annual International Symposium on Computer Architecture*, pp. 15-26, May 1990.

[4] P. Keleher et al., "TreadMarks: Shared Memory Computing on Networks of Workstations," *IEEE Computer*, pp. 18-28, Feb. 1996.

[5] P. Keleher, "Distributed Shared Memory Using Lazy Release Consistency," PhD dissertation, Rice University, 1994.

[6] P. Keleher, A. L. Cox, S. Dwarkadas, and W. Zwaenepoel, "An evaluation of software based release consistent protocols", *Journal of Parallel and Distributed Computing*, Vol 29, pp. 126-141, October 1995.

[7] P. Keleher, "CVM: The Coherent Virtual Machine", http://www.cs.umd.edu/projects/cvm, November 1996.

[8] S. Woo, M. Ohara, E. Torrie, J. P. Singh, and A. Gupta. "The SPLASH-2 Programs: Characterization and Methodological Considerations," *Proceedings of the 21st Annual International Symposium on Computer Architecture*, June 1995.

[9] L.R. Monnerat and R. Bianchini. "Efficiently adapting to sharing patterns in software DSMs," *Proceedings. Of the 4th International Symposium on High-Performance Computer Architecture*, Feb. 1998.

[10] C. Amza, A. Cox, S. Dwarkadas, and W. Zwaenepoel, " Software DSM protocols that Adapt Between and single Writer and Multiple Wirter," *Proceedings of the 3rd International Symposium on High Performance Computer Architecture*, Feb 1997

[11] C. Amza, A. Cox, K. Rajamani, and W. Zwaenepoel, "Tradeoffs Between False Sharing and Aggregation in Software Distributed Shared Memory," *Proceedings of the 6th ACM SIGPLAN Symposium on Principles and Practice of Parallel Programming*, Jun 1997.

CACHE-ONLY WRITE-DETECTION FOR NAUTILUS DSM

M. Marino, G. Campos

Abstract   The cache-only write detection technique consists in maintaining the pages writable only on the home nodes and only detecting writes on the cache copies in a page-based DSM. A consequence, this technique generates a less number of page faults and page requests, consequently better speedups can be achieved. In this paper, the traditional write detection mechanism is compared to the cache-only write detection technique, when both are applied to Nautilus DSM. In addition, in order to have a fair and homogeneous comparison, TreadMarks DSM was included in this study. keywords: distributed, shared, memory, DSM

1.   INTRODUCTION

The Distributed Shared Memory (DSM) paradigm[2][7], which has been largely discussed for the last 9 years, is an abstraction of shared memory which permits to view a network of workstations as a shared memory parallel computer.

Some important DSMs like TreadMarks[7], JIAJIA[3][4], CVM[8] and Nautilus[9] are page-based DSM systems.

The multiple writer technique[2], for page-based DSMs, allows two or more processors to write on the same page at different variables, minimizing the false sharing effect. The multiple writer protocols technique is based on diffing[2] (diffs: codification of the modification suffered by a page during a critical section) and twinning techniques[2], which requires a write detection mechanism.

Hu[5] has proposed a cache-only write detection for JIAJIA[4]. In this scheme, in home nodes, pages are protected at the beginning of an interval to detect writes in it, and a write to a shared page is detected and this page will remain to be written by the home node until it is written by another node. Thus, in this interval, the page only is written by its home node and no write detection is necessary, decreasing the number of page faults and the overhead, thus improving its speedup.

The main contribution of this paper is to evaluate the cache-only write detection proposed by Hu[5] scheme on Nautilus's speedup, verifying how this technique can help to decrease the overheads.

TreadMarks[7], a reference of optimal speedups by the scientific community, is included in the comparison in order to have a reference parameter of speedups. Unhappily, the results from cache-only write-detection technique applied to TreadMarks DSM will not be showed nor compared here because the version 1.0.3 used in this study is a demo version, therefore, the source is not available.

The evaluation comparison for cache-only write-detection is done by applying two benchmarks: LU (kernel from SPLASH-2)[10] and SOR (from Rice University). The environment of the comparison is a 8PC's (K6-233MHz, 64MB) network running RedHat 6.0,interconnected by a fast-Ethernet shared media (hub) and completely isolated from any other external networks.

2.   NAUTILUS AND CACHE-ONLY WRITE-DETECTION

Nautilus is a scope consistency[6] and home-based DSM.

Following other important DSMs, such as TreadMarks and JIAJIA, also it is a page-based DSM. In this scheme, pages are replicated through the several nodes of the net, allowing multiple reads and writes, which improves the performance. Nautilus distributes its shared pages across all nodes and each shared pages has a home node. When home nodes access their home pages, no page faults occurs. When remote pages are accessed, page faults occur, and these pages are fetched from their home node and cached locally. So, virtual memory is used to detect writes to shared pages.

Through the mprotect() primitive, in Nautilus pages can be in RO (read-only), INV (invalid) or RW (read-write) states, thus their states can be changed easily.

A write detection is an essential mechanism to identify writes to shared pages. Hu [5] proposed a cache-only write detection for JIAJIA, where shared pages protected at the beginning of an interval (several critical sections). When the first write to a shared page occurs, a SIGSEGV signal is delivered, and in this moment the page can be written without protection. As it can be seen, a signal and several system calls (significant overheads) are necessary to produce it, as several studies [1][5] showed.

The study of Amza[1] showed that in many applications, single-writer constitutes the dominant part of the sharing behavior and shared pages are normally written by the home node (owner) for a certain interval. Thus, it is possible to conclude that for applications with large shared data set and good data distribution, if the write-detection would be eliminated from the home node, a great overhead can be decreased.

And going further, it is not necessary to become the page from the read-write state to read-only state[5] if only the home node writes to this page. Also, only in cache copies (remote nodes), writes are detected and, when this occur, the pages go from read-write to read-only state.

Concluding, if the home page is written in some interval, several mprotect() and SIGSEGV handlers calls are saved, improving the DSM's speedup. If the home page is not written by its home in the interval, some unnecessary invalidations of remote cached pages can occur, thus more remote accesses.

Table 1   comparing TreadMarks and Nautilus

application	LU	SOR
t(1)	350.90	29.10
t(8).Tmk	55.45	8.66
t(8).NautV	54.32	7.66
t(8).NautCO	49.60	4.37
Sp.Tmk	6.33	3.36
Sp.NautV	6.46	3.80
Sp.NautCO	7.07	6.66
SG.NautV	7980	12425
SG.NautCO	440	927
gp.NautV	1528	118
gp.NautCO	340	74

3.   EXPERIMENTAL ANALYSIS

From table 1, for eight nodes and LU benchmark, the cache-only write method improved the speedup of Nautilus up to 9.44% The increasement of the speedups can be justified by the reduction of the number of SIGSEGVS and the number of page requests by an order of magnificence lower, when comparing NautCO to NautV. Comparing with TreadMarks, for eight nodes, NautV outperforms it by 2.05% and NautCO outperforms it by 11.69%. Also, an adequate choice of the page owners (data distribution) of Nautilus improves data locality and gives a lower cold start up time to distribute shared data. In addition, the elimination of SIGIO signals minimizes the overheads of Nautilus.

By looking at table 1, for SOR, the cache-only write detection technique improved Nautilus's speedup up to 75.26%. The increasement of the speedups can be justified by observing the number of SIGSEGVS from table 1, an order of magnificence lower for the NautCO version compared to NautV. The number of page requests were reduced too. When compared to TreadMarks, NautV outperforms it up to 13.10% and NautCO outperforms it up to 98.21%, the last an excellent speedup. The better choice of the page owners, the multi-threading and the SIGIO's elimination help to improve Nautilus's speedup.

4.   CONCLUSION

This study shows that the cache-only write detection improved Nautilus's speedup up to 9.44% for LU application, and 75.26% for SOR benchmark, which showed that these benchmarks had shared data and single-writer behavior. A reduction of one order of magnificence of number of SIGSEGVs and the number of request page faults were observer when the studied technique was applied.

In future works, other benchmarks and other DSMs will be evaluated in this comparison. Also, the speedups of TreadMarks and Nautilus DSMs were compared with different programs.

References

[1] Amza C., Cox A. L., Dwarkadas S., Jin L. J., Rajamani K., Zwaenepoel W., *Adaptive Protocols for Software Distributed Shared Memory*, Proceedings of IEEE, Special Issue on Distributed Shared Memory, pp. 467-475, March 1999.

[2] Carter J. B., *Efficient Distributed Shared Memory Based on Multi-protocol Release Consistency*, PHD Thesis, Rice University, Houston, Texas, September, 1993.

[3] Eskicioglu, M.S., Marsland T.A., Hu W, Shi W.; *Evaluation of the JIAJIA DSM System on High Performance Computer Architectures*, Proceeding of the Hawai'i International Conference on System Sciences, Maui, Hawaii, January, 1999.

[4] Hu W., Shi W., Tang Z., *JIAJIA: An SVM System Based on a new Cache Coherence Protocol,* technical report no. 980001, Center of High Performance Computing, Institute of Computing Technology, Chinese Academy of Sciences, January, 1998.

[5] Hu W., Shi W., Tang Z., *Write Detection in Home-based Software DSMs*, to appear in Proceedings of Euro-Par'99, August 31-September 2, Tolouse, France.

[6] Iftode L., Singh J.P., Li K; *Scope Consistency: A bridge between release consistency and entry consistency*. Proceedings of the 8th ACM Annual Symposium on Parallel Algorithms and Architectures (SPAA'96), pp. 277-287, June, 1996.

[7] Keleher P. , *Lazy Release Consistency for Distributed Shared Memory*, PHD Thesis, University of Rochester, Texas, Houston, January 1995.

[8] Keleher P., *The Relative Importance of Concurrent Writers and Weak Consistency Models*, in Proceedings of the 16th International Conference on Distributed Computing Systems (ICDCS-16), pp. 91-98, May 1996.

[9] Marino M. D.; Campos G. L.; *A Preliminary DSM Speedup Comparison: JIAJIA x Nautilus*, HPCS99, Kingston, Canada, June, 1999.

[10] Woo S., Ohara M., Torrie E., Singh J.P., Gupta A.; *The SPLASH-2 programs: Characterization and methodological considerations. In Proceedings of the 22th Annual Symposium on Computer* Architecture, pages 24-36, June, 1995.

HIVE: IMPLEMENTING A VIRTUAL DISTRIBUTED SHARED MEMORY IN JAVA

Fabrizio Baiardi, Gianmarco Dobloni, Paolo Mori and Laura Ricci
Department of Computer Science, University of Pisa
Corso Italia 40 - 56125 Pisa
{baiardi,mori,ricci}@di.unipi.it

Abstract   Hive is a Java library implementing a distributed shared memory on a cluster of workstations. The memory is structured as a set of variable size areas and a user can exploit two consistency models, sequential and release consistency. Hive defines original strategies to implement the consistency models and to synchronize concurrent processes. Synchronization is implemented through tokens, i.e. privileges. Preliminary performance figures are discussed.

Keywords: workstation cluster, distributed memory, consistency model, JAVA, parallelism

Introduction

A fundamental issue of software, distributed shared memory systems (DSM) on a cluster of workstations (COW) is the *consistency model*. The *sequential* model is not suitable for a COW due its large overhead. For this reason, *release consistency models* tolerate some degree of *inconsistency* among the copies of shared data because the updates are notified only upon a process synchronization. The *eager release model* [3] propagates the updates when a process either releases a critical section or it synchronizes with other processes.

This paper presents Hive, ·a Java library implementing a distributed shared memory consisting of a set of areas. An area is a sequence of consecutive positions whose size is chosen by the user. Hive enables Java programs to exploit both the sequential model and the eager release consistency one. With respect to other proposal, Hive introduces neither *a centralized manager* for each shared data nor the notion of *probable owner* of a shared data. The latter requires the definition and the scan of a distributed list to obtain either the privilege to acquire the lock on shared data, or the shared data itself. Hive defines a new synchronization strategy together with a protocol to guarantee the consistency of shared data in the case of unsynchronized accesses.

1.   THE HIVE ABSTRACT MACHINE

Hive shared memory is structured as a user defined set of *areas*,where an area is a sequence of contiguous positions whose size is fixed at run time. To avoid false sharing, the user can freely choose the size of an area.

The functions of Hive may be classified into *notification, synchronization* and *access* functions.

Notification functions declare the set of shared areas and signal the end of the operations on an area.

Serialization functions acquire or release a shared area through a *multiple reader/single writer* scheduling. Hive also supports *synchronization barriers.*

Access functions either read or update an area. For each function f, Hive defines two versions f_{sc} and f_{rc}, that implement, respectively, the sequential and the release consistency model. To update an area, if a data is accessed within a critical section or if races among updates are not possible because of process synchronization, the $write_{rc}$ function should be used. In this case, consistency is guaranteed at the release of the critical section or at the first synchronization, i.e. a barrier, after the $write_{rc}$. The $write_{sc}$ function, instead, immediately notifies any update to any copy. In this way, user defined synchronization strategies may be implemented.

Furthermore, Hive defines *blocking* access functions, i.e. the invoking process is blocked till the operation is completed, and *non blocking* functions.

Distinct phases of the same progam may exploit distinct consistency models provided that these phases are separated by a barrier.

2.   THE CONSISTENCY MODELS

Since most applications adopt the release consistency model, we focus on it to optimize the implementation.

Hive adopts the invalidation model and it exploits the notion of owner of an area, but it minimizes the number of attempts to find the owner by recording, whenever it is possible, the real owner of the area rather than the probable one.

We have defined a protocol that assure that a *unique owner* for each area always exists.

To implement the release consistency model, each process notifies the invalidations of the modified data and updates the owner before releasing the critical section or when executing a barrier. Furthermore, the process waits for an acknowledgment from any other process before releasing the critical section or passing the barrier. In this way, when a process accesses an area, it always knows its real owner. Hive does not to implement complex *write shared protocols* to avoid false sharing, because it should be minimized by properly choosing the size of each area.

Serialization functions are implemented in a decentralized way based upon the definition of a *unique privilege* for each area. Hive exploits *a virtual ring* among the processing nodes and a token for each area is initially injected into this ring. To implement a *multiple reader/single writer protocol*, each token carries a numerical value V: $V = 0$ denotes that the area is free, $V = n, n > 0$ that the area is currently read by n processes, while $V = -1$ denotes that the area is currently updated. To access an area, first of all, a process has to acquire the token. Then, it deduces from the token value whether the operation can be executed. If the area cannot be accessed, the process forwards the token along the ring. Otherwise, it forwards the token after updating it according to the pending operation.

Two versions of *Hive* have been implemented, $Hive_s$ and $Hive_m$, that exploit, respectively, a distinct token for each area and one data structure, the *tokenvector*, that stores all the tokens. $Hive_s$ increases the degree of parallelism in the acquisition of the areas, but its overhead is larger than that of $Hive_m$, because of the time to set up the communications. As a counterpart, $Hive_m$ is simpler than $Hive_s$, because just one structure is transmitted along the ring. In $Hive_s$, a process updating an area holds the corresponding token.

3.   EXPERIMENTAL RESULTS

Hive has been implemented on a COW including 10 nodes running $Linux$ and interconnected by a 100 Mbit fast Ethernet. Each node includes a Pentium II at 266 Mhz and 128 Mbytes of local memory. Hive is implemented in Java and exploits the $DatagramPacket$ and $DatagranSocket$ classes.

The run time support of each node includes a pair of threads, the *AreaFaultManager, AFM*, and the *TokenServer, TS*, created during the system start up and always active. An area is transferred from a local memory to another one by further threads created by the *AFM*.

When the *AFM* receive a request for an area coming from a local process, it deduces the owner O of the area from its local information, and it sends a message to O to acquire the area. Then, *AFM* creates a thread, the *LocalRequestManager, LRM*, to manage the communication to receive the area. To recover the possible loss of information due to UDP, the protocol exploits both a time out and a unique identifier of each message. If the *AFM* of a node N_1 receives a request for an area, from a process of a node N_2, it creates a thread *RemoteRequestManager, RRM* which cooperate with the *LRM* of N_2 to transfer the area. Both *LRM* and *RRM* terminate as soon as the transfer has been completed. *AFM* also accepts invalidation requests from a remote node.

TS receives the synchronization token from the ring and, if it has been locally requested, it either updates or holds the token before forwarding it along the ring. In the case of $Hive_m$ the tokenvector is never held. The experimental results show that in $Hive_m$ the time to acquire the token increases with the number of nodes, but is independent of the number of areas. In this case, a larger number of areas results in a larger size of the *tokenvector* but not in a larger number of communications. In $Hive_s$, instead, the time is strongly influenced by the number of areas, that is by the number of tokens transmitted along the ring. Hence, $Hive_m$ should be preferred when a few nodes share a large set of areas.

The first problem we have considered is the parallel matrix multiplication $C = AB$. The scalability, in the case of a 1000×1000 matrix, ranges from 2.5 to 7 when the processing nodes range from 3 to 10.

We have also solved the traveling salesman problem through a branch and bound approach [2]. A *threshold T* determines the portion of each path which is expanded sequentially and it is modified to tune the degree of parallelism. The solution exploits the release consistency model. Even in the case of a 9 city problem, the experimental results confirm the effectiveness of Hive because the best scalability is achieved by the lowest values of T, that is by the largest degree of parallelism.

The results of other applications are shown in [5].

References

[1] Adve S.,Cox A.,Gharachorloo K.,Gupta A., Hennessy J, Hill M.,"Programming for Different Memory Consistency Models", *Journal of Parallel and Distributed Programming*, 15, 1992.

[2] Amza C.,Cox A.,Dwarkadas S.,Keleher P.,Lu H., Rajamony R., Yu W. and Zwaenepoel W., "ThreadMarks:Shared Memory Computing on Network of Workstations",*IEEE Computer*, Feb. 1996.

[3] Bennett J.K., Carter J.B., Zwaenepoel W., "Techniques for Reducing Consistency-Related Communication in Distributed Shared-Memory Systems", *ACM TOCS*, Vol.1, No. 3, Aug. 1995.

[4] Bennett J.K., Carter J.B., Zwaenepoel W., "Implementation and Performance of Munin",*13th ACM Symp. on Operating Systems Principles*, Oct. 1991.

[5] Dobloni G., Romano T., "Memoria Virtuale Condivisa su Architetture a Memoria Distribuita: rassegna di modelli ed implementazione di una proposta", *Master Thesis*, in Computer Science, Univ. of Pisa, Oct. 1999.

[6] Li K., Hudak P. "Memory Coherence in Shared Virtual Memory Systems", *ACM TOCS*, Vol. 7, No. 4, Nov. 1989.

Part IV

WEB AND CLUSTER COMPUTING

ANALYZING ALGEBRAIC CURVES BY CLUSTER COMPUTING

Wolfgang Schreiner, Christian Mittermaier, Franz Winkler
Research Institute for Symbolic Computation (RISC-Linz)
Johannes Kepler University, Linz, Austria
http://www.risc.uni-linz.ac.at
FirstName.LastName@risc.uni-linz.ac.at[*]

Abstract   We describe a parallel solution to the problem of resolving non-ordinary singularities of a plane algebraic curve. The original sequential program is implemented in the software library CASA on top of the computer algebra system Maple. The new parallel version is based on Distributed Maple, a distributed programming extension written in Java. We evaluate the performance of the program in a cluster environment and compare it to that on a massively parallel multiprocessor.

Keywords: Computer algebra, Maple, parallel algorithm, cluster, Java.

1.   INTRODUCTION

We describe a parallel solution to the problem of resolving non-ordinary singularities of a plane algebraic curve. The starting point of our work is the library CASA (computer algebra software for constructive algebraic geometry) which has been developed since 1990 by various researchers under the direction of the third author [5]. CASA is based on the computer algebra system Maple.

In order to parallelize a number of CASA functions, the first author has developed "Distributed Maple", a system that allows to implement parallel algorithms in Maple and to execute them in any networked environment [6, 7]. Its core is a scheduler program written in Java which is in charge of coordinating the activities of the Maple kernels running on various machines. The system

---

[*] Supported by the FWF grants P11160-TEC (HySaX) und SFB F013/F1304.

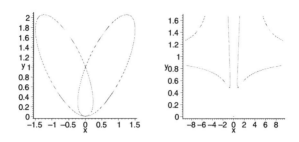

Figure 1   The Tacnode Curve and its Transformed Version

has evolved from our own experience in the development of parallel computer algebra environments [3] and from related work of other researchers [9, 2, 1].

On the basis of Distributed Maple, we have parallelized several algorithms from algebraic geometry, mostly in the frame of the diploma thesis of the second author [4]. In this paper, we present one of these parallel solutions.

2.   RESOLUTION OF SINGULARITIES

The basic objects of the software library CASA are algebraic sets represented e.g. as systems of polynomial equations [5]. Algebraic sets represented by bivariate polynomials model plane curves; an important problem is to determine whether such a curve has a *rational parameterization* [8], i.e., whether there exist rational functions $X(t), Y(t)$ such that, for almost all parameters $t \in \mathbb{R}$, the point $(X(t), Y(t))$ is on the curve and, for almost every point (x, y) on the curve, there exists some $t \in \mathbb{R}$ such that $(x, y) = (X(t), Y(t))$.

A curve has such a parameterization only if $(d-1)(d-2) = \sum_{i=1}^{n} m_i(m_i - 1)$ where d is degree of the polynomial p defining the curve and n is the number of curve singularities with multiplicities $m_1, \ldots, m_n$, respectively. A singularity is a curve point P such that both partial derivatives $\frac{\partial p}{\partial x}$ and $\frac{\partial p}{\partial y}$ vanish at P; the multiplicity of P is the largest m such that all derivatives $\frac{\partial^{u+v} p}{\partial x^u \partial y^v}$ with $u + v < m$ vanish at P; the curve then has at most m tangents at P.

Above decision criterion only holds, if every singularity is ordinary, i.e., if its multiplicity m denotes m tangents. If a curve C has a non-ordinary singularity, we may however transform it into some C_1 where the non-ordinary singularity is resolved into ordinary ones (see the right curve in Figure 1 that resolves the non-ordinary singularity $(0, 0)$). By repeating this transformation, we thus compute a sequence $C_1, C_2, \ldots, C_n$ such that C_n has only ordinary singularities and we may decide from C_n whether C has a rational parameterization [8].

Each C_i is given in projective space, i.e., it is defined by a homogeneous polynomial $p(x, y, z)$. A part of the transformation is the computation of all singularities of p of the form $(x, 1, 0)$. We solve this problem in two steps:

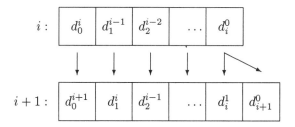

Figure 2   Computation of Derivatives of Total Order $i + 1$

1. $(b, n) :=$ **derivatives(p)**

Let $d_u^v \in \mathbb{Q}(x, z)$ denote $\frac{\partial p(x,1,z)^{u+v}}{\partial x^u z^v}$ of total order $u + v$. Our goal is to compute a sequence $[b_i]_{i=0}^n$ where b_0 is the greatest square free divisor (gsfd) of $p(x, 1, 0)$, $b_{i+1}(x)$ is the greatest common divisor (gcd) of $b_i(x)$ and of all $d_v^u(x, 0)$ with $u+v = i+1$, and n is the smallest order such that $\deg b_n = 0$. The roots of $b_i(x)$ are the x-coordinates of all singularities $(x, 1, 0)$ of order at least $i + 1$. The x-coordinates of all singularities $(x, 1, 0)$ of order i are thus the roots of $\frac{b_{i-1}(x)}{b_i(x)}$ for $1 < i \leq n$.

The partial derivatives of total order $i + 1$ are generated from (and overwrite) the derivatives of order i as illustrated in Figure 2:

$(b, n) :=$ **derivatives(p)**
$\quad i := 0$
$\quad d_0(x, z) := p(x, 1, z)$
$\quad b_0(x) := \text{gsfd}(d_0(x, 0))$
$\quad$ **while** $\deg(b_i) \neq 0$ **do**
$\quad\quad d_{i+1}(x, z) := \frac{\partial d_i(x,z)}{\partial z}(x, z)$
$\quad\quad$ **for** j **from** 0 **to** i **do**
$\quad\quad\quad d_j(x, z) := \frac{\partial d_j(x,z)}{\partial x}(x, z)$
$\quad\quad b_{i+1}(x) := b_i(x)$
$\quad\quad$ **for** j **from** 0 **to** $i + 1$ **do**
$\quad\quad\quad b_{i+1}(x) := \gcd(b_{i+1}(x), d_j(x, 0))$
$\quad\quad i := i + 1$
$\quad n := i$
end

2. $S :=$ **singularities(b, n)**

Let q_i denote b_{i-1}/b_i for $2 \leq i \leq n$. Every root a of q_i is the x coordinate of a singularity $(a, 1, 0)$ of multiplicity i; S is the set of all such $(i, (a, 1, 0))$.

The first step accounts for most of the computation time of each curve transformation. Our goal is therefore to speed up **derivatives** by parallelization.

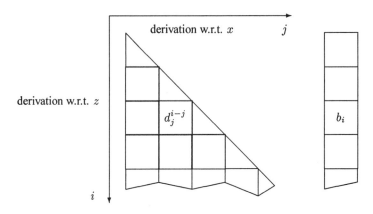

Figure 3   The Matrix of Partial Derivations

3.   THE PARALLELIZATION APPROACH

Figure 2 suggests to organize the computation of all d_u^v in a triangular matrix shown in Figure 3: each line i contains all d_u^v with $u + v = i$, each column j contains all d_j^v, i.e., the matrix holds at position (i, j) the derivative d_j^{i-j}. The basic parallelization idea is to compute all those positions (i, j) with $i \geq j$ in parallel whose data dependencies have been resolved, i.e., for which $(i - 1, j)$ is available (if $i > j$) respectively $(i - 1, j - 1)$ is available (if $i = j$).

However in order to increase its granularity, a task should compute multiple matrix elements, i.e., we have to *block* the computation accordingly. We achieve this by partitioning the triangular matrix into square blocks of size $m * m$ (for some blocking factor m) that comprise all partial derivatives that are computed by the same task. The blocks along the diagonal boundary of the triangular matrix are themselves triangular and only have to compute $\frac{m^2 - m}{2}$ elements.

The tasks are created by a main program which itself computes iteratively the d_u^0, i.e., the derivatives along the diagonal boundary of the matrix. When it has computed all those derivatives that represent the diagonal boundary of a triangular block, it starts a corresponding task that computes the values of this block. Whenever a task (computing a triangular block or a square block) has terminated, the main program starts a new task for computing that square block that is adjacent to the lower boundary of the result block.

Actually, the result of a task need not be the values of all d_u^v in the corresponding block because we are only interested in

1. the last line of the block which is required by the task computing the adjacent block (this result need not be returned to the main program but can be put into a shared space from which the other task can retrieve it);

$(b, n) :=$ **derivatives**(p)
$\quad T := \emptyset$
$\quad$**for** i **from** 0 **to** $m * p - 1$ **by** p **do**
$\quad\quad$compute $d^0_{i+k}(x, z)$ for $0 \le k < m$
$\quad\quad T := T \cup \{$**start**$(\text{task}, i, i)\}$
$\quad$**end**
$\quad n := \deg(p)$
$\quad$**while** $T \ne \emptyset$ **do**
$\quad\quad (t, T) := (\text{any element of } T, T - \{t\})$
$\quad\quad (b', i, j) := $ **wait**(t)
$\quad\quad$**for** k **from** 0 **to** $m - 1$ **do**
$\quad\quad\quad$**if** $b_{i+k}(x)$ is initialized
$\quad\quad\quad\quad$**then** $b_{i+k}(x) := \gcd(b_{i+k}(x), b'_k(x))$ **else** $b_{i+k}(x) := b'_k(x)$
$\quad\quad\quad$**if** $\deg(b_{i+k}) = 0 \wedge i + k < n$ **then** $n := i + k$
$\quad\quad$**end**
$\quad\quad$enable $(i + m, j)$
$\quad\quad$**if** $i = j$ **then** enable $(i + m, j + m)$
$\quad\quad$**do**
$\quad\quad\quad$select enabled (i, j) with minimum i and disable it
$\quad\quad$**while** $i \ge n \wedge$ some block is enabled
$\quad\quad$**if** $i < n$ **then**
$\quad\quad\quad$**if** $i = j$ **then** compute $d^0_{i+k}(x, z)$ for $0 \le k < m$
$\quad\quad\quad T := T \cup \{$**start**$(\text{task}, i, j)\}$
$\quad\quad$**end**
$\quad$**end**
$\quad$**for** i **from** 0 **to** $n - 1$ **do** $b_{i+1}(x) := \gcd(b_i(x), b_{i+1}(x))$
end

Figure 4   The Parallel Algorithm

2. the greatest common divisor of each line of the block which is required to compute the greatest common divisor of the whole matrix line (this result is returned to the main program).

Since the gcd is commutative and associative, the program may receive in any order the results computed by the tasks of line i and combine them with the current value of b_i. In a final step, b_{i+1} is then combined with b_i.

To let the algorithm efficiently execute on a machine with a limited number of processors, we have to adopt an appropriate *scheduling strategy*. In particular, as soon as we have detected, for some i, the termination criterion $\deg(b_i) = 0$, only the results of those tasks are required any more that operate on lines with index less than or equal i. In order not to let superfluous tasks compete with required tasks for the p processors available, the main program does therefore not immediately start all tasks whose data dependencies have been resolved but schedules at most p tasks for execution at any time.

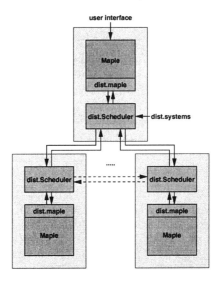

Figure 5   Distributed Maple Architecture

Initially, tasks are created for computation of the first p triangular blocks. Whenever a task terminates, we "enable" the adjacent square block whose computation thus becomes possible; if the terminated task has computed a triangular block (and it was not one of the p initial tasks), we also enable the subsequent triangular block. Among all enabled blocks, we choose a block with minimum line index (its computation may make the computation of blocks with larger indices superfluous). When the termination criterion is detected in line i, only those tasks will be started that operate on lines with indices less than i; when no more task is active, the algorithm terminates.

4.   DISTRIBUTED MAPLE

Distributed Maple is an environment for writing parallel programs on the basis of the computer algebra system Maple [6]. It allows to create tasks and to execute them by Maple kernels running on various machines of a network. Each node connected to a session comprises two components (see Figure 5):

Scheduler The Java program `dist.Scheduler` coordinates node interaction. The initial scheduler process (created by the Maple kernel attached to the user frontend) reads all system information from file `dist.systems`; it then starts instances of the scheduler on other machines.

Maple Interface The file `dist.maple` read by every Maple kernel implements the interface between kernel and scheduler. Both components use pipes to exchange messages (which may embed any Maple objects in the compact linear format that Maple uses for library files).

After a session has been established, every scheduler instance accepts tasks from the attached computation kernel and schedules these tasks among all machines connected to the session. During the execution, additional socket connections between remote scheduler instances are created on demand.

The user interacts with Distributed Maple via a (text or graphical) Maple frontend. Maple commands establish a session in which tasks are created for execution on any connected machine, e.g.:

```
> read 'dist.maple';
Distributed Maple V1.0.7 (c) 1998 Wolfgang Schreiner (RISC-Linz)
See http://www.risc.uni-linz.ac.at/software/distmaple
> dist[initialize]([[gintonic,linux], [andromeda,octane]]):
connecting gintonic...
connecting andromeda...
> dist[all]("Integrate := proc(e, x) int(e, x) end:"):
> t1 := dist[start](Integrate, x^n, x):
> t2 := dist[start](Integrate, x^n, n):
> dist[wait](t1) + dist[wait](t2);
```

The file dist.maple implements the interface to the distributed backend as a Maple package dist. The command dist[initialize] asks the system to start the backend and create two additional Maple kernels on machines gintonic and andromeda of types linux and octane, respectively.

The following operations represent the core programming interface:

dist[all] (*command*) lets the Maple statement *command* be executed on every Maple kernel connected to the session. If this command refers to a file, this file must be visible on every machine connected to the session.

dist[start] (*f, a, ...*) creates a task evaluating *f(a, ...)* and returns a task reference *t*. Tasks may create other tasks; arbitrary objects (including task references) may be passed as arguments and returned as results.

dist[wait] (*t*) blocks the execution of the current task until the task represented by *t* has terminated and returns its result. Multiple tasks may independently wait for and retrieve the result of the same task *t*.

This parallel programming model is essentially based on functional principles which is sufficient for many kinds of computer algebra algorithms [3]. In addition, the environment supports a non-deterministic form of task synchronization for speculative parallelism and shared data objects which allow tasks to communicate via a global store. The later facility was applied in the implementation of the algorithm presented in this paper for storing the last line of each block computed by one task and required as input for another task.

5.   EXPERIMENTAL RESULTS

We have benchmarked the parallel variant of the derivatives computation with four examples for which the sequential computation takes 552s, 198s, 402s, and 1798s, respectively (the times refer to execution on a PIII@450MHz Linux PC). The examples were extracted from the resolution of the singularities of four artificially generated curves in which they represented the most time-consuming part (88%, 85%, 95%, and 95% of the total runtime). The program has been executed in two environments consisting of 24 processors each:

- a Silicon Graphics Origin multiprocessor (64 R12000@300 Mhz, 24 processors used) located at the university campus;

- a cluster of 4 SGI Octanes (2 R10000@250Mhz each) located in our institute and of 16 of the Origin processors; the Octanes are linked by two 10 Mbit Ethernet subnetworks connected via ATM to the campus.

The raw computing power of the Origin and of the cluster are 18.7 and 17.2, respectively; these numbers (measured by a Maple benchmark) denote the sum of the processor performances relative to a PIII@450MHz. In the cluster, the frontend was executed on an Octane such that the configuration behaved as if each Origin processor was executing on a separate workstation. We had to exclude our Linux PCs from the cluster, because their Java 1.1 did not support native threads, which severely downgraded the communication throughput of the multithreaded scheduler (we verified by a test installation that the forthcoming Java 2 port with native threads solves this problem). On the Origin, we achieved much better performance by using green threads.

The top diagram in Figure 6 generated from a Distributed Maple profile illustrates the execution of Example 3 in the cluster configuration with 8 Octane and 8 Origin processors (top and bottom half of the diagram, respectively). Each line represents a task being executed on one of the processors.

The table in Figure 6 lists the execution times in both environments for each input and varying numbers of processors. The subsequent row of diagrams visualizes the absolute speedups $\frac{T_s}{T_n}$ (where T_s denotes the sequential execution time and T_n denotes the parallel execution time with n processors), the second row visualizes the scaled speedups, i.e., the absolute speedups multiplied with $\frac{n}{\sum_{i=1}^{n} p_i}$ (where p_i denotes the performance of processor i), the third row visualizes the scaled efficiency, i.e., $\frac{T_s}{T_n \sum_{i=1}^{n} p_i}$. The scaled speedups and efficiencies of the Origin (marker $\times$) and of the cluster (marker $+$) are almost the same.

The scaled efficiencies with up to 4 processors are greater than one because of two effects: first, the new way in which the greatest common divisors of lines of derivatives are computed turns out to be more efficient for this input (which is a hint for a general algorithmic improvement); second, the overall increase of available Maple memory considerably reduces the garbage collection times.

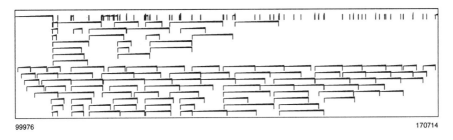

99976   170714

Example	System	1	2	4	8	16	24
1 (552s = 88%)	Origin	560	294	190	113	83	80
	Cluster	817	436	233	155	100	101
2 (198s = 85%)	Origin	192	123	70	44	41	45
	Cluster	214	142	91	64	45	49
3 (402s = 95%)	Origin	371	218	128	70	59	62
	Cluster	518	265	153	107	71	73
4 (1798s = 95%)	Origin	2199	928	574	348	239	228
	Cluster	3015	1222	703	469	275	241

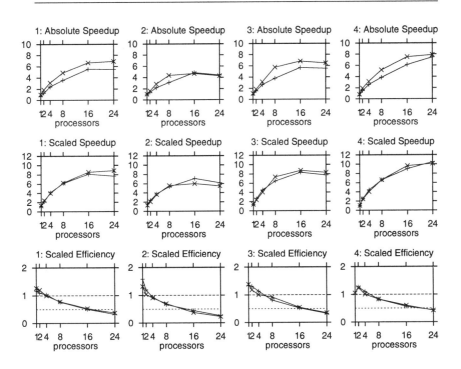

Figure 6   Experimental Results

6.   CONCLUSIONS

We have demonstrated that also in distributed environments the parallel implementation of a computer algebra algorithm can achieve significant speedups which compete with those on a standalone massively parallel multiprocessor. We have faced super-linear speedups caused by subtle algorithmic changes and by reduced garbage collection times due to more memory available. The algorithm operates on large amounts of data, which made it necessary to carefully tune the parallelization: to select an appropriate blocking strategy and to place data into a virtually shared space. The implementation also exhibited some problems with the Java thread support on Linux PCs and on the Origin.

References

[1] L. Bernadin. Maple on a Massively Parallel, Distributed Memory Machine. In *PASCO '97 — Second Int. Symp. on Parallel Symbolic Computation*, pages 217–222, Maui, Hawaii, July 20–22, 1997. ACM Press.

[2] A. Diaz and E. Kaltofen. FoxBox: A System for Manipulating Symbolic Objects in Black Box Representation. In O. Gloor, editor, *ISSAC '98 Int. Symp. on Symbolic and Algebraic Comp.* ACM Press, New York, 1998.

[3] H. Hong, A. Neubacher, and W. Schreiner. The Design of the SACLIB/ PACLIB Kernels. *Journal of Symbolic Computation*, 19:111–132, 1995.

[4] C. Mittermaier. Parallel Algorithms in Constructive Algebraic Geometry. Master's thesis, Johannes Kepler University, Linz, Austria, 2000.

[5] M. Mnuk and F. Winkler. CASA - A System for Computer Aided Constructive Algebraic Geometry. In *DISCO '96 — Int. Symposium on the Design and Implementation of Symbolic Computation Systems*, volume 1128 of *LNCS*, pages 297–307, Karsruhe, Germany, 1996. Springer, Berlin.

[6] W. Schreiner. Distributed Maple — User and Reference Manual. Technical Report 98-05, Research Institute for Symbolic Computation (RISC-Linz), Johannes Kepler University, Linz, Austria, May 1998.

[7] W. Schreiner. Developing a Distributed System for Algebraic Geometry. In B. H. Topping, editor, *EURO-CM-PAR '99 Third Euro-conference on Parallel and Distributed Computing for Computational Mechanics*, pages 137–146, Weimar, Germany, March 20-25, 1999. Civil-Comp Press.

[8] R. J. Sendra and F. Winkler. Symbolic Parametrization of Curves. *Journal of Symbolic Computation*, 12(6):607–631, 1990.

[9] K. Siegl. Parallelizing Algorithms for Symbolic Computation Using ‖MAPLE‖. In *Fourth ACM SIGPLAN Symposium on Principles and Practice of Parallel Programming*, pages 179–186, San Diego, California, May 19-22, 1993. ACM Press.

A NOVEL PROGRAMMING STRATEGY CONSIDERING PORTABLE WIRELESS NODES IN A HETEROGENEOUS CLUSTER

E. M. Macías-López, A. Suárez, C. N. Ojeda-Guerra, L. Gómez

Grupo de Arquitectura y Concurrencia (G.A.C.)*

Dpto. de Ingeniería Telemática (U.L.P.G.C.)

{elsa,alvaro}@cic.teleco.ulpgc.es

Abstract   In the past, the most common way of network-based computing was through wired networks. However, with advances in wireless communication technology, the Wireless Local Area Network (WLAN) has become a viable option for performing distributed computing. Taking this novel scenario into account, in this paper we present a cluster based on wireless and wired nodes. In this cluster, the wireless nodes can appear and disappear dynamically in a controlled way. We define a communication protocol in order to achieve an efficient load balance and a reasonable execution time of parallel or distributed programs.

Keywords: wireless clusters, programming model.

1.   INTRODUCTION

In the recent years, high speed networks and the performance of improved processors are making network of workstations an appealing vehicle for parallel computing. Clusters/networks of workstations built using commodity hardware or software are playing a major role in redefining the concept of Supercomputing [11]. A cluster consists of a collection of interconnected commodity stand-alone computers working that can act together as a single, integrated computing resource [8]. Applications appropriate for clusters are not restricted to those traditionally run on supercomputers or other high-performance systems [9].

*This research is supported in part by Spanish CICYT under Contract: TIC98-1115-C02-02.

Currently, the number and types of applications using clusters are increasing all the time.

In recent Local Area Networks (LANs), the communication speed of wired networks can be of the order of Gigabits per second [3]. There are also high speed communication devices that can manage communications efficiently [4]. On the other hand, with the rapid evolution of wireless communications, an explosion of communication devices and mobile processors have been developed. With these advances, the Wireless Local Area Network (WLAN) has become a viable option to perform distributed computing. WLAN technology is rapidly becoming a crucial component of computer networks, and its use is growing by leaps and bounds. The maximum data rate can be from 1 Mbps [5] to 23,5 Mbps [6]. Taking these advances into account, some authors have thought in clusters with wireless communications. We have found two different solutions to integrate wireless communications in a cluster. In [1] are presented some of the application environments for Mobile Cluster Computing (MCC) and a generic architecture for MCC. In this kind of clusters there is cellular communication among mobile computers. These nodes are communicated with fixed computers attached in a Wide Area Network. In [7] is studied the feasibility of using a WLAN as a platform to perform parallel computing. The wireless environment consists of two Ethernet LANs segments connected through two wireless bridges. Since the wireless bridges separate the wireless LAN in two segments, it can be reduced the bandwidth competition of simultaneous group communications among workstations. An analytical model is given to show the possible improvement.

We are interested in the implementation of clusters using a WLAN and a LAN. The WLAN can work indoor (with radio or infrared transmission) or outdoor in a short-distance (if physical level is built with radio transmission technology). In this kind of heterogeneous cluster it is important to consider an efficient programming model. We have measured how affect the wireless nodes physical allocation on communication speed and transmission errors for indoor infrared transmissions [2] and we have developed a technique for parallel programming based on the overlapping of computations and communications [10]. In this paper we present a protocol of communication in order to consider the efficient load balancing and execution time of parallel or distributed programs, that is used as a basis of a novel programming model for our WLAN-LAN based cluster.

The rest of the paper is organized as follows. In section 2, the chosen cluster architecture is defined. In section 3, we propose the programming model. In section 4, a performance model of program execution is explained, and finally, we sum up some conclusions and we present future work.

2.   THE PROPOSED CLUSTER

At present, there are a lot of different technologies for LANs and WLANs. The technology most widely used in LANs is Ethernet with rates from 10 Mbps up to 1 Gbps (Gigabit Ethernet). On the contrary, in WLAN lower speed communication can be achieved because two different physical technologies are used: Infrared radiation and Radio signal. Although the computing over LAN is up to now more efficient than the computing over WLAN due to its higher communication speed, we are interested in testing which are the limits using a WLAN. We limit our scope to a short area network over wireless and wired links. Moreover we study the influence of the portability of the wireless nodes, which in any moment can be or not be connected with the wired network.

In [7] a wireless connection for two segments of Ethernet LANs and a logical communication ring over the cluster is presented. We consider a cluster with one wired Ethernet segment and an arbitrary amount of portable nodes. In our cluster the parallel programs are harder to design due to the consideration of portability. For this reason we have designed a general strategy for parallel programs implementation. Moreover, our architecture presents more flexibility.

Figure 1 shows the cluster architecture. The wired nodes are connected through any typical wired interconnection and the wireless ones employ Network Interface Cards (NICs) which are connected to an external radio or infrared transmitter. The interconnection of both types of nodes is done by an access node which is connected to both networks using wired and wireless NICs. Besides, the access node makes the following actions:

- the dynamic distribution of data to each node present in the cluster,

- the reception of results calculated by those nodes,

- the coordination of the wireless medium access implementing a Point Coordination Function similar to that defined by the IEEE 802.11 standard, and

- the invocation of the association and disassociation services to allow that the wireless nodes can appear and disappear dynamically in the cluster in a controlled manner. In this way, the access node has knowledge of the number of nodes at the cluster and so it can make an efficient load balancing.

3.   THE PROGRAMMING MODEL

In order to develop an efficient programming strategy, it is important to take the high transmission latency of the wireless media into account. For that reason, we hide this communication latency overlapping communications

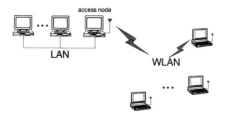

Figure 1   The cluster architecture

and computations. To do this we have identified two different overlapping strategies: 1. while access node does computations, it can overlap its communications, and 2. the computations and communications of wireless and wired nodes can be overlapped (we can suppose a logical communication bus or ring connecting the wired nodes and another one connecting the wireless nodes). While the first overlapping is not difficult to implement, the second one is a hard task and several studies for efficient dynamic data distribution have to be done. At present, we consider the first type of overlapping and we are in phase of implementing the second one.

We have developed an automatic tool which analyses the dependence graph of a sequential algorithm and helps us to carry out the best embedding (and initial data distribution) to overlap computations and communications over logical ring and torus topologies [10]. Focus on this target, we have parallelized different numerical algorithms using our code generation methodology. But due to the wireless nodes can appear and disappear dynamically of the cluster in a controlled way, we can not distribute data among nodes (wired and wireless) in compilation time because the number of wireless nodes are unknown. Because of our methodology in [10] only distributes data at compilation time, in this paper we present a new dynamic data redistribution methodology (in execution time) and the corresponding code generation methodology.

Figure 2 shows a high level communication protocol that makes feasible the first type of overlapping described previously. Notice that computations made by access node, e. g. computations made with the results coming from the wired and wireless nodes, can be overlapped with communications. In this figure, the parameters np and nw represent the number of wired and wireless nodes respectively. While the former is a constant value, the latter can vary during the execution time of the parallel algorithm due to the association and disassociation of wireless nodes. For example, initially in the association point there are nw wireless nodes associated with the cluster. This number of nodes can increase or decrease in the association/disassociation point. Both parameters np and nw can change their values from application to application. The parameters gp and gw represent the data packet size in bytes which are sent to the wired and wireless nodes. Their values are variable during the execution time of the parallel algorithm to let the access node to perform an efficient load balancing.

The access node starts the program execution sending an association message to wireless nodes and data message size gp to the wired ones. Let us mention that the wireless communications are slower than the wired ones. So if we throw two threads in the access node to perform the wired and wireless communications we can even overlap both communications. Besides, if the access node were a computer with two processors, the threads would be executed in parallel. In this protocol there can be also several association and disassociation messages. The final message is an end one that means that the access node has finished the program execution.

Notice that the proposed communication protocol is based on a centralized controller. This scheme could prevent the scalability of the strategy for a large number of machines. In a such situation the distributed schemes help to solve this problem. The sequential load balancing decision in the centralized approach is made in parallel (replicated) in the distributed schemes. However, we consider that the adopted centralized solution performs well in our architecture.

Next we present the general skeleton of the algorithm to be implemented by the wired nodes, the wireless stations and the access node respectively. These nodes work in the implementation of iterative parallel algorithms.

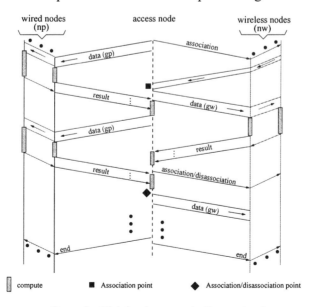

Figure 2   High level communication protocol

3.1   Algorithm in the Wired Nodes

Initially, the wired nodes determine their identifier my_id, with $1 \leq my\_id \leq np$ (table 1). Then, each node waits for data sent by the access node which sends p data segments, of k elements, so that $gp = p \times k$ with $1 \leq p \leq np$. The processor with identifier 1 ($P1$) works with the first segment received, $P2$ with the second one, etc. Processor i makes computation with the $i - th$ data segment if the identifier of the processor is minor or equal to the number of data segments sent by the access node (variable p). In other case ($my\_id > p$) the processor does not participate in the computation during the present iteration. Then, each processor sends its results to the access node. The steps above are repeated until no more data are sent by the access node.

Table 1   Skeleton for the wired nodes

```
determine my_id
repeat
    receive(data,p)
    if my_id ≤ p then
        compute()
        send(access_node,result)
    end if
until no more data
```

3.2   Algorithm in the Wireless Nodes

Initially, the wireless nodes try to associate to the cluster after they have received an association message sent by the access node (table 2). During the association interval, the wireless stations contend to gain access to the wireless medium using CSMA/CA protocol. The station which gains the medium, sends a message to the access node, which replies to it by sending another message that contains the processor identifier (initially this identifier is 1). When the association interval finishes, the access node knows the number of wireless nodes present at the cluster. Notice that it could be possible the existence of more wireless nodes which could not be able to associate to the cluster (the current association interval has finished and some wireless nodes do not have gained the medium). These stations must wait the next interval association to try again the association. Next, the wireless nodes previously associated receive data from the access node. Now, we can not consider that processor i associated computes with the $i - th$ data received due to the presence of disassociations, e.g., if a processor with identifier smaller than i is disassociated, the processor i computes with $(i - 1) - th$ data segment received.

Because of disassociation process is implemented in a centralized manner (like the association process), only the access node can know the identifiers (processors) active. For that reason, together with the data sent, the access node sends a vector of integers (we denote it by ID). $ID[j]$ equal to 1 means that station with identifier j is associated and it participates in the computations. On the contrary, if $ID[j]$ is 0 means that station j does not take part in the calculations due to this is a disassociated node. With this vector, processor i determinates its data segment. It could happen that the processor i does not receive a data segment to work with, i.e., for this processor the expression is true. In this case, processor i does not participate in the current iteration of the computation process. On the contrary, it takes part actively if the processor receives a data segment to make computations.

To gather results, the access point initiates a polling interval in which take part the stations that have contributed on the computations. Immediately later, a disassociation interval starts. During this period, one o more stations can try to disassociate of the cluster. The complete algorithm presented above is repeated until no more data are sent by the access node.

Table 2   Skeleton for the wireless nodes

```
repeat
    while not(associated) and not(end association interval) do
        receive an association message
        if medium==free then
            send association request
            receive identifier
        end if
    end while
    if associated then
        receive(data,p,ID)
        if data to compute with then
            make computations
            receive a polling message
            if my turn then send results
            else wait my turn
            end if
        end if
        if disassociation then
            receive a disassociation message
            send a disassociation request
        end if
    end if
until no more data or disassociated
```

3.3   Algorithm in the Access Node

Initially, the access node determines the number of wired and wireless nodes in the cluster (table 3). The former can be read in a configuration file, and the latter can be calculated after the association interval finishes. For each association request, it generates a new identifier (initially 1) which is sent to the applicant wireless node and updates the ID vector. At the same time the access node receives these requests, it sends data to the wired nodes. After the association interval ends, the access node sends data plus ID vector to the wireless nodes. It also receives results coming from the wired nodes. The access node initiates a period of polling in which it receives data coming from wireless processors. After that, a disassociation interval takes place in which the wireless nodes contend for the medium if they want to request its disassociation of the cluster. For each request received, the access node updates the number of wireless nodes and the vector ID. At the end of this interval, the algorithm above is repeated until there are not more data to be distributed to the wired and/or the wireless network.

Table 3   Skeleton for the access node

```
compute number of wired nodes (np)
repeat
    do_overlapped
        for wireless network
            send an association message
            receive requests,update ID and send identifiers
            compute number of wireless nodes (nw)
        end for
        for wired network
            send data
        end for
    end do_overlapped
    barrier
    do_overlapped
        for wireless network
            send data + ID to wireless nodes
            send a polling message
            receive results
            initiate a disassociation service
            update number of wireless nodes and vector ID
        end for
        for wired network
            receive results
        end for
    end do_overlapped
    barrier
until no more data to be distributed
```

4.   EXECUTION TIME EVALUATION

Let be $t_{com}(k) = t_{wles}(k_1) + t_{wred}(k_2) + t_{ad}$ the communication time for sending k bytes in the parallel algorithm, where $k = k_1 + k_2$, $t_{wles}(k_1)$ is the communication time to send k_1 bytes to the wireless nodes, $t_{wred}(k_2)$ is the communication time to send k_2 bytes to the wired nodes, and t_{ad} is the time spent in the association and disassociation of wireless nodes. Let us note that we suppose that there is no overlapping among wired and wireless communication. In general $t_{wles}(k_1)$ can be calculated as $t_{wles}(k_1) = A_1 + k_1 \times A_2$ and $t_{wred}(k_2)$ as $t_{wred}(k_2) = B_1 + k_2 \times B_2$, where A_1 and B_1 represent the message startup overhead in the wireless and wired communications respectively, and A_2 and B_2 are the transfer times for a byte. With the current communication technologies we have the following values for our parameters: $A_2 > 7,6\ \mu s$ (1 Mbps) or $A_2 < 0,4\ \mu s$ (23,5 Mbps), and $B_2 > 762$ ns (10 Mbps) or $B_2 < 8$ ns (1 Gbps). Due to we have to send a lot of messages when the size of the problem is high, then we do not take the terms A_1, B_1 and t_{ad} into account.

In order to balance the communications among wireless and wired nodes we will try: 1. optimize the number of bytes to (from) the wireless nodes from (to) the access node, because the time spent in this part of the cluster is higher than the one in the wired nodes, and 2. calculate the optimal number of wireless nodes such as the communication time be not declined and the speed-up be greater than in the case of using only wired nodes.

We formulate this problem considering that k_1 and k_2 depend on np, nw and the size of the problem (global amount of bytes to be sent). But nw is not known in compilation time which means that its value along the time can be any positive integer number. Moreover the number of bytes to be sent to the wireless nodes depends on the distribution along the time of nw.

To optimize the number of bytes the objective is making that $k_1 < k_2$. To calculate the optimum number of wireless nodes we have to take the size of the messages into account, the communication time when there is no wireless nodes and when $nw > 0$, and estimating the minimum value such as $t_{wles}(k_1)$ is close to $t_{wred}(k_2)$.

For example, let us suppose that we implement the matrix per vector algorithm, $A(m \times n) \times b(n) = c(m)$, in which we distribute rows of matrix A among the processors. And suppose that nw is constant along the time, i. e., there is no dissasociation and association of wireless nodes after the initial association interval. In this situation, the communication time to send k bytes in the parallel algorithm is $t_{com}(k) = 3,8 \times k_1 + 0,762 \times k_2$ considering a 2 Mbps transmission speed in the wireless network and 10 Mbps in the wired one. To balance the communication latency of the wireless network, k_2 must be at least 5 times greater than k_1. The problem is to determine how high or low must be the term k_2 (or k_1) such as the terms A_1, B_1 and t_{ad} be not important in the communication time above. This is a task it must be put into practice.

5.   CONCLUSION AND FUTURE WORK

With the recent advances in wired and wireless LANs, it is apparent that it could be feasible to perform distributed computing over such heterogeneous networking environment. In this paper we have presented a WLAN-LAN based cluster, where the wireless nodes can associate and disassociate of the cluster during the parallel algorithm execution. A programming model to programme iterative applications on the above architecture was also presented.

Nevertheless, many things remain to be done. We are in process of testing the programming model proposed and evaluating the optimal number of messages to be sent to the wired and wireless nodes to balance the communications. In ongoing work, we are in phase of discussing how adapt a MPI/PVM application for our architecture.

References

[1] Haihong, Z., Rajkumar, B., Bhattacharya, S.: Mobile Cluster Computing and Timeliness Issues. Informatica 17. (1999)

[2] Hernández, M.: Parallel Computing for the Search of Global Minimums and its Application in the Design of Wireless MAC Protocols. Master Thesis to be presented in year- 2000 (in Spanish)

[3] Information available in: www.gigabit-ethernet.org

[4] Information available in: http://ibm.tc.cornell.edu/ibm/pps/sp2/sp2.html

[5] Information available in: http://grouper.ieee.org/groups/802/11/

[6] Information available in: http://www.hiperlan.com/hiper_white.pdf

[7] Janche, S., Lin, C-H M., Wang, M-C: Experiences with Network-Based Computing over Wireless Links. International Journal of Parallel and Distributed Systems & Networks, vol. 2, no. 2. (1999) 79-87

[8] Mark, B.: Cluster Computing White Paper. Draft version 0.915. (1999)

[9] Mark, B., Rajkumar, B., Hyde, D.:, Cluster Computing: A High-Performance Contender. Technical Activities Forum. (1999) 79-83

[10] Ojeda-Guerra, C. N.: Methodology of Parallelization of Algorithms Based on Coloured Graphs. PhD Thesis to be presented in May-2000 (in Spanish)

[11] Rajkumar, B.: High Performance Cluster Computing: Architectures and Systems, vol. 1. Prentice Hall. (1999)

QUALITY-AWARE PROXY CACHING FOR WEB VIDEOS

Stefan Podlipnig, László Böszörményi
Institute of Information Technology
Universität Klagenfurt, Klagenfurt, Austria
{spodlipn,laszlo}@itec.uni-klu.ac.at

Abstract   The growing number of web videos have caused an increasing demand on new approaches for a better video delivery over the Internet. Video caching is seen as a possibility for improving video delivery. In this paper we present a comprehensive view on video caching approaches proposed in the literature. We introduce the notion of quality-aware video caching and discuss how video scaling techniques can be integrated into a video cache. Besides proposing a combination of quality reduction and replacement strategies we present a basic structure for a video proxy. Additionally we discuss further video caching topics.

Keywords: Proxy, caching, quality-awareness, web videos, replacement.

1.   INTRODUCTION

Proxy caching is seen as an important factor in providing large scale access to web objects on the Internet. It is known that web access patterns show frequent requests for a small number of popular objects at popular servers. Such popular objects and popular servers form hot spots in the network that influence the overall performance significantly. To overcome this problem proxy caches have been introduced to cache popular objects near to the clients.

During recent years Internet content has changed from simple text based documents to rich multimedia content including text, images and continuous media data. Especially, continuous media data is growing dramatically. Although currently audio data dominates, video data will be the dominating factor in the future. Because web videos are much larger than normal web objects they introduce an especially high load when delivered over the Internet. Therefore it is an important question how web videos can be cached near to clients.

Despite the success of proxy caching, caching of web videos has not been considered in depth. Due to special properties of web videos, video caching is not a straight forward task. In this paper we give an overview of different video caching approaches described in the literature (section 2.). We introduce the notion of quality-aware video caching (section 3.) and discuss the combination of quality reduction and replacement strategies. Furthermore, we propose a basic structure for a video proxy and point out further research topics.

2.   RELATED WORK

The growing number of web videos on the Internet has influenced the development of different techniques for the delivery of video data. We distinguish two techniques for sending stored video data from a server to a client:

- Download-and-play: Video data is transferred completely to the client site before display. Due to the large size of web videos, this results in large space usage and long start-up at the client. Besides this some client software allows a playback as soon as a certain amount of data has been received. Nevertheless the whole video is downloaded.

- Streaming: The client software plays the video as soon as a certain amount of data has been received. The client software uses a small buffer for the incoming data and does not have to store the whole video.

Generally, downloading the whole file is accomplished over reliable transport mechanisms. For streaming applications a number of streaming protocols and systems have been introduced. Although there exist standard protocols for streaming applications (Real Time Transport Protocol, Real Time Streaming Protocol) the current environment of internet streaming is influenced by a number of commercial companies which use proprietary implementations. We do not want to concentrate on this. Our main aim is to present concepts that do not rely on special techniques.

Due to the growing interest in web videos a growing number of video caching strategies have been proposed recently. These strategies can be divided into two categories: Full video caching (the whole video is cached) and partial video caching (a certain part of the video is cached). Full video caching can be found in many available caching products. Video files are handled like normal web objects (download-and-play). To our knowledge there are only few vendors (e.g. Inktomi [7], NetworkAppliance) that have special solutions for caching continuous media (video/audio content). They also cache whole videos[1].

In the research literature, caching of whole videos is handled in different ways. In [1] complete video sequences are stored, with their tails being removed from the cache when it fills up (combination of full and partial caching). A different view of video caching is presented in [12]. They assume that the caching proxy is an efficient video server. It conducts admission control and resource reservation to provide statistical quality of service. To ensure a good stream quality the proxy uses replication and striping of videos. Such a proxy is thought as a support for many concurrent interactive video streams.

Because videos tend to be much bigger than typical web objects, a partial caching strategy can be applied. Such partial caching strategies have been proposed recently. These strategies cache a certain part (depending on a criterion) of the videos. [14] proposes caching of the initial frames (prefix) of a video sequence at the proxy. This prefix is used for work-ahead smoothing and hides the initial start-up delay of the work-ahead transmission schedule. A more general approach is proposed in [9]. Besides the prefix also additional parts are stored. Given an appropriate cost function, it can generate the solutions presented in [1, 14]. Another scheme [16] prefetches and stores bursty portions of a stream in proxy servers and uses them to smooth the stream during playback.

A comprehensive approach to multimedia streaming is presented in [6]. It combines a special form of partial caching (segmentation), serving multiple multimedia requests through one stream (like patching in Video-on-Demand Systems) and cooperation among caching systems. In [13] a proxy caching mechanism is combined with a congestion control mechanism and layered coding. With layered coding the compressed video is split into a base layer, which contains the most important video information, and enhancement layers, which are used for improving video quality. The basic idea of this approach is to cache layers according to the congestion situation in the Internet and the popularity of the video. The more popular a video, the more layers are cached.

3.   QUALITY-AWARE PROXY CACHING

Our caching strategy is based on the fact that videos can be presented (transmitted, stored) with different quality levels. Depending on the actual situation a specific part of the video information may be sufficient for an acceptable video delivery. We call a caching proxy that uses media scaling techniques a quality-aware caching proxy. We see two forms of quality awareness:

- Quality reduction: The removal policy chooses videos in a web cache. Their quality is reduced and they are stored again. Initial ideas about this topic were presented in [10]. In [11] a comprehensive framework for caching quality-reduced JPEG-images (soft caching) is presented.

- Quality adaptation: The quality of cached videos is adapted according to a specific optimization criterion (for example popularity). A comprehensive approach for adaptive video caching is presented in [13].

Note that quality reduction could be seen as a special form of quality adaptation. We prefer to distinguish between these concepts because they influence the design of caching policies in different ways. Therefore we use the overall notion of quality awareness to subsume these concepts.

The main points of our proposal can be summarized as follows:

- Quality awareness: The basic idea is based on quality reduction. Initially, the whole video is cached at the proxy. When the cache fills up, the replacement policy starts. To get enough storage space for new videos, the policy selects videos according to a specific strategy. Instead of removing these videos like in typical replacement policies for proxy caches, their quality is reduced and they are stored further with a lower quality. A video is removed from the cache when its quality reaches a level that is not acceptable.

- Metadata: The combination of web objects and corresponding metadata has not been considered very often. Due to the small size of traditional web objects metadata would introduce a high overhead. Videos tend to be much bigger and therefore a few kilobytes of metadata do not introduce much overhead. Such metadata can describe special video information that can be used for a more intelligent cache management.

- Caching Architecture: We want to integrate our cache into a specific architecture that supports efficient video delivery.

In the following sections we will focus on three parts. First, we give a justification of using full or partial caching. Second, we show that quality aware video caching introduces new interesting questions. At last, we describe a cache architecture.

3.1   Full versus Partial Caching

Many recent proposals for video caching try to apply a partial caching strategy. The main argument against caching of whole videos is that videos tend to be much bigger than typical web objects. Therefore, a normal sized cache will be filled with a small number of videos and that will reduce the hit rate. Although this is true it does not give a complete view of video caching. To give a more differentiated view of video caching we rely in our following discussion on the expected advantages of original web caching.

According to [15], web caching reduces bandwidth consumption, access latency and the workload of the remote web server. Furthermore, it enhances robustness and provides possibilities to analyze usage patterns. In the following discussion we will concentrate on the first three points. The reduction of bandwidth consumption, access latency and load on remote servers are the main advantages of original web caches. Traditional caches assume that the whole web object is stored at the cache. This is not true for partial video caching strategies. Storing only a specific part of the video has a great advantage. At the beginning more videos can be served from the cache. Therefore, the start-up latency can be reduced for more videos. This is the original motivation for introducing partial video caching [14]. However, every video delivery involves the original server and the network between original server and proxy cache. Therefore, if we talk about pros and cons of video caching proposals we have to take into account this trade-off. It depends on the aim of the video caching proxy whether the full video or a part of it is cached.

We consider full caching as a special case of partial caching (caching all parts of a video). Suppose that each video consists of different parts. Each part is characterized by a benefit value and its corresponding size. We use a simple greedy algorithm for choosing the parts that should be cached at the proxy. This algorithm sorts the parts according to their benefit/size ratio in descending order. Then it picks the parts according to their benefit/size ratio in descending order until the cache is full. It is likely to cache the entire video if the following holds: The benefit is nearly uniform for all parts of the video, the size is nearly uniform for all parts of the video and the benefit is very high for the video. If the benefit and size are nearly uniform for all parts, these parts will have similar benefit/size ratios. They will be placed near each other in the sorting order. If the benefit is very high (compared to other videos), the whole video will be cached.

It is likely that the benefit and size values for parts of an entire video are not uniform. If the video parts are different video objects (like in MPEG-4) the size can vary significantly. If the benefit includes access frequencies, uneven access frequencies caused by uneven playback (users prefer to watch the beginning of videos, limited use of quality information due to special network conditions etc.) of video parts can cause non uniform benefit values. Due to this the parts of one video can have very different benefit/size ratios and only the most beneficial parts will be stored at the proxy cache. Therefore many videos will be cached in a partial state.

3.2   Quality-Aware Video Caching

Although our initial idea is based on the simple approach of quality reduction we still have to face a lot of new problems and interesting questions. We distinguish two possible video classes: structured and unstructured videos. In the former case there exists a certain structure. Structured videos consist of certain parts and an application can use these parts separately. Unstructured videos do not have this structure. Note that unstructured videos are a special case of structured videos, i.e. they consist of one part which constitutes the whole video. The following methods for quality reduction can be applied to unstructured videos.

- Recompression: The video is decompressed and compressed with a higher quantization value.

- Filtering[2]: Filtering operates on compressed data and means arbitrary manipulation (discarding of information) of compressed data streams.

As noted above structured videos consist of certain parts. On the one hand these parts can be used for quality reduction (removing one or many parts) and for quality adaptation (removing or reloading one or many parts). On the other hand the granularity of these parts determine the granularity of the quality adaptation process. An example for this is layered coding.

In the following we concentrate on the integration of quality reduction and proxy caching. We assume that the cache uses an appropriate method for quality reduction that results in smaller sized videos. We further assume that the quality reduction is applied in discrete steps (limited number of resulting quality levels) to the set of videos that is determined by the replacement strategy. To be consistent with the usual terminology we talk about replacement strategies although a real removal of a video only takes place when a quality reduction results in a video with unacceptable quality.

The main topic in connection with video caching is the integration of the quality reduction process and existing replacement strategies. There are many studies about replacement strategies in web caches (see for example [2, 15, 17]). They were developed for original web objects and do not consider quality reduction. One example for the integration of quality reduction and replacement is presented in [8]. The basic idea is the following. The quality reduction is considered as a part of the replacement strategy (LRU in the specific case) because otherwise a cache object is repeatedly recompressed until the lowest quality level is reached. Therefore, the access time of the recompressed object needs to be adjusted as a function of the quality level. The new access time *new* is calculated as

$$new = old + \frac{remaining\_quality\_levels}{maximum\_quality\_levels}(current\_time - old) \quad (1)$$

where *old* is the time of the last reference. The new access time (LRU value) for an object that has been recompressed a few times is close to the current time which increases its priority in the LRU algorithm. A strongly recompressed object is probably not useful and its new access time is set closer to its old access time. However, there are still some problems with this version of LRU. It does not take into account the non-linear relationship between visual quality and quality level. Therefore an additional factor should be added to the second term to represent this non-linearity. Determining the visual quality is not an easy task. Sophisticated methods are very complex and time consuming.

To overcome the described problems we assume that special information (metadata) is provided with the original video. This metadata can be stored in a separate file in connection with the video (video object) or can be encoded in the video (video object). It can include any form of quality information (e.g. quality levels, relationship between quality level and visual quality, quality level and corresponding file size, cost for quality adaptation), access statistics collected at the server of the video or special video properties (video category etc.). The metadata is given by the provider of the video and is used for intelligent cache management. We are aware of potential problems concerning metadata provision (e.g. tools that provide this information, additional server load when collecting access statistics). Therefore, the evaluation of metadata for video caching has to focus on two points: Which metadata can be supplied realistically and how does metadata influence cache management?

One important hint for a quality-aware proxy cache is the relationship between potential quality levels and visual quality. In the following we assume, that a given video consists of one or more video objects. We assume that each video object has two ore more quality levels. Removing (through scaling techniques) some information from the video object results in reduced video object size (memory requirement) and reduced visual quality (lower quality level). The relationship between video object size and visual quality can be characterized by some sort of quality function. Typically a decrease in video object size does not increase the visual quality making the quality function a nondecreasing function on video object size. We assume discrete quality curves which model discretely adaptive video objects, i.e. a limited number of scaling operations (with resulting quality levels) is used . A simple implementation would use metadata in the form of an order of scaling operations o together with the resulting size s and resulting quality q, e.g. $(o_1, s_1, q_1), ..., (o_n, s_n, q_n)$. Note that this simplification assumes that a scaling operation results in equal quality for the whole video object. Although in reality the quality will fluctuate over time such an approach limits the metadata that has to be used by the cache and simplifies the caching decision. A quality-aware proxy cache can integrate this metadata (size and video quality information) into its replacement strategy.

3.3   Video Proxy Proposal

Caching videos near to the clients is one possibility for improving video delivery (smaller start-up latency, better network conditions). Adapting the quality of videos to a certain amount is an additional aid in improving the hit rate of such a video cache. However, this form of caching is still similar to normal web caching. We think that a video cache has to be supported by additional components thus forming a powerful video proxy. Such a proxy cache should consist of three components: caching component, buffering component and video delivery component (Figure 1).

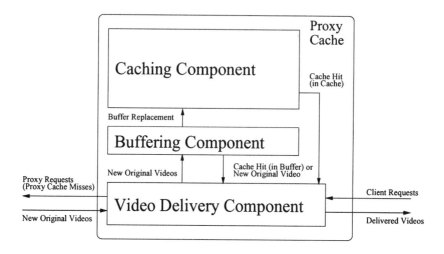

Figure 1   Proxy cache architecture

The caching component handles the storage of video files on disk. It is responsible for the whole cache management (quality reduction, adaptation, removal etc.). The buffering component buffers downloaded videos in main memory. The video is downloaded in a loss-less fashion (e.g. TCP). Depending on the current network situation between the original server and the proxy the buffer has to be filled to a certain amount before the video delivery component begins its transmission to the client. After the transmission the video remains in the buffer as long as there is enough space for new incoming videos (main memory cache). Therefore the buffering component needs its own replacement strategy, e.g. videos have to be moved to the caching component. The video delivery component handles client requests. If a client requests a video file in the caching component or in the buffering component (cache hit) the video delivery component performs an admission control. This admission control checks if the new stream from the proxy to the client overloads the proxy. If the admission control fails the client has to retrieve the video from the original server. Otherwise, the video is delivered from the video proxy. We assume that such a video proxy resides near to the clients in the sense that there is a fast network between the proxy and the potential clients.

4.   CONCLUSION AND FUTURE WORK

The emerging topic of video caching was discussed. We gave a survey of proposed video caching approaches and introduced the notion of quality-aware video caching. We presented some initial ideas about quality-aware video caching. Especially, we discussed the combination of quality reduction and replacement strategies. The discussed ideas have to be evaluated in a real implementation. Additionally, we are going to investigate the following topics:

- Quality-aware replacement strategies: The integration of known replacement strategies and quality awareness is not straight forward. More sophisticated replacements strategies have to be considered in future work.

- Quality adaptive replacement: We discussed aspects of quality reduction and cache replacement. The next step is to consider real quality adaptation and cache replacement. With quality adaptation the quality of a video (video object) can decrease or increase according to the actual situation at the proxy cache (fluctuating overall load etc.).

- Cache admission control: With an admission control a cache can evaluate which incoming videos should be stored in the cache. Additionally, the admission control can be combined with quality adaptation, i.e. only a low quality version is accepted for the cache.

- QoS (Quality of Service): Web caching is a best-effort service. The inevitability of cache-misses implies that caches cannot be relied upon to deliver cache objects on a predictable basis. The lifetime of a cache object is a function of its popularity and the load seen by the cache. To introduce some sort of QoS new forms of caching have to be introduced [3].

Besides these scientific questions the realization of a caching proxy has to be considered in a real environment based on standard protocols. Such a realization introduces new problems and questions (see for example [4, 5]). We have to evaluate whether our initial ideas can be integrated in such environments.

Notes

1. Although there is no special technical information about these products, they seem to simply relate the idea of caching to multimedia streams
2. This definition is different from the usual one used in electrical engineering, where it means discarding parts of the signal (low-pass filtering) or refining the signal (noise reduction).

References

[1] S. Acharya. "Techniques for Improving Multimedia Communication over Wide Area Networks". PhD thesis, Cornell University, 1999.

[2] P. Cao and S. Irani. "Cost-Aware WWW Proxy Caching Algorithms". In Proceedings of USENIX Symposium on Internet Technologies and Systems, pages 193-206, December 1997.

[3] J. Chuang and M. Sirbu. "stor-serv: Adding Quality-of-Service to Network Storage". In Workshop on Internet Service Quality Economics, 1999.

[4] J. Geagan, M. Kellner and A. Pariyannan, "Caching Support in Standards-based RTSP/RTP Servers", Internet Draft, February 2000.

[5] S. Gruber, J. Rexford and A. Basso. "Protocol Considerations for a Prefix-Caching Proxy for Multimedia Streams". In Proceedings of the 9th International World Wide Web Conference, May 2000.

[6] T. Hofmann, T. S. E. Ng, K. Gue, S. Paul and H. Zhang. "Caching Techniques for Streaming Multimedia over the Internet". Technical report, Bell Laboratories, April 1999.

[7] Inktomi. "Streaming Media Caching White Paper". Technical report, Inktomi Corporation, 1999.

[8] J. Kangasharju, Y. G. Kwon, A. Ortega, X. Yang and K. Ramachandran. "Implementation of Optimized Cache Replenishment Algorithms in a Soft Caching System". In IEEE Signal Processing Society 1998 Workshop on Multimedia Signal Processing, December 1998.

[9] Z. Miao and A. Ortega. "Proxy Caching for Efficient Video Services over the Internet". In 9th International Packet Video Workshop (PVW 99), April 1999.

[10] M. Oguchi and K. Ono. "A Study of Caching Proxy Mechanisms Realized on Wide Area Distributed Networks". In IEEE Symposium on High Performance Distributed Computing, pages 443-449, 1996.

[11] A. Ortega, F. Carignano, S. Ayer and M. Vetterli. "Soft Caching: Web Cache Management Techniques For Images". In IEEE Signal Processing Society 1997 Workshop on Multimedia Signal Processing, June 1997.

[12] M. Reisslein, F. Hartano and K. W. Ross. "Interactive Video Streaming with Proxy Servers". In Proceedings of First International Workshop on Intelligent Multimedia Computing and Networking (IMMCN), February 2000.

[13] R. Rejaie, H. Yu, M. Handley and D. Estrin. "Multimedia Proxy Caching Mechanism for Quality Adaptive Streaming Applications in the Internet". In IEEE INFOCOM 2000, March 2000.

[14] S. Sen, J. Rexford and D. Towsley. "Proxy Prefix Caching for Multimedia Streams". In IEEE INFOCOM 99, March 1999.

[15] J. Wang. "A Survey of Web Caching Schemes for the Internet". ACM Computer Communication Review, 29(5):36-46, 1999.

[16] Y. Wang, Z. Zhang, D. H. C. Du and D. Su. "A Network-Conscious Approach for End-to-End Video Delivery over Wide-Area Networks Using Proxy Servers". In IEEE INFOCOM 98, April 1998.

[17] S. Williams, M. Abrams, C. R. Standridge, G. Abdulla and E. A. Fox. "Removal Policies in Network Caches for World-Wide Web Documents". In ACM SIGCOMM 96, pages 293-305, 1996.

CLUSTER COMMAND & CONTROL (C3) TOOLS SUITE

Ray Flanery[1], Al Geist[1], Brian Luethke[2], and Stephen L. Scott[1]

[1] *Computer Science and Mathematics Division, Oak Ridge National Laboratory, Oak Ridge, Tennessee 37830-6367, USA.*   [2] *Computer Science Department, East Tennessee State University, Johnson City, Tennessee 37614-0718*

contact author: scottsl@ornl.gov

Abstract   The computation power of PC clusters running the Linux operating system rivals that of supercomputers of just a few years ago at a fraction of the purchase price. However, the lack of good administration and application tools represents a hidden operation cost that is often overlooked when proposing a cluster. This paper presents a number of command line tools developed at Oak Ridge National Laboratory for use in operating the HighTORC cluster. These same tools provide the "backend" connection to the cluster for our web based GUI tool suite M3C (Monitoring and Managing Multiple Clusters).

Keywords: PC cluster tools, cluster administration

1.   INTRODUCTION

While there are numerous tools and techniques available for the administration of clusters, few of these tools ever see the outside of their developer's cluster. Basically they are developed for specific inhouse uses. This results in a great deal of duplicated effort among cluster administrators and software developers. Thus, after building HighTORC[1], a 64-node – 128 processor – Beowulf cluster in the Summer of 1999, it was decided to make an effort to develop and collect a suite of system administration cluster tools that could be released to the cluster community so that others may benefit from our effort as well.

To simplify administration some cluster builders simply NFS mount one master file system to all nodes. While the "one file system" approach does greatly simplify configuration management and application development, it also provides the least scalable model and lowest performance for cluster computing due to machine and network constraints. Our approach is to decentralize every aspect of the cluster configuration in HighTORC to promote scalability. This resulted in every node hosting its own independent operating system with the remaining local disk space used as temporary application and data storage. Of course, this approach generated the need for tools to hide the fact that HighTORC consists of 64 independent machines. Using a number of freely available tools; rsync[2], tomsrtbt[3], ssh2[4], DHCP[5], and Systemimager[6] we developed a suite of cluster command and control (C3) tools to easily move information into and out of the cluster as if it were a single machine rather than a group of loosely coupled independent machines. These tools are similar in function to those developed by Gropp and Lusk [7] for use on MPPs.

One of the main criteria of the tools is that, they provide the look and feel of commands issued to a single machine. This is accomplished through using lists, or configuration files, to represent the group of machines on which a command will operate. While this requires the building of machine lists, or cluster node lists, it still presents the typical user with a single machine interface. This occurs as generally a cluster is configured and used in its entirety at any given instance by a single user. Thus the cluster node list containing all cluster nodes may be built once and then forgotten. However, a strength of the C3 tool suite is that an individual user may dynamically customize and use their cluster configuration list without affecting any other cluster users.

A second criterion is that the tools be secure. Generally security inside a cluster, between cluster nodes, is somewhat relaxed for a number of practical reasons. Some of these include 1) improve performance, 2) ease programming, and 3) all nodes are generally compromised if one cluster node's security is compromised. Thus, security from outside the cluster into the cluster is of utmost concern. Therefore, user authentication from outside to inside must be done in a secure manner.

The third criterion is tool scalability. A user may tolerate an inefficient tool that takes a few minutes to perform an operation across a small cluster of 8 machines as it is faster than performing the operation manually 8 times. However, that user will most likely find it intolerable to wait over an hour for the same operation to take effect across 128 cluster nodes. Further complicating matters is that many cluster sites are now hosting multiple clusters that are or will eventually be combined into federated computation clusters. Extending even further is the computation Grid[8] where combining federated clusters from multiple sites is the norm.

Toward this effort, this paper describes the command line interface tools for cluster command and control (C3) developed for use on HighTORC. These same tools are used to provide the back end services for the web based M3C tool.

2.   REQUIRED SOFTWARE ENVIRONMENT

A number of tools developed and freely published on the web were collected to facilitate the development of our C3 tool suite. The following section briefly describes and provides information where each of these tools may be obtained.

Rsync is a method for mirroring drives similar to rdist[9]. It operates by: 0) get the list of files to be transferred from a source, 1) split the target file into small fixed-size blocks, 2) generate a checksum – both a weak "rolling" 32-bit checksum and a strong 128-bit MD4 checksum, 3) transfer both checksums, 4) remote system uses the checksums to generate a sequence of instructions used to request blocks to be updated, 5) send requests to update blocks. A more detailed explanation of the rsync algorithm may be found at the rsync web page. This tool is used in C3 to effect the movement of files between server and node. Systemimager uses rsync to move disk images from image server to client node. Rsync simplifies file movement between cluster nodes.

Tomsrtbt is self proclaimed as "the most linux on one floppy". Tomsrtbt is used to build a bootable diskette to initially boot a new cluster node prior to using the cl_pushimage command to install and restart the node as a fully functioning cluster node.

OpenSSH is an open source tool that uses the ssh 1.5 protocol. OpenSSH requires the **openSSL** package to work. OpenSSH uses a digital signature generated by OpenSSL for authentication purposes. This eliminates the need to send passwords across the network to remote machines. OpenSSH is an enabling tool that provides a secure means for C3 to connect to remote cluster nodes from outside the cluster's internal network. Without such security the C3 tool suite would either not be permitted to execute or at the very least would be restricted by security policy. C3 uses OpenSSH for a secure means to eliminate the need to login to each cluster node when invoking a command. OpenSSH is used to both execute a remote command (like rsh) and is used by rsync to transfer files.

Dynamic Hosts Configuration Protocol (DHCP), is used to allocate IP addresses to machines on a given network. It can do this dynamically within a given range of IP addresses or statically by associating a NIC's MAC address with a specific IP address. Dynamic allocation of IP addresses makes it easy to swap out machines with little operator intervention. Static allocation of IP address makes it easier to troubleshoot machine/network problems and subsequently debut distributed cluster codes.

Dynamic IP allocation allows DHCP to "lease" an IP address to a client for a specified time period. This time period may be set from a few seconds to forever. Forever in this case ends when the client gives up the IP address – like on a reboot. A short lease will be detrimental to cluster performance, as it will require the cluster nodes to continually access the DHCP server to obtain a new IP address. A forever lease will produce stability at least until a node crashes or reboots. However, periods of instability in clusters tend to affect more than one node thus making debugging using the IP address useless, as they will shuffle on many nodes simultaneously. Our recommendation is to initially dynamically allocate IP addresses within a specified range in order of cluster node identifier (number). Then use the systemimager tool, described later, to change the dynamic allocation to a static allocation scheme. Thus, ease of initial installation with troubleshooting and debugging capabilities is retained. In practice, the static allocation of IP address on clusters eases the replacement of a cluster node.

Systemimager is a cluster system administrator tool, run from root, that enables a cluster node to *pull* the current cluster node image from an outside cluster image server. This proves to be very valuable when initially installing the cluster environment and for subsequent cluster wide operating system and software environment updates.

When combined with tomsrtbt, Systemimager provides a simplified technique to place the initial cluster image on each cluster node. As each machine is booted from the tomsrtbt diskette, it will *pull* the current image from the image server. The image is downloaded, installed, and now the machine may reboot as a cluster node. The only task remaining is to assign a network IP address to the node.

Systemimager requires DHCP to be installed and run on the outside cluster image server. Configuration options include both dynamic and static assigned IP addresses. DHCP dynamically assigns IP addresses by default as machines boot. However, statically assigned addresses are generally advocated for cluster use as it facilitates node debugging and trouble shooting. However, one can not store statically assigned IP addresses on a cluster image when pushing the same image across a number of machines. To do so would produce disastrous results as all machines would then try to use the same IP address. The alternative is to manually change the IP address of each machine after initial startup and then reboot with the correct IP address. This is not very practical as it is time consuming, error prone, and becomes rather annoying after about four machines. Systemimager provides a solution to this problem via it's makedhcpstatic utility. Simply boot cluster nodes in order of desired IP address as DHCP will sequentially assign the IP number to each machine as it comes on line. Next run makedhcpstatic which will rewrite the /etc/dhcpd.conf file to associate each node's MAC address with it's host name. Last, restart DHCP. Now each time a node requests an IP address, the same number will be assigned. This technique works great for installing a large number of machines with contiguous IP addresses. However, if a machine or NIC is replaced, you must manually set the IP address on the node and in the /etc/dhcpd.conf file. However, this is a small price to pay for the occasional machine or NIC failure compared to the effort required to initially build and configure a large cluster.

The only shortcoming of Systemimager is that it requires the cluster node to request an image from the outside cluster image server. While this technique avoids the security problems of an outside machine forcing new software on a cluster node, perhaps taking control of the machine, it also restricts the usefulness of the image update to preplanned updates (*pulls*) driven by coordinated node cron jobs. Our desire was to augment the features of Systemimager such that a system administrator may effectively *push* a new system image in a secure manner across the entire cluster or any portion of the cluster. Thus, the creation of cl_pushimage.

3.   C3 TOOLS SUITE

Eight general use tools have been developed in this effort thus far. Cl_pushimage is our single machine *push* answer to the Systemimager *pull* image solution. Like Systemimager, cl_pushimage and cl_shutdown are both root user system administrator tools. The other six tools, cl_push, cl_rm, cl_get, cl_ps, cl_kill, and cl_exec are tools that may be employed by any cluster user both at the system and application level. Cl_push will let you push individual files or directories across the cluster. Cl_rm will permit the deletion of files or directories on the cluster. Cl_get copies cluster based files to a user specified location. Cl_ps returns the aggregate result of the ps command run on each cluster node. Cl_shutdown will shutdown nodes specified in command arguments. Cl_kill is used to terminate a given task across the cluster. Cl_exec is the C3 general utility in that it enables the execution of any command across the cluster.

Cl_pushimage enables a system administrator logged in as root to *push* a cluster node image across a specified set of cluster nodes and optionally reboot those systems. This tool is built upon and leverages the capabilities of Systemimager. While Systemimager provides much of the functionality in this area it fell short in that it did not enable a single point *push* for image transfer. Cl_pushimage essentially *pushes* a request to each participating cluster node to *pull* an image from the image server. Each node then invokes the *pull* of the image from the outside cluster image server.

Cl_pushimage uses a PERL script to iterate through a series of IPs provided by the user. The default cluster configuration file /etc/c3.conf specifying all cluster nodes is used if the user does not provide their own IP address or configuration file. At each iteration, IP address, cl_pushimage uses OpenSSH to call the Systemimage tool updateimage on the cluster machine. Thus, effectively pushing an image to the specified nodes. OpenSSH is employed to provide secure root access to each of the cluster machines from the outside cluster image server. Of course this description assumes that Systemimager has already been employed to capture and relocate a cluster node image to the outside cluster image server machine.

SYNOPSIS

　　cl_pushimage [OPTIONS]... --image=[list:]imagename

OPTIONS

　　--help　　　　　display help message

    --nolilo   don't run lilo after update

    --reboot   reboot node after update completes

GENERAL

There are two different ways to call cl_pushimage :

-using the default list of clusters

"cl_pushimage –image=imageName

-using a subset of the cluster from a given file

"cl_pushimage –image=list_of_nodes:imageName

While cl_pushimage has the ability to push an entire disk image to a cluster node, it is too cumbersome as an application support tool when one simply desires to push files or directories across the cluster. Furthermore, cl_pushimage is only available to system administrators with root level access. From these restrictions grew the desire for a simplified cluster *push* tool, **cl_push**, providing the ability for any user to *push* files and entire directories across cluster nodes. Cl_push uses rsync to push files from server to cluster node. *Caution – do not use cl_push to push the root file system across nodes. Systemimager provides a number of special operations to enable cl_pushimage and updateimage to operate properly.*

SYNOPSIS

cl_push [OPTIONS]… --source=Source --destination=[list:]destination

OPTIONS

    -d,--delete   removes any file that are on the nodes but not on the server

    -s,--source   the directory, file, or pattern to move

    -d,--destination the destination directory or the destination file on the nodes. Using the list option allows you to send to a subset of nodes specified in the file.

GENERAL

There are several different ways to call cl_push, below are some of the ways:

-for moving whole directories

"cl_push –source=/home/* --destination=/home/"

        the use of the backslash before the "*" prevents the shell from trying to expand the special character before the call is made.

-for a single file

"cl_push –source=/home/filename –destination=/home/"

-for a single file and renaming that file on the nodes

"cl_push –source=/home/filename1 –destination=/home/filename2"

-to move a set of files mathing a pattern

"cl_push –source=/home/*.*c –destination=/home/"

        again, notice the backslashes proceding the special characters to prevent the shell from expanding them.

-to move a file to a subset of your nodes

"cl_push –source/home/filename –destination=list_of_nodes:/home/

cl_rm is the cluster version of the rm delete file/directory command. This command will go out across the cluster and attempt to delete the file(s) or directory target in a given location across all specified cluster nodes. By default, no error is returned in the case of not finding the target. The interactive mode of rm is not supplied in cl_rm due to the potential problems associated with numerous nodes asking for delete confirmation.

SYNOPSIS

    cl_rm [OPTIONS]... --files=[list:]pattern

OPTIONS

--help	display help message
-r	recursive delete
-v	verbose mode, shows error message from rm
-files	the file or pattern to delete

GENERAL

    There are several different ways to call cl_rm :

-to delete a directory (must be done recursively)

    "cl_rm –r –files=/home/usr/*"

        notice the use of a \ before the special character. The shell try's to expand the wildcards before the program is called and this forces the shell not to expand them.

-to delete a single file

    "cl_rm –files=/home/filename"

The converse of cl_push is the **cl_get** command. This command will retrieve the given files from each node and deposits them in a specified directory location. Since all files will originally have the same name, only from different nodes, each file name has an underscore and IP or domain name appended to its tail. IP or domain name depends on which is specified in the cluster specification file. Note that cl_get operates only on files and ignores subdirectories and links.

SYNOPSIS

    cl_get --target=target --source=[list:]pattern

OPTIONS

    None.

GENERAL

    There are two basic ways to call cl_get :

-to get a given pattern(in this case a whole directory)

    "cl_get --target=/home/usr/ --source=/home/usr/*"

        notice the use of a \ before the special character. The shell trys to expand the wildcards before the program is called and this forces the shell not to expand them.

-to get a single file

    "cl_get –target=/home/ --source=/home/usr/filename"

        notice that target is always a directory as this is the file destination.

The **cl_ps** utility runs the ps command on each node of the cluster with the options specified by the user. For each node the output is stored in /$HOME/ps_output. A cl_get is then issued for the ps_output file returning each of these to the caller with the node ID appended per the cl_get command. The cl_rm is then issued to purge the ps_output files from each of the cluster nodes.

SYNOPSIS

cl_ps –options=ps options [–list=cluster list]

OPTIONS

--options = Put the options you want ps to use here, any option ps reconizes
is fine here

--list = this is an optional list of clusters

GENERAL

An example useage of cl_ps is as follows:

"cl_ps –options=A"

runs ps with the –A options on all nodes. If more than one option is
needed, use --options=ABC for the ABC options.

Without a cluster shutdown command it is very time consuming to log onto each node and perform an orderly shutdown process. If the direct approach of simply powering down machines is taken, the penalty will be paid on the subsequent startup as each machine will then spend time checking its respective file system. Although most clusters are not frequently shutdown in their entirety, clusters that multi-boot various operating systems will most definitely benefit from such a command as will all clusters after updating the operating system kernel. Also, on those rare occasions where a cluster must be brought down quickly, such as when on auxiliary power due to a power outage, the **cl_shutdown** is much appreciated. Thus, the cl_shutdown was developed to avoid the problem of manually talking to each of the cluster nodes during a shutdown process. As an added benefit, many motherboards now support an automatic power down after a halt - resulting in an "issue one command and walk away" administration for cluster shutdown.

SYNOPSIS

cl_shutdown --options=options -t=time [–list=cluster_list --message="message to
send"]

OPTIONS

--options = Put the options you want shutdown to use here, any options
shutdown reconizes is fine here

--list = this is an optional list of clusters, see below for the file format.

--t = time before shuting down

--message = message to display on each node

GENERAL

An example useage of cl_ps is as follows:

"cl_shutdow –options=h –t=1 –message="system shutting down""

Halts each machine in one minute displaying the given message on each node.

The **cl_kill** utility runs the kill command on each of the cluster nodes for a specified process name. Unlike the kill command, the cl_kill must use process name as the process ID (PID) will most likely be different on the various cluster nodes. Root user has the ability to further indicate a specific user in addition to process name. This enables root to kill a user's process by name and not affect other processes with the same name but run by other users. Root may also us signals to effectively do a broad based kill command.

SYNOPSIS

cl_kill –signal=signal –process=[list:]process name [--user=username]

OPTIONS

--signal   = use the same format and signals you would normally use with kill

list: = this is an optional list of clusters

--process = the name of the process being killed(not the PID or job number)

--user   = the name of the user whose process to kill. this can only be used by root. ALL specifies all users. This searches /etc/passwd for a UID.

GENERAL

An example useage of cl_ps is as follows:

"cl_kill –signals=9 –process=a.out –user=ALL"

does a kill –9 (unconditional kill) on all a.outs(--user=all specifies that all a.outs running on a system be killed, regardless of the user.

The **cl_exec** is the utility tool of the C3 suite in that it enables the execution of any command on each cluster node. As such, cl_exec may be considered the cluster version of rsh. A string passed to cl_exec is executed "as is" on each node. This provides a great deal of flexability in both the format of command output and arguments passed in to each instruction.

SYNOPSIS

cl_exec [OPTIONS] --command="[list:]string"

OPTIONS

--help   = display help message

--command -c = The string to be passed the each node in the cluster

-p   = print the name of the node before executing the string

--list -l   = file containing a list of nodes to send the string to.

GENERAL

There are two basic ways to call cl_exec:

-to execute a command

"cl_exec -command "mkdir temp""

notice the use of the "'s. this allows perl to interpret what is inside the quotes as a single string.

-to print the machine name and then execute the string

"cl_exec -p -c "ls -l""

> this allows the ability to read the output from a command such as ls
> and to know which machine the message came from.

4.   CONCLUSION

Although clusters are relatively inexpensive to build while providing good performance in comparison to recent supercomputers, the lack of good administration and application tools represents a hidden cost to cluster owners and users. This paper presented a number of command line tools developed as part of the Oak Ridge National Laboratory's HighTORC cluster project that are designed to reduce the cost of cluster ownership. These same tools provide the "backend" connection to the cluster for our web based GUI tool suite M3C (Monitoring and Managing Multiple Clusters) [10]. Both the C3 and M3C may be found at http://www.epm.ornl.gov/torc.

Of the three criteria set forth for our tools at the beginning of this paper – single machine look and feel, secure, scalable – the one we acknowledge falling short of is scalability. The current implementation of some of our commands iterate through a list of nodes on the server side. While we acknowledge this is a problem – we are very pleased with performance and cost savings resulting from use on our small 64-node HighTORC cluster. Furthermore, we are presently working on two competing techniques that are expected to greatly improve the scalability of our tools not only on large clusters but also on federated clusters and across the computation Grid.

Research sponsored by the Laboratory Directed Research and Development Program of Oak Ridge National Laboratory (ORNL), managed by UT-Battelle, LLC for the U. S. Department of Energy under Contract No. DE-AC05-00OR22725.

Brian Luethke is a participant in the Office of Science, DOE Energy Research Undergraduate Laboratory Fellowships, Spring 2000.

References

[1] The HighTORC system page, http://www.epm.ornl.gov/torc
[2] Rsync system documentation, http://www.rsync.samba.org
[3] Tom's root boot utility, http://www.toms.net/rb
[4] OpenSSH Specifications, http://www.openssh.com/
[5] ISC Dynamic Host Configuration Protocol, http:// www.isc.org/products/DHCP
[6] Systemimager documentation, http://www.systemimager.org
[7] Ptools project, http://www-unix.mcs.anl.gov/sut/
[8] The Grid: Blueprint for a New Computing Infrastructure, Morgan Kaufmann Publishers, Inc., San Francisco, 1999.
[9] Rdist home page, http://www.magnicomp.com/rdist
[10] M3C Tool, http://www.epm.ornl.gov/~jens/m3ctool

SEARCHING THE WEB AS AN ELEMENTAL SEMI-STRUCTURED INFORMATION SYSTEM OF TODAY

Dávid Fülep
Dept. of Information Technology, University of Miskolc, Hungary
fulepdav@freemail.hu

Abstract   The World Wide Web has become a prime platform for disseminating online information. The information stored on the Web is extremely distributed, a particular type of data may be distributed across thousands of independent information sources in many different formats. We can say, the main problem of the Internet or any other semi-structured information media today is finding the proper information. When the user finds something, never knows whether he/she has found the 'best' information and what has been missed. It becomes more obvious day by day that currently available search services are not capable to keep in line with the ever-growing complexity and size of the Web. The problem with most current Internet search services is that the search results are mostly based on information coded into web pages that are the results of the query. This paper deals with the problems of searching the Web. At first, it gives a general overview of the current methods, analyses the problems occurred, and than suggests some solution to solve the main problems.

Keywords: searching the Web, search engine, ranking methods, World Wide Web

1.   INTRODUCTION

The amount of information available online has grown fast over the past decade. Simultaneously, the computing power, disk capacity and network bandwidth have also increased. The World Wide Web has become a basic platform for disseminating information [7]. The Web is a very rich data source of the HTML code itself, natural language text within the HTML code and embedded images, voices, videos, etc.

On the top of this data there is *a well-defined link structure*, which is mathematically a directed graph over all the Web pages. The edges are labelled (with the text of the anchors on the links). In this data model labels are arbitrary atomic values, such as strings or different types of numbers or pictures. Efficiency problems can turn up during the use of the flexible graph repository, compared to the structured databases, such as relational or object-oriented database systems. In addition, the structure of real sites makes it hard to manage them easily, this is one reason why I call the Web not a structured but a semi-structured information system. The other reason is also easy to understand: there are quite a few structures inside the particular pages, as they store loose, natural language-based information.

The information stored on the Web is extremely distributed. A particular type of data may be scattered across thousands of independent information sources in many different formats. Instead of searching the Web itself in real time, which would be very slow, the common way of searching is storing the web pages in a database and then search in that database, using indexes and all known database management methods. The next section gives an overview and evaluation on the present search engines, the most successful methods and new proposals based on them are described in the third one.

2.   SEARCH ENGINES OF TODAY

We can say, the main problem of the Internet or any other semi-structured information media today is finding the proper information. It is very difficult to find all the relevant information we look for that is available somewhere on the Internet. When the user finds something, never knows whether the 'best' information has been found and what has been missed. It becomes more obvious day by day that currently available search services are not capable to keep in line with the ever-growing complexity and size of the Web [1]. Search engines can generally classified into 3 types that will be described next. The term "search engine" is often used to describe both true search engines and directories. These are basically different in the way of collecting and sorting information.

2.1   True Search Engines

Search engines crawl the web, and create their listings automatically. They eventually check all the web pages looking for changes. Search engines have three main elements. First is the motor of the engine, it is called spider. The spider loads the web page, reads it and follows the links found to other pages. Everything the spider finds and collects goes into the second main part of the search engine, the database (also called index or catalogue) [4]. The contents of this giant database are updated on a regular basis. When the spider returns to the site, i.e. every month, it looks for new or changed information. It is possible to inform the spider on the expiry date of a given page so the spider should update its database on that date. The database is not simply a collection of web pages, it contains many different types of indexes (in its original meaning used in database technology). Sometimes it takes some time that the information about 'spidered' web pages (pages visited by the spider) gets into the index. The third main part of the search system is the search engine itself. This program retrieves the matches to a search, sifting through millions of pages recorded in the database. Generally, there are many search results: the search engine has to order the list of matches. It does its job with so-called *ranking* the web pages. All search engines have the main parts described here, and work basically in the same way, the differences are only in how these parts are implemented and tuned. The main difference is how the web pages are ranked.

Whenever a search engine is used, it will present a long list of search results, which is ordered in such a way that the best results are placed in the beginning of the list. Most of users do not search deep [8]. The fact is that the relevant information has to appear in the first three pages of search results. Otherwise no one will find it, for example, on the 1000th place of the list. When a search engine informs the user about millions of matches, it is assumed that the user will not check through that list. It is indicated just for orientation, the user knows that he/she would determine his query with additional conditions. The advantages and drawbacks of the well-known ranking techniques will be mentioned in this paper.

Due to the theoretically infinite number of automatically generated HTML pages, it is impossible to store the whole Web in a local database. All that developers can do is to collect a part of the Web into a large repository, but they aim to have the largest set of static pages to be indexed. There are some efforts to create so-called meta search engines, these carry out their searches using more than one other search engine. Their success is based on the fact that individual search engines cover only 5-20% of web space. It is an interesting question, how we can determine the subset of the Web to store. The search engine's database can be of general purpose, or can be focused on a particular field of interest.

2.2   Directory-type Search Engines

A directory search strategy depends on humans for its decisions. There are human experts, editors, who are responsible for reviewing and classifying the sites. In this case the search engine looks for matches only in the descriptions submitted. As collecting information is not automatic, changing in web pages has no effect on the hand-made listings until an editor takes action manually. The main penalty with using directories that it is impossible to employ enough experts who are able to categorise *properly* web pages in all the fields of human knowledge. There is no guarantee that the categorisation by these experts is not affected by their personal taste. In the opinion of the writer of this paper, directories will find their particular field of usage, on some general and frequently searched fields, for example, travel information, sport facilities or cultural events. There are other types of human-assisted search engines, mainly pilot models, some of them are of quite great promise, and some seem to be a total breakdown and are not worth dealing with. These research projects are beyond the scope of this paper and will not be discussed here.

2.3   Hybrid and other Mixed Type Search Engines

These search engines are some kind of mixture or variation of the two basic types. For example, search engines maintain an associated directory, and anyone can submit a site for review just like at directories. But the search method based on the true search engine, the software uses directory as a complementary [4]. The most of these search engines can be grouped into one of the previously described two types, if we make some simplification.

3.   NEW APPROACHES TO SEARCH THE WEB

As mentioned before, the existing search engines need to be improved to get better results. Some of the techniques that can be used are presented in this section as follows.

3.1   Collecting information automatically

At first, let us try to determine what should be automated and what will require human intervention. Should a search engine be developed, which *automatically collects and sets out* all the information needed from the web sites? The answer will be a definite yes for the time being, because of the large number of web pages. It seems that only the use of autonomous and computerised search engines shall be able to be in steps with the growing of the Internet. It needs some (artificial) intelligence for the search engines. Although, at this time it is worth using several cases of searchable web page collections generated by directory-type search engines or other human effort. This paper only deals with autonomous search engines.

3.2   Ranking methods

Analysing the current methods of web searching, and trying out some well-known search services, shows that there are many things to do in this area. Users usually get responses to their queries, but the results are rarely satisfying. The search result is a set of links of amazing extent in most cases. The best-ranked results should appear among the first dozens of matches, and it is disappointing to discover how small percentage of the links is useful. Many of them do not relate to the topic the user was looking for, and the rest of the remaining pages are of low quality from the problem's point of view. In this paper a method is suggested for ranking the web pages, and storing strategy of the search engine is discussed.

3.3   Responsibility of Web site management

Managing a Web site with its large amount of data has a great importance from the searching point of view. Recent research results on information integration and managing semi-structured data can play a key role in web site management, because it is possible to extend and adapt these concepts to the problem of managing sites. It is not clear yet, if it is the responsibility of the web-masters to make efficient search possible on their web material and how they can help the search engine's work. In most cases it is not useful to search by only the file type, file size or the modification date of the file, but these can complement other search criteria. The problem with most current Internet search services is that the search results are mostly based on information coded into web pages that are the results of the query. This statement does not hold for the directory services as they have other problems that will be discussed later. This principle could work well only if each Web developer in the whole Internet community describes his/her web pages correctly and accurately. Everybody should fill in the title and keyword areas accordingly to the real contents and value of the web pages, which is rather utopian. If this condition cannot be satisfied, – and it cannot! – no one can rely only on information stored in a particular web page while designing and then using a web search service. In addition, HTML does not have the built-in facility to really help searching with its, come to that, compulsory tags in page definition. There are many efforts made to extend the HTML description language with these facilities, but no search engine or no authority can enforce that all the web page authors describe their pages accurately [3]. And all that the authors write into the HTML page, will reflect their own judgement of values and own opinions. Despite of these disadvantages, it is worth developing and using these methods to inform the search engine what does the given page consists of. Most of methods based on utilising the <META> HTML tag and providing the robots.txt file to instruct the spider visiting the site. Most search engines use both types together. Although, way of using of <META> tag is not standardised yet.

3.4   Reliance on keywords

It seems that the biggest weakness of both the human and automated approaches is the reliance on keywords. There are some efforts to overcome using only keywords [11,12]. Trying to look at the meaning of the keyword can help to find relevant sites even if the keyword does not appear on them.

3.5   Number of backward links

Every page has some number of (zero or more) forward links and backward links (sometimes called backlink). If the user downloads a particular page, he/she knows all of its forward links, but never knows all of the backward links have been found. Because of the theoretically infinite number of web pages, it is impossible to collect all the backward links of a given page [7]. But generally we can say if a large number of backward links of a page is found, this highly linked page is considered as important. After defining the rank of pages, it can be used for selecting and then ranging the search results. Ranking pages by the method based on the number of backward links has been implemented by an independent group Google, but their implementation seems to give some erroneous results and needs to be improved [13].

3.6   Placement of keywords

In line with these approaches, there is a lot to do with developing search methods based on keywords. Documents containing the *keyword* can be weighted more if the keyword occurs *in an important place,* for example, in the title or in a headline. If two words occur close together in a document, that document should be weighted much more heavily than if they appear far apart. Checking the text of the link anchors pointing to a given page can be helpful, because it contains important information coming from other web pages. Unfortunately, the text of the anchor is totally unusable or does not exist in many cases, and it is tedious to distinguish automatically between useful and useless information. Unfortunately, current search engines give little information about using these possibilities because of proprietary reasons.

3.7   Using synonyms

The known literature mostly deals with the keyword itself while discussing keyword based searching. *Using synonyms* besides the keywords given by the user should make possible to achieve much more reliable ranking methods. The search engine should look for the occurrences of not only the given keyword but of its synonyms too. Of course, it enlarges the number of matches but the large amount of search results is the common problem of all search engines, and they can handle this question well. A deeper problem is that using synonyms may introduce false results as well. The point is ranking the results, or, to be more accurate, selecting the most highly ranked pages that will be enumerated in the first places.

If the search engine find different occurrences of synonyms for the same keyword in the document, it possibly means that the page really deals with the theme the user is just searching for.

It is worth counting the occurrences of the different synonyms of a keyword in the text: where these numbers are relatively high, that page should get a high rank. The longest the text of the page with the more repetition of the keyword and its synonym, the best result this page will be. We can say, that papers dealing with a theme deeply contain the most important keywords of their topic many times. And, to be bolted and sophisticated, they use almost all the synonyms of these words. (And it is a pity that many times they do not: it can happen that the page does not contain the keywords or their synonyms of the topic at all. That is why there is no one good separate method for searching, we have to use more different methods at the same time.) Replacing a keyword with its synonym may decrease the importance of finding good (the best!) keywords for searching. Without this it can happen that the user does not find a page containing really relevant information. It is because he/she has not tried exactly that word which was used in an important place of the page (for example, in the title field or in a headline), but he/she used its synonym instead.

Looking for synonyms can be much more useful when using more than one keyword in the search query: In this case the search engine can summarise the weight of all the keywords and their synonyms during the ranking procedure. It can assume that the set of the given phrases to look for is more extent, which means that it is more possible to find the documents really corresponding to the original query. If some of these words occur close together in a page, that document should have higher rank than if they appear far apart.

Also, there is another thing worth dealing with about synonyms: when the spider downloads the pages and sets out the information out of them, it should be beneficial to group all the words into sets of synonyms and store these sets themselves as synonyms. In such a system, a much more efficient synonym-based keyword-searching algorithm could be realised. At the moment, there is no search service that has realised this method and has made it common to the public.

3.8   Determining what to store about the pages

The question of essential importance, namely *determining what to store about the text of web pages,* can be restated in some other ways. We can raise the question: Should the web search engine store the *whole web page* or just some meta information about it? This question should be analysed deeper. There are advantages and disadvantages of storing the whole document as-is in the database of the search engine. The main benefit is that there is a possibility to draft new types of searching queries on the available data, we are not limited into the constraints of the predefined indexes. In addition, the search engine can be used as a cache or proxy server which can be applied because of security reasons or to save the throughput capacity of the Internet connection. Some sites are not accessible for shorter or longer periods, in this case getting the file from the search engine itself may be beneficial. A drawback of storing the whole web page can be, for example, the need for higher disk and computing capacity. If disk capacity problems occur, we can make a decision on a file size, under which the server should store the file itself, and above it stores only a link (URL) to the original place of the file.

At the moment the writer of this paper is constructing a new experimental search engine, which - because of the lack of the gigantic amount of necessary disk capacity - will use the database of more than one other well-known search engines. This type of search engine is called a meta-search one. Its most important benefits are the small demand of disk space and simplicity. (We do not have to deal with the spider, "only" with retrieving information out of the databases of others.) It is planned to apply two or three search engines at the beginning, which will be increased to at least a dozen. The new meta-search engine will use the new principles of using synonyms described in this paper. The details of this project will be published along with the first experiences in a follow-up paper.

4.   CONCLUSIONS

This paper has reviewed the most current questions arising when designing search engines for the World Wide Web. It has given an overview on how the current search engines work, what are the conditions they agree and what are the main problems with using them. This paper has suggested some solutions, which can decrease these disadvantages experienced by the users of search services. These new approaches to searching the Web are under implementation, results (including the details of the project and experiences of practical implementation and usage) will be published in due course.

References

[1]   J. Hammer, H. Garcia-Molina, J. Cho, R. Aranha, A. Crespo: Extracting Semistructured Information from the Web
[2]   P. Atzeni, G. Mecca, P. Merialdo: Semistructured and Structured Data in the Web: Going Back and Forth
[3]   Maxim L. Lifantsev: The Open GRiD Project, http://www.cs.sunysb.edu/maxim-cgi-bin/OpenGRiD
[4]   Danny Sullivan: How Search Engines Work, Search Engine Watch, http://searchenginewatch.interet.com
[5]   M. Fernandez, D. Florescu, A. Levy, D. Suciu: Reasoning about Web-Site Structure
[6]   M. Fernandez, D. Florescu, A. Levy, D. Suciu: A Query Language and Processor for a Web-Site Management System
[7]   S. Brin, R. Motwani, L. Page, T. Winograd: What can you do with the Web in your Pocket?
[8]   Danny Sullivan, The Search Engine Report: Counting Clicks and Looking at Links
[9]   Danny Sullivan, How Search Engines Rank Web Pages, http://www.searchenginewatch.internet.com
[10] Clever Project, IBM, http://www.almaden.ibm.com/cs/k53/clever.html
[11] Oingo, http://www.oingo.com
[12] Simpli.com, http://www.simpli.com
[13] Google, http://www.google.com

PROTOTYPING CLUSTER-BASED DISTRIBUTED APPLICATIONS

Václav Dvořák, Rudolf Čejka

Department of Computer Science and Engineering

Brno University of Technology

http://www.fee.vutbr.cz/UIVT/

{dvorak,cejkar}@dcse.fee.vutbr.cz[*]

Abstract: A simple CSP-based model of cluster computing is presented. A Transim simulation tool, originally intended for simulation of transputer networks, can be used to simulate various parallel applications running on workstation clusters. Since communication latency is quite high in clusters, prediction of processor utilization, obtainable speedup and execution time are of interest. The Transim tool enables to find all these figures in minimum time and with minimum effort. As an example, a solution of a large system of (1000+) linear equations on up to 8 workstations connected via fast Ethernet to a hardware router is simulated and results are compared to real execution based on MPI.

Key words: Cluster computing, CSP-based modeling, parallel performance prediction, MPI, linear equations benchmark.

1.   INTRODUCTION

This paper introduces the well-known technique of CSP into modeling of cluster computing based on a multiport switch. Modeling is important to categorize which jobs are most conductive to this environment and to select proper system parameters (number of nodes, CPU speed, link speed, communication protocol etc.) for required

[*] Supported by the grant No. CEZ: J22/98: 262200012 Research of the Information and Control Systems

performance. The CSP-based simulation and prototyping tool Transim is used throughout this study [1]. The input file for Transim simulator contains Occam-like descriptions of software, hardware and mapping to one another. Simulated time moves ahead due to special timing constructs SERV( ) replacing CPU execution, and due to implicit communication overhead based on the default parameters or on a user-defined communication model. Explicit overhead can be represented directly by WAIT( ) construct. Hardware is described by NODE construct and the mapping between software and hardware is made through the MAP construct.

2.   MODEL OF A WORKSTATION CLUSTER

We have chosen to model fast Ethernet (100 Mbit/s) network of workstations with star topology, Fig.1a. Node processors are modeled in Transim by processes $cell[i]$ running on processors $cpu[i]$, whereas a hardware multiport router is modeled by processes $in[i]$ and $out[i]$ running on processing elements $cross[i]$ and $bar[i]$, respectively. Each processor $cpu[i]$ is connected to the multiport switch via a pair of channels $ch[i][fcb]$ (from crossbar) and $ch[i][tcb]$ (to crossbar); 2D-array of channels among processes in and out within a crossbar are denoted $i2o[i][j]$ (input-to-output). Nodes are Ultra 5 stations with UltraSPARC II processors running at 270 MHz. The hardware multiport router has been Summit48 (from Extreme Networks), Fig.1a. HW latency of the hardware router is below 10 μs and can be neglected with respect to the SW latencies (160 μs for send and 260 μs for receive operation at clock speed 270 MHz). Interesting parameters of processing elements simulating the crossbar switch and workstations (configurable in Transim) are clock speed SPD, link speed LS, external channel delay ECD and internal channel delay ICD.

We have used a linear time model for point-to-point as well as for broadcast communications, whose parameters have been obtained by measurement communication overhead in MPI. E.g. the total latency of MPI broadcast depends on a number of nodes. Measured values of broadcast latencies are about 500, 750 and 1000 μs for 2, 4 and 8 nodes whereas related transfer rates have been 10, 5 and 3.5 Mbyte/s respectively. From the input of the multiport switch to its output and on to the receiver node, the latency of 3 external channels will be seen. We have taken zero latency for each processing element $cross[i]$ and $bar[i]$ and full measured values of broadcast latencies for processors $cpu[i]$.

Since in Transim each message transfer passes only a single integer between the sender and receiver, we can use it as a message header to indicate the destination address or a type of group communication (e.g. one-to-all broadcast). But since receivers (processes "in" and "out") have to pass the message on, they have to determine the message size, defined by the sender, from the message itself. Therefore we combine a message header and a message size into one integer.

Processing elements (PEs) "$cross$" and "bar" included in a crossbar network have to be excluded from the total count of 20 PEs when efficiency of node processors is analyzed. Since Transim tool reports speedup, average efficiency of all processing elements and individual efficiencies as well, the right value has to be figured out by averaging individual efficiencies of only a subset of "*cpu*" PEs.

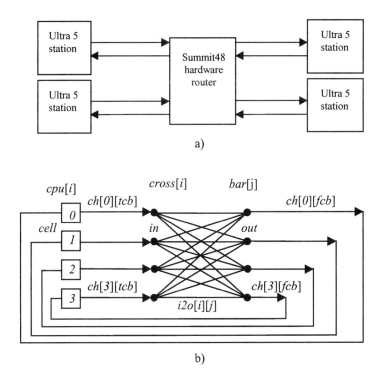

a)

b)

Figure1. a) Cluster of P ≤ 48 Ultra 5 stations and Summit48 HW router
b) Process graph implemented in the Transim model (P = 4)

3.   RESULTS AND CONCLUSIONS

To illustrate performance prediction of cluster computing, we have used a large system of *n* linear equations which was solved by the Gauss-Jordan method with no back-substitution phase. A parallel version of the Gauss-Jordan method for *P* processors assigns each processor *n/P* consecutive equations. Each processor takes its turn as a "leader" and sequentially broadcasts one of its *n/P* equations (a pivot row) after another to all other processors. Following each broadcast, all processors modify their equations by subtracting a certain multiple of the pivot row from each equation. Only the pivot row is left intact by the leader processor.

The model of cluster computing is obtained by combining the crossbar switch model with the description of algorithm for solution of linear equations. An 8 × 8 version of a crossbar switch has been investigated with store & forward (SF) routing with parameters selected as suggested above. As for the computation times, duration of inner loops has been measured and the obtained values used in simulation (SERV commands). Tables 1 and 2 show results of simulations.

The goal of simulation of parallel computations on a cluster of workstations was to predict the performance of parallel applications and to find out if parallel implementation makes sense at all, before a parallel program (e.g. in C with MPI directives) is written in detail and debugged. The effort was fruitful, since successful simulation has been demonstrated and the obtained accuracy has been quite satisfactory (± 10%). Simulations can be run under various parameters settings, with number of processors from 1 up to low tens (PC version of Transim). Simulations made possible to model various cluster technologies, various types of crossbar switches and interconnection networks (made of smaller crossbars 2x2, 8x8). Workstation clusters with bus topology can also be simulated using strategy developed for SM architectures [2].

Table 1. Efficiency [%] / processing time [s] of real execution (MPI)

no. of eqns →	200	400	600	800	1000	1200
P = 1	100 / 0.17	100 / 1.61	100 / 5.64	100 / 13.5	100 / 26.5	100 / 46.1
P = 2	43.3 / 0.20	76.8 / 1.05	85.2 / 3.31	90.1 / 7.45	92.9 / 14.2	94.4 / 24.4
P = 4	20.3 / 0.21	54.1 / 0.74	71.8 / 1.96	79.3 / 4.27	83.4 / 7.96	85.0 / 13.6
P = 8	9.2 / 0.23	32.3 / 0.62	52.2 / 1.35	63.2 / 2.68	69.1 / 4.80	73.4 / 7.85

Table 2. Efficiency [%] and speedup of simulated execution

no. of eqns →	200	400	600	800	1000	1200
P = 2	50.5 / 1.01	79.0 / 1.58	88.8 / 1.78	93.0 / 1.86	95.1 / 1.90	96.4 / 1.93
P = 4	24.9 / 0.99	54.5 / 2.18	71.3 / 2.85	80.3 / 3.21	85.6 / 3.42	88.9 / 3.56
P = 8	10.9 / 0.87	30.6 / 2.45	47.6 / 3.81	59.9 / 4.79	68.4 / 5.47	73.7 / 5.89

Further development of this work will be done in direction of creating models of other emerging cluster architectures and technologies (clusters of SMPs, Remote Store Architecture RSA, etc.) using the same methodology with the goal of fair performance comparison.

References

[1] Hart, E.: TRANSIM - Prototyping Parallel Algorithms. London, Univ. of Westminster Press (2nd edition), 1994.

[2] Cejka, R. - Dvorak, V.: "CSP-based Modeling of SM Architectures". Proceedings of conference Computer Engineering and Informatics CE&I'99, Kosice - Herlany, Slovakia, pp. 163-168, FEI TU Kosice Publ., 1999. ISBN 80-88922-05-4.

RESOURCE MANAGEMENT IN A JINI-BASED METACOMPUTING FRAMEWORK*

Zoltan Juhász
Department of Information Systems, University of Veszprem, Hungary
Department of Computer Science, University of Exeter, England
Z.Juhasz@exeter.ac.uk

Laszlo Késmárki
Department of Information Systems, University of Veszprem, Hungary

Abstract   This paper describes the overall structure of a Jini -based metacomputing environment. The working mechanism and details of the resource management philosophy are described.

Key words: Metacomputing, Java, Jini, Resource Management

1.   INTRODUCTION

Cluster and metacomputing environments are of great interest these days. Several research projects, e.g. [1-6], are underway aiming to provide seamless access to the vast number of computers connected by the Internet, and to create better, more efficient and useful computing services. Our work focuses on the use of Jini Technology [7] as a potential infrastructure for metacomputing systems. Jini has been designed to create autonomous, ad hoc network of digital devices. It is a service-based system featuring automatic discovery of the network and its available services, providing fault

* Work supported by the Hungarian National Science Fund under Grant No. F 20839.

tolerance, transactions and distributed event mechanism. In this paper we report on the resource management aspects our prototype.

2.   THE JINI METACOMPUTING PROTOTYPE

The structure of our system is shown in Figure 1. The environment consists of three types of participants, Clients, Brokers and Hosts. A *Client* represents a parallel application to be executed on the metasystem. The *Broker*'s responsibilities are monitoring resources and selecting a set of suitable hosts for executing the client's tasks. Monitoring is performed through *Host* services (representing the computing hosts) that provide state information and, as generic compute engines, execute tasks allocated to them by the broker service.

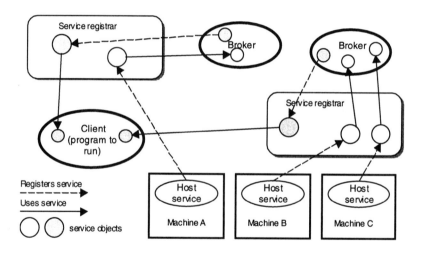

Figure 1. Overall system structure

3.   RESOURCE MANAGEMENT

On startup, the Host and Broker services register themselves on the lookup service as Jini services and as a result upload a copy of their service objects. When clients join the federation, they look for brokers to service their execution request. The located, then selected brokers discover potential resources by finding Host services in the registrar, and after downloading, they extract information from the host services. Both clients and brokers can use attributes to locate the most suitable broker and host service, respectively.

The responsibility of the Broker service is to take an execution request from the Client, then allocate and run tasks on suitable machines. Allocation is based on requirements received as part of the execution request (e.g. required performance, maximum number of tasks, maximum allowed cost of execution to be paid for, etc) as well as on machine information extracted from Host services. Scheduling the tasks is based on the rule of minimising the number of processors used and maintaining geographical locality of the selected machines. This can only be violated if such a parallel supercomputer is available that can handle the execution of the complete problem itself.

Broker services can be stored with attributes, too. They can specify e.g. whether a broker is specialised in a particular application area (e.g. scientific computation, simulation) or deals with a particular set of computer types (e.g. parallel supercomputers, clusters).

The client has several alternatives for program execution. In automatic mode, through the broker's execute() method, it can delegate the machine selection, task allocation and execution to the broker. Should there be more than one brokers, the client can ask the brokers to bid (using the bid() method) for the execution of the program (semi-automatic mode). The returned bid result can include the estimated execution time, cost of machine use. The client then can decide which broker's bid to accept and proceed. Clients can also ask the broker(s) to only select available machines for task execution with the findMachines() method (manual mode). This method returns a set of machine list–cost pairs. The client can then allocate and run the subtasks explicitly by invoking the execute() method of the Host service.

For host services we have abstracted out attributes such as Host, Processor, Network and Memory. The Host attribute stores general information, such as host URL and the number of processors. The Processor and Memory attributes refer to building blocks of the given computer, while the Network one describes the interconnect parameters of the machine.

Jini uses exact matching for attributes. Consequently, it is not possible to match e.g. interval values – to find machines with processor number e.g. $64 \le p \le 1024$. To achieve this effect, all machines must be retrieved and the calling object must check the interval. We believe this is not a major drawback in our case, since these attributes are static, and brokers can easily build up a table of these parameters for interval checking to eliminate the need for frequent lookup operations.

4.   CONCLUSIONS

This paper reported on our ongoing project, whose aim is to develop a Jini-based metacomputing environment. It showed the basic structure and operation of the system as well as the framework for resource allocation, management and program execution. The prototype shows that Jini technology offers effective support for creating reliable metacomputing systems.

In the near future we will be looking at how multi-agent technology can be exploited e.g. in the negotiation process between clients and brokers under conflicting goals. Other key areas of our investigation are examining scalability aspects of such metasystems and evaluating the performance of Jini systems.

References

1. I. Foster and C. Kesselman, The Globus project: a status report, *Future Generation Computer Systems* 15 (1999) pp 607-621.
2. A. Grimshaw, W. Wulf et al. The Legion Vision of a Worldwide Virtual Computer. *Communications of the ACM*, vol. (40)1, January 1997.
3. M. Beck, J. Dongarra, G. Fagg, A. Geist, P. Gray, J. Kohl, M. Migliardi, K. Moore, T. Moore, P. Papadopoulos, S. Scott, and V. Sunderam, HARNESS: A Next Generation Distributed Virtual Machine, Special Issue on Metacomputing, Future Generation Computer Systems, Elsevier Publ. Vol 15, No. 5/6, 1999.
4. M.O. Neary, B.O.Christiansen, P. Capello and K.E.Schauser, Javelin: Parallel Computing on the Internet, *Future Generation Computer Systems* 15 (1999) pp 659-674.
5. T. Haupt, E. Akarsu, G. Fox and W. Furmanski, Web based metacomputing, *Future Generation Computer Systems* 15 (1999) pp 735-743.
6. L.F.G Sarmenta and S. Hirano, Bayanihan: building and studying a web-based volunteer computing systems usign Java, *Future Generation Computer Systems* 15 (1999) pp 675-686.
7. K. Edwards, *Core Jini*, Prentice Hall, 1999.

Author Index